YUMMY Easy QUICK
Around the World
T0290226

This book is dedicated to anyone who ever taught me anything – and to everyone who still wants to learn more.

Thank you to Valli Little, Antonio Carluccio, Tony Bourdain, John Lermayer, Paul Bocuse, Darren Simpson, Jeremy Strode, Joël Robuchon and, above all, Ted Bennison for your wisdom.

YUMMY Easy QUICK Around the World

MATT PRESTON

CONT

ENTS

WELCOME TO THE WONDERFUL WORLD OF FAKING IT!

The first *Yummy Easy Quick* book was all about super-tasty and super-simple recipes for dinner that minimised the amount of time you spent in the kitchen, because there might be something more fun or more pressing you could be doing.

This book takes the same approach but whisks you around the world to find yummy, easy and quick ways to cook favourite dishes from 11 of the world's great cuisines: China, Japan, Thailand, Vietnam, France, Spain, Greece, Italy, the Middle East and North Africa, India and Mexico.*

This is not, however, some dull, cheffy tome loaded with tedious, time-consuming and dusty techniques dating back to a time when your nonna's nonna had to spend all day in the kitchen to make dinner, but a book that will show you how to fake unique flavours from around the world, so you can knock up a tasty and thoroughly convincing pad thai or a samosa pie in less time than it takes to find the local takeaway menu or scroll through your choice of takeaway app.

This time, we've also added desserts (which might take a little longer to make, but will result in a show-stopping end to a meal) and specific shopping lists that will help give your recipes those hallmark flavours of authenticity if you want to take 'faking it' to another level, even if, when it comes to food, 'authenticity' is a bit of a myth. True authenticity can obviously only exist in the country, village and, perhaps, even the kitchen where an original dish was created, made with exactly the same ingredients and techniques.

Authentic and authoratitive this book is not. Really the title of this book should be 'FAKING IT', because you'll soon realise that by combining certain key ingredients a dish quickly starts to take on the unique feel of one or another corner of the world ... so when family or friends ask what's for dinner, you can proudly proclaim Chinese, Indian, French, Italian, Mexican or Middle Eastern!

These days, everyone is very sensitive to cultural appropriation. However, when it comes to food, almost every country's national cuisine has great swathes that have been appropriated. It's the nature of humans and their kitchens that wherever we are we want to make the best dinner we can. Imagine Japanese food without sushi, Italian food without tomatoes or Australian food without anything other than indigenous ingredients. That is an unnatural world without the joys of cross pollination of ideas and ingredients.

To help you find the right recipe faster and more easily, there are loads of different indexed lists at the back of the book, so you can find the fastest recipes, the fanciest recipes (ideal for showing off with) and even the ones that are best for those people in your life who favour a 'plant-based cuisine' (cos you can't call them filthy vegans or vegos any more, as that's wrong).

*DISCLAIMER: This book shamelessly focuses on the 11 most popular and most requested cuisines in Australia, but that's not to say that I don't have a profound love for food from all over the world, whether it be Portuguese, Turkish, Korean, Malaysian, Sri Lankan, Bangladeshi, Pakistani, Dutch, German, Swiss, South African, Peruvian, Venezuelan, any of the Nordic countries, Brazilian, Irish or any other of the world's great cuisines.

FLAVOUR PALATES – AND HOW THEY'LL HELP YOU FAKE IT

If you were painting a picture of the sea, you'd need to have plenty of blues, greens and whites on your artist's palette. If it was a desert, then you'd be sure to have lots of yellows, browns and ochres. Use a colour that doesn't occur in those environments, and not only will it stand out discordantly, but it could also ruin your picture. (Mind you, that's how Impressionism started if you want to get all Year 11 Art Class about things ... but no one will thank you for that.)

Painting a desert and making a dessert have a lot in common. When you are cooking, you are painting with flavours, and adding the wrong ingredient or taste can ruin a great dish. It will stand out as much as that uncharacteristic colour in your painting or a bum note in a *Voice* audition, maybe.

There are chemical, geographical, historical, cultural, climatic and social reasons why certain ingredients seem to belong together. This is especially true when it comes to the flavours of a particular country's cuisine. The good news is that these bonds are so tight and the connections so instinctive that a smart cook can use a different palette (or palate) of flavours to create a convincing recreation of any national flavour.

Don't believe me? Look at the below shopping lists and see if you can pick the nationality of the kitchens these ingredients belong to:

- Soy sauce, mirin, rice, wasabi, miso, seaweed, raw fish
- Garlic, cream, wine, Dijon mustard, soft herbs, such as tarragon, thyme and chervil
- Tomatoes, basil, olive oil, cured pork, mascarpone, pasta, parmesan
- Spring onions, ginger, rice, soy sauce, oyster sauce, five spice powder
- Limes, tomatoes, coriander, avocados, chillies, corn, tortillas
- Fish sauce, lemongrass, palm sugar, coconut milk, limes, galangal.

While many of these individual ingredients exist in different cuisines, when listed together like this I'm sure you immediately saw which list belonged to Japanese, French, Italian, Chinese, Mexican and Thai kitchens respectively.

So, when it comes to changing up the flavours of your favourite meatballs, pumpkin soup or Sunday roast, remember that using ingredients from one of the dedicated flavour palates that follow in this book will give that cherished dish a whole new lease of life and a distinctly more international outlook. You might marinate that chicken in a spice paste of coriander stalks and roots, limes and galangal (to later serve with chewy rice cakes and Thai basil slaw), or rub it with a spice mix of two-parts ground coriander, one-part cumin seeds and lemon or orange zest, and stuff it with couscous, pistachios and dates for a fuzzy North African touch.

Here, we will teach you to paint in broad brush strokes of flavour but, please, once you have mastered a basic understanding of the flavours used, dive deeper into each cuisine to uncover the wonderful regional variations that exist in each and every one of these countries. Enjoy!

Now, let's cook ...

FAKING IT IS LARGELY ABOUT not using clashing flavours or ingredients. So avoid putting pork in your tajine, peanuts on top of your French Lyonnaise salad or a crunchy slab of fried polenta in a betel leaf with chilli fish sauce caramel pineapple.

So it is with oils. Always try and use the right (aka regionally appropriate) fat for your cooking when faking it. This means using olive oil when you want to emulate dishes from southern Italy and France, especially if they use ingredients, such as capers, zucchini or capsicum, and then butter or cream for dishes from the north. Similarly, peanut oil or coconut fat is the way to go for Vietnamese or Thai dishes, which use peanuts or coconut in them respectively.

ASIA

From the warming claypots, delicate dumplings and hearty braises of China's west and north to the steamy southeast of the continent with its vibrant, spicy herb-driven cuisine, Asia is a rich playground when it comes to finding something tasty and easy for dinner. Throw in Japan and you have some of my favourite cuisines all in one, albeit rather large, place. In this section you will find 46 flavour-packed Asian dishes that are perfect to make for family and friends.

Note: For selfish personal reasons, I have included India and the Middle East into the Rest of the World section (see pages 226–307). I know this is a cardinal sin for a bloke descended from a geographer grandfather who was employed to draw borders, but I feel India is a cuisine that deserves to stand alone, and we had a row about whether we should split the food of the Middle East out of the North African and Middle East section, but that seemed silly given that it was only a couple of recipes. I share this in the interests of transparency, and because I know it will anger geography pedants, which is rather fun.

CHINA
JAPAN
VIETNAM
THAILAND

CHINA

A huge land mass and rich history make the Chinese kitchen one of the most diverse, but when drawing the cuisine in simplistic primary colours, it's wheat in the north and rice in the south. Much of China's culinary contribution to the world has been set by its diaspora, which often means loads of slippery wok-fried Cantonese dishes, but in this section we have plundered the whole country for ideas, whether from the wok, oven or steamer basket.

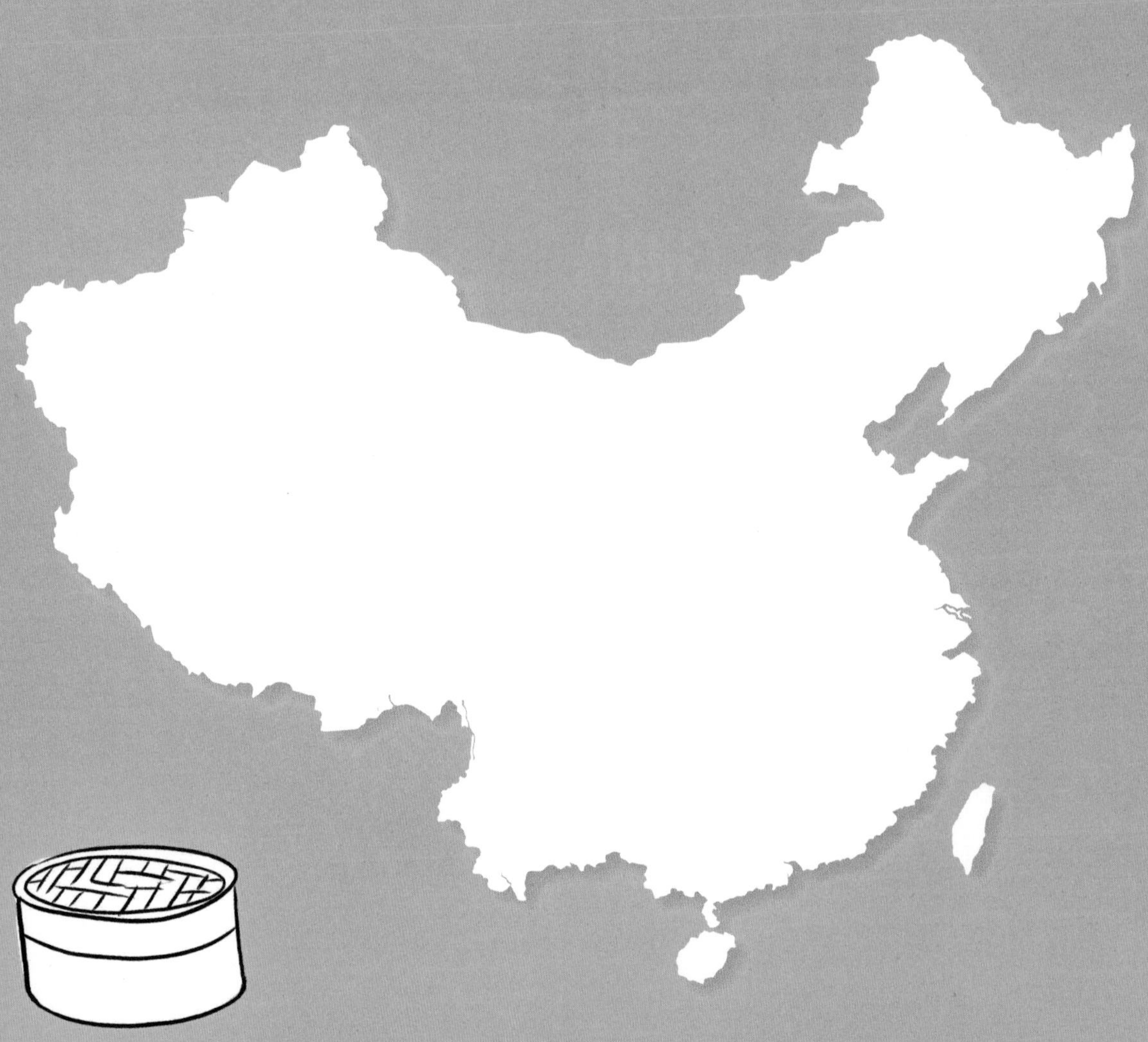

In Chinese cuisine, you'll find that pork, duck, chicken, seafood and freshwater fish are the most popular proteins, along with all manner of tofu products and mushrooms. Goose, beef and local venison also feature.

Then there's the signature flavour of the Chinese kitchen – that heady combination of fennel seeds, star anise, cloves, Chinese cinnamon (cassia) and Sichuan pepper ground together into five spice powder. In the south of the country, dried mandarin peel might replace the cloves for a tangier result.

The backbone of Chinese cuisine is further bolstered by the use of garlic, ginger and spring onion, along with bottled sauces and vinegars, such as oyster, hoisin, plum, black vinegar and, of course, soy and Shaoxing rice wine. In addition, fermented chilli bean pastes and fancier XO sauces are simple umami bombs that will make even steamed rice taste special, but they may require a special visit to an Asian grocer if you don't have a great supermarket.

Finally, nuts, such as peanuts, cashews and almonds, sesame seeds and oil, and fresh ingredients, including sugar snaps, bean sprouts, water chestnuts and all manner of Asian greens – kangong (water spinach), bok choy and Chinese broccoli – are all employed to add a crisp, bitey texture to dishes.

FAKING IT TIPS

1. Cut ingredients small for stir-fries. Cook them separately, and keep the wok dry so you don't stew the ingredients. Finish with Shaoxing rice wine and hoisin sauce, and add noodles at the end if you are not serving with rice.
2. A wet crisp texture is prized, whether this comes from water chestnuts or steamed bok choy. Try frying your bok choy halved and cut-side down in a pan. Finish with soy sauce to caramelise the underside of the bok choy with salty stickiness.
3. Flavour plain steamed veg with oyster sauce or chilli pastes, or simply stir-fry with garlic and perhaps a few threads of ginger. You might baulk at buying bottled sauces, but I once made my own oyster sauce; it took all day, cost $60 a bottle and didn't taste as good as a quality store-bought one. And it was available immediately.
4. Rub pork belly, duck or chicken with five spice powder before roasting, clay-potting or grilling. Serve with plum sauce, fresh chilli sauce or a mash of spring onions, salt and a little ginger. You'll find my recipes for those last two online if you search my name and the words 'Chinese red chilli sauce'. These also go with steamed seafood and chicken poached with Chinese aromats.
5. Use good-quality bottled XO sauce as the base for butters and bespoke sauces for seafood. Add fresh orange or lemon juice and herbs, such as coriander, for freshness. These sauces are great to finish off vegies, too.
6. Add fried lap cheong to pretty much everything.
7. Always use white pepper rather than black.

SHOPPING LIST

Take a trip to your local Asian grocer and look to set up your pantry with sesame oil, funky fermented chilli and soy bean pastes, such as 'doubanjiang' (which will lift any stir-fry), black beans and chilli oils. Also stock up on black vinegar, Shaoxing rice wine and better-quality soy, oyster, hoisin and char siu sauces than you might find in your local supermarket.

Also look for long-lasting Chinese rock sugar, an expensive jar of XO sauce with loads of dried scallops called 'compoy' (and Yunnan ham if that's your thing), Asian pancakes and frozen steamed buns, as well as a good selection of dried mushrooms, such as wood ear, cloud and the best shiitake. If they have any dried mandarin peel buy it, as it's wonderful in pretty much anything. I tend to find that if I want to add some brightness to a Chinese-inspired dish, even grated fresh mandarin peel and juice or a little orange will help with Chinese vinegars that feel too dark and heady.

While Chinese lap cheong is widely available in supermarkets these days, you may find your local Asian grocer has a fancier version you want to experiment with. And also remember there is no shame in buying roast or char siu pork or Peking duck from your local Chinese supermarket or restaurant to share with the family.

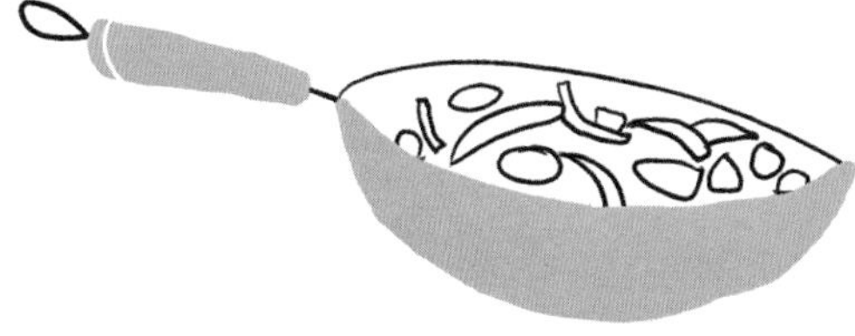

SICHUAN BOLOGNESE

(AKA DAN DAN NOODLES WITH CHICKEN MINCE)

I'd love to say I first encountered this classic street food dish on a hiking tour of Sichuan in the far west of mainland China, where the winters are savage and the spicy food sings with chilli and mouth-tingling Sichuan peppercorns. Actually, it was in a little hole in the wall in deepest Springvale.

Springvale is a Melbourne suburb blessed with fewer tourist attractions than most. Sure, there are a couple of Buddhist temples and a greyhound track – which covers most of life's requirements – but the real attraction is the dizzying selection of Thai, Cambodian and regional Chinese restaurants and grocery stores.

SERVES: 4 PREP: 15 MINS COOKING: 10 MINS

1 tablespoon peanut oil
500 g chicken mince
60 ml (¼ cup) hoisin sauce
1 tablespoon light soy sauce
1 tablespoon Shaoxing rice wine (or dry sherry – but Chinese rice wine is cheap and readily available)
½ teaspoon Chinese five spice
500 g fresh or dried wheat noodles
150 g snow peas, sliced diagonally
50 g (¼ cup) coarsely chopped roasted unsalted peanuts
2 spring onions, white and dark green parts thinly sliced
2 tablespoons Chinese-style chilli oil, such as chiu chow (see TIPS)

PEANUT SAUCE

60 ml (¼ cup) salt-reduced chicken stock or water
95 g (⅓ cup) unsweetened smooth peanut butter
2 large garlic cloves, crushed
2 tablespoons Chinese-style chilli oil, such as chiu chow (see TIPS)
2 tablespoons light soy sauce
1½ tablespoons black vinegar
1 tablespoon dark soy sauce
1 tablespoon Sichuan peppercorns, toasted, ground using a mortar and pestle
1 tablespoon sesame oil
2 teaspoons brown sugar

To make the peanut sauce, place all the ingredients in a bowl and stir to combine. Well! That was easy, wasn't it?

Heat the oil in a large frying pan over high heat. Add the chicken mince and cook, breaking up any lumps with the back of a wooden spoon, for 5 minutes or until browned and cooked through. Add the hoisin, soy sauce, Shaoxing rice wine and five spice and stir to combine. Remove from the heat and set aside.

Bring a large saucepan of water to the boil over high heat. Add the noodles and cook for 2 minutes, stirring occasionally to separate the noodles. Add the snow peas and cook for a further 1 minute. Drain.

Divide the noodles and snow peas among serving bowls. Top with some of the peanut sauce, followed by the chicken, peanuts and spring onion. Blob some more peanut sauce over the top, drizzle over some chilli oil and serve.

TIPS

To bulk this dish up even further add some pan-wilted Asian greens, such as bok choy or Chinese broccoli, which is what we decided to do at the photoshoot and can be seen pictured here!

If you can't find chiu chow chilli oil, substitute 1 finely chopped bird's eye chilli.

Leftover peanut sauce will keep stored in a jar in the fridge for up to 2 weeks.

PEKING DUCK PANCAKES WITH QUICK CUCUMBER PICKLE

I call it 'the pistachio effect' – those foods that are so delicious you can't stop eating them. Hot chips have that addictive allure, as does chocolate, and ice-cream when someone leaves the tub right in front of you. So, too, do young brussels sprouts tossed in a fish sauce caramel (check out page 83). Or is that just me?

Sometimes it's down to the heavenly but rather wicked 'golden ratio' of animal fat and sugar, and I suspect that this – along with my natural greed – is part of the reason I find it hard to stop eating Peking duck pancakes. But there is more than just the sweet sauce, crispy maltose-glazed duck skin and duck fat going on here. The perfect Peking duck pancake is all about the journey of the teeth: through soft pancake, crispy skin, a thin layer of juicy, yielding fat that has almost been totally rendered away, then meat and the refreshing crunch of cucumber and spring onion, all bound together with a thin coating of sweet sauce – usually hoisin.

Traditionally in Beijing, the duck meat will be cut into over 80 slices, each with a little bit of skin, and served with shredded leek or spring onion (cucumber is a more recent arrival). And pickles can add a nice little difference. These traditions inspired our 'at home Peking duck' – which is convenient because making Peking duck the traditional way is a three-day process of drying, glazing, pumping up the duck with a bicycle pump to help the skin separate from the flesh, and roasting! Ideally, it also requires a Peking duck from Nanjing. Yummy, yes; easy and quick, no!

SERVES: 4 (MAKES 12 PANCAKES) **PREP:** 20 MINS **COOKING:** 20 MINS

4 × 200 g duck breast fillets
finely grated zest and juice of 1 small orange
2 tablespoons hoisin sauce, plus extra to serve
½ teaspoon Chinese five spice
12 store-bought Asian pancakes (see TIPS)
½ bunch spring onions, white and dark green parts shredded into strips
½ bunch coriander, leaves picked

QUICK CUCUMBER PICKLE

2 Lebanese cucumbers
1 long red chilli, thinly sliced (optional)
2 star anise
1 garlic clove, crushed
2 tablespoons black vinegar
2 tablespoons light soy sauce
2 teaspoons caster sugar
½ teaspoon sesame oil

Preheat the oven to 240°C/220°C fan-forced (the high temperature helps to render the fat). Line a baking tray with foil.

Pat the duck dry with paper towel and use a sharp knife to score the skin on an angle at 5 mm intervals. Set aside.

Pour the orange juice into a small saucepan and simmer over medium heat for 4 minutes or until reduced by half. Transfer to a large heatproof bowl and set aside to cool slightly.

Add the hoisin, five spice and orange zest to the reduced orange juice and stir to combine. Add the scored duck breasts and toss to coat. Transfer to the prepared tray, skin-side up, and roast for 12 minutes or until the fat has rendered, the sauce is sticky and the duck is cooked through. Set aside, uncovered, to rest for 5 minutes.

It's now time to make the cucumber pickle. Halve the cucumbers lengthways and use a teaspoon to remove the seeds. Slice the cucumber diagonally into slices. Place in a bowl with the remaining pickle ingredients and stir until the sugar has dissolved. Set aside for 5 minutes.

Warm your pancakes in the microwave for 15 seconds. Slice the duck and serve with the pancakes, pickled cucumber, shredded spring onion, coriander and extra hoisin sauce.

TIPS

To save time, buy a roast Peking duck from your Asian butcher and ask them to slice it and remove the bones for you.

Asian pancakes are available from Asian grocers. If unavailable, try using soft tacos or make some crepes at home.

CHICKEN & CASHEW NUT STIR-FRY WITH SUGAR SNAP PEAS

Contender for the dullest intro in this book #4:

Chicken and cashew nut stir-fry is a classic Chinese dish often served at takeaway restaurants, and it has also been absorbed into Thai cuisine. The slight crunch of the cashew nuts works perfectly with the tender chicken and slightly sweet and salty sauce.

SERVES: 4 PREP: 15 MINS COOKING: 10 MINS

500 g chicken thigh fillets, cut into 3 cm pieces
1 tablespoon cornflour
1 tablespoon peanut or vegetable oil
1 brown onion, halved, cut into thin wedges
2 garlic cloves, finely chopped
200 g sugar snap peas, sliced in half diagonally, smaller ones left whole
100 g baby corn, halved lengthways
110 g (⅔ cup) roasted unsalted cashews
steamed rice, to serve

SAUCE

2 tablespoons light soy sauce
2 tablespoons oyster sauce
1 tablespoon Shaoxing rice wine or dry sherry
2 teaspoons cornflour
1 teaspoon yellow rock sugar, ground using a mortar and pestle (or raw caster sugar)
⅛ teaspoon ground white pepper

To make the sauce, place all the ingredients in a small bowl, add 125 ml (½ cup) water and stir to combine.

Combine the chicken and cornflour in a bowl and toss to lightly coat.

Heat the oil in a large frying pan or wok over medium–high heat. Add the chicken and cook, tossing, for 5 minutes or until golden and cooked through. Transfer to a bowl.

Add the onion and garlic to the pan and cook, stirring, for 2 minutes or until starting to colour.

Add the sugar snaps and baby corn and cook, stirring, for a further 2 minutes. Pour in the sauce and cook for 1 minute or until starting to thicken.

Return the chicken to the pan and toss to combine. Stir through the cashews and serve with steamed rice.

TIP

Replace the cashews with peanuts, swap out the corn for red capsicum pieces, and add a handful of dried and roasted red chillies for a simple twist that takes chicken and cashews halfway to kung pao chicken. To refine it further, replace the oyster sauce with a mix of hoisin and black vinegar.

CHARGRILLED PRAWNS WITH XO BUTTER

XO sauce is a rich and complex Chinese sauce made from dried scallops, shrimps, smoked Chinese ham and chilli. Invented in Hong Kong in the last days of disco, it was designed to be something decadent and obviously expensive to slather on your lobster. Its name even comes from the brandy classification in the hope that this would add extra kudos. Making your own XO is both time-consuming and expensive, so I buy it in jars from fancier supermarkets or Asian grocers. It's still pretty darn tasty, as you'll find out when you make this recipe! Mixing XO sauce with butter was the inspired brainwave of Karlie Verkerk who helped me develop all these Chinese recipes. Watch her star rise.

SERVES: 4 **PREP:** 15 MINS **COOKING:** 5 MINS

150 g unsalted butter, chopped
95 g (⅓ cup) XO sauce (see TIPS)
2 garlic cloves, crushed
1 tablespoon fish sauce
juice of 1 lemon, plus extra lemon wedges to serve
⅛ teaspoon ground white pepper
1.5 kg unpeeled green king prawns
½ bunch coriander, leaves picked and coarsely chopped

Place the butter in a microwave-safe bowl and heat on medium for 30 seconds or until just melted. (Alternatively, melt in a small saucepan over low heat.) Add the XO sauce, garlic, fish sauce, lemon juice and pepper and whisk with a fork to combine. Set aside to cool slightly.

Preheat a barbecue grill or large chargrill pan over medium–high heat. Use a sharp knife to cut along the back of each prawn through the shell. Remove the vein and discard, then use the palm of your hand to lightly flatten out the prawns. Place in a shallow dish.

Pour half the XO butter mixture over the prawns and toss to coat. Lay the prawns, flesh-side down, on the grill and cook for 2 minutes or until the flesh is opaque and the prawns have nice char marks. Use tongs to turn the prawns over and brush with more XO butter. Cook for a further 1 minute or until the shells have turned bright orange. Immediately remove from the heat and arrange on a serving plate.

Drizzle over the remaining XO butter, top with coriander and serve with lemon wedges.

TIPS

Make the XO butter ahead of time and store in a jar in the fridge. Simply transfer to a microwave-safe bowl and melt in the microwave for 30 seconds before using.

There are many uses for leftover XO sauce:

- *Use a dollop to add intense flavour to grilled salmon, brussels sprouts or any other green vegetables.*
- *Stir XO generously through clams, wok-steamed with Shaoxing rice wine, along with spring onion, red chilli and thinly sliced (top and tailed) snow peas or sugar snaps. Serve with steamed rice.*
- *Once on the* MasterChef *set I mixed XO sauce with a rubble of crushed toasted almonds to make a crunchy dressing for a chook salad. Arrange a bed of lettuce leaves or steamed rice on a serving platter. Top with torn meat from a bought barbecued chicken sprinkled with sliced spring onion, torn coriander, fried slices of lap cheong sausage and rings of red chilli. Drizzle over the XO dressing and top with a zig-zag of Kewpie mayonnaise. It actually looks like you've gone to some effort to make dinner!*

SOUP DUMPLINGS?!?

FILLED WITH GINGER, PORK &, MAGICALLY, SOUP – OBVIOUSLY!

The Chinese are the masters of the impossible when it comes to food. I mean, how could you pipe soup into a xiao long bao dumpling without it spilling out? Usually, making Chinese soup dumplings is a bit of a palaver but this cheat's version makes the process a whole lot easier – especially if you enlist the whole family to form their own dumplings! The secret is using an ice-cube tray to set the filling.

The pay-off is placing one of these dumplings on a spoon, biting into the silky skin at the side near the top and sucking out the piping-hot soup before popping the entire thing in your mouth. *Beware:* this age-old technique was developed after countless foolish tourists tried to eat a dumpling in one bite, scalding their mouths on the sizzling soup inside! Luckily, this is less likely to happen with these dumplings, as there will probably only be a moderate amount of liquid inside the ones you make.

MAKES: 48 PREP: 45 MINS (PLUS 45 MINS COOLING & SETTING)
(Less if you get the whole family involved to help you fold!) COOKING: 15 MINS

2 titanium-strength gelatine sheets
250 ml (1 cup) chicken stock
1 tablespoon light soy sauce
48 fresh gow gee wrappers

PORK FILLING

250 g pork mince (not lean)
3 spring onions, white part only, finely chopped
1 garlic clove, crushed
1 tablespoon finely grated ginger
1 teaspoon light soy sauce
1 teaspoon Shaoxing rice wine or dry sherry
1 teaspoon sesame oil
⅛ teaspoon ground white pepper

DIPPING SAUCE

2 tablespoons light soy sauce
2 tablespoons black vinegar
2 teaspoons Chinese-style chilli oil, such as chiu chow (optional)
3 cm knob of ginger, peeled and thinly sliced into matchsticks

Place the gelatine sheets in a bowl of cold water and set aside for 5 minutes until soft.

Pour the chicken stock and soy sauce into a small saucepan over medium heat. Bring to a simmer, then remove from the heat. Use your hands to squeeze the excess water from the gelatine. Add the gelatine to the stock mixture and stir until dissolved. Transfer to a jug and set aside for 15 minutes to cool completely.

To make the pork filling, combine all the ingredients in a bowl.

Place four 12-hole ice-cube trays on a baking tray. Fill each hole with 1 teaspoon of the filling, then pour over enough cooled chicken stock mixture to just cover the filling. Cover with plastic wrap and place in the fridge for 30 minutes or until the stock has set.

To make the dipping sauce, combine all the ingredients in a small bowl.

Remove one ice-cube tray from the fridge. Place a gow gee wrapper on a flat surface. Use a teaspoon to carefully remove one block of filling from the tray and place in the centre of the wrapper. Dip your finger in water and lightly wet the edge of the wrapper. Holding the wrapper and filling in one hand, use your forefinger and thumb to pleat the wrapper in a circular motion to completely enclose the filling. Pinch the pleats together in the centre of the dumpling to seal. Set aside and repeat with the remaining wrappers and filling.

Bring a large saucepan of water to the boil. Working in batches, place the dumplings in a steamer basket lined with baking paper, leaving some space between each dumpling. Carefully set it over the saucepan, then cover and steam for 3 minutes or until the filling feels soupy and the wrappers are opaque.

Serve the dumplings with the dipping sauce. Remember: the soup filling will be piping hot!

TIPS

You can make the filling a day or two in advance to help save time. When it's time for dinner, simply remove the ice-cube trays from the fridge and assemble the dumplings.

If you're on a roll, make extra dumplings and freeze them in an airtight container – they will keep for up to 6 months. Steam for 8–10 minutes from frozen.

BARBECUED RUMP WITH PIMPED-UP BLACK BEAN SAUCE & CHARRED BROCCOLINI

It was once rather well argued that Peking duck pancakes and a bottle of good pinot should be Australia's national dish, given that the Chinese and Europeans were among the first new settlers of the colonial era. I'd like to suggest a slightly more down-to-earth suburban alternative – beef and black bean with beer (or tea for the teetotallers out there). After all, beef and black bean, along with sweet and sour, and chicken and cashew, make up the holy trinity of the great Australo–Chinese* takeaway. By enlisting the barbecue for the rump steak, I feel we've taken beef and black bean even deeper into the Australian psyche, with the saltiness of the black bean sauce making the perfect marinade.

Ed: Did you make this word up ...?!

Me: Yup! Sounds suitably anthropological, doesn't it?

Ed: No ... it just sounds like you made it up.

Some very small-print background on Sino-Australian relations in the fledgling colonies and birth of the first Chinese restaurants ...

Maybe while sharing a meal like this, we could paper over such unpleasant cracks in the friendship between those of European and Chinese heritage, such as the White Australia Policy and the discrimination of the gold-rush years, as Chinese miners arrived at New Gold Mountain hoping to make their fortune – or at least a little money to send home to people who'd clubbed together to pay their passage to the new Victorian gold rush.

Once at the diggings, fear and hatred fostered by misunderstandings of culture and language saw tensions spring up almost immediately, as the Chinese sunk their round pits alongside the square-cornered pits of the Europeans. Chinese superstition dictated demons lurked in corners; however, the real demons at the diggings were their fellow miners and the government that represented them. In 1855, the *Act to Make Provision for Certain Immigrants* levied a £10 arrival tax on Chinese miners arriving by sea. This meant new arrivals too poor to pay had to walk from Robe in South Australia to Bendigo, Ballarat and Beechworth with their pick and shovel. The Act also specified extra taxes to be paid by any Chinese people residing on the goldfields. This legislation did little to calm the anti-Chinese sentiment at the diggings. After a vicious riot where 100 of the 700 European miners in the Buckland Valley tried to drive 2000 Chinese miners out of their camp, anti-Chinese leagues rose in other Victorian goldfields and in New South Wales.

There were other demons at the diggings, too. Ned Kelly's right-hand man and Cantonese speaker, Joe Byrne, and his best friend and eventual betrayer, Aaron Sherritt, regularly smoked opium with Chinese miners along the Woolshed Valley outside of Beechworth. Many of the Chinese arrivals, whether coming from the fading Californian gold rush or direct from China, earned a living not mining but by establishing market gardens, catching and drying fish, selling opium or even setting up Chinese cook shops to feed the rag-tag diaspora panning, digging and sluicing for gold. I like to think that something good came from these ugly early days: what would eventually become Australia's love of the suburban Chinese restaurant.

SERVES: 4 PREP: 15 MINS (PLUS 10 MINS MARINATING) COOKING: 15 MINS

125 ml (½ cup) black bean sauce
1 tablespoon fermented chilli bean paste, such as doubanjiang (or gochujang or sriracha)
2 teaspoons brown sugar
3 cm knob of ginger, peeled and finely grated
2 garlic cloves, crushed
⅛ teaspoon ground white pepper
2 × 400 g beef rump steaks
2 bunches broccolini, woody ends trimmed
1 bunch spring onions, white parts only, cut into 10 cm lengths
3 teaspoons sesame oil
¼ teaspoon sea salt
1 tablespoon sesame seeds

Place the black bean sauce, chilli bean paste, sugar, ginger, garlic and pepper in a large glass or ceramic bowl and stir to combine. Remove 60 ml (¼ cup) of the sauce and reserve for later.

Add the steaks to the bowl and toss until well coated. Cover and set aside to marinate for 10 minutes; this also allows time for your steaks to come to room temperature.

Place the broccolini and spring onion in a bowl, drizzle with 2 teaspoons of the sesame oil, season with salt and toss to coat.

Preheat a barbecue grill or chargrill pan over medium–high heat. Chargrill the steaks for about 4 minutes each side for medium. You will need to check the steaks while they cook, as the cooking time will depend on the thickness of the steaks, their core temperature when they hit the barbecue and the heat of the grill.

It's done! Huge pat on the back for correctly cooking the steak, given the dizzying world of variables. Transfer to a plate and set aside, uncovered, to rest for 5 minutes.

While your steaks rest, grill the broccolini and spring onion mixture for 2 minutes or until lightly charred and cooked to your liking. Transfer to a bowl. Sprinkle with sesame seeds, drizzle with the remaining sesame oil and toss to coat.

Cut the steaks into 2 cm thick slices and serve with the charred broccolini and spring onion, and reserved black bean sauce drizzled over the steak.

VEGETARIAN MAPO TOFU WITH CRISPY LENTILS

Here's another hot and numbing classic from the Sichuan province. While you would normally find it made with pork mince, this recipe uses black lentils instead for a delicious vegetarian version.

SERVES: 4 PREP: 15 MINS COOKING: 45 MINS

105 g (½ cup) dried black lentils
2 tablespoons peanut or vegetable oil
1 tablespoon Sichuan peppercorns, toasted, ground using a mortar and pestle
1 tablespoon cornflour
4 large shiitake mushrooms, finely chopped
3 garlic cloves, crushed
3 cm knob of ginger, peeled and finely grated
6 spring onions, white part finely chopped, dark green part thinly sliced
2 tablespoons fermented chilli bean paste, such as doubanjiang (or gochujang or sriracha)
1 tablespoon light soy sauce
2 teaspoons dried chilli flakes (optional)
1 teaspoon yellow rock sugar, ground using a mortar and pestle (or raw caster sugar)
800 g firm silken tofu, cut into 2 cm cubes
1½ tablespoons Chinese-style chilli oil, such as chiu chow (see TIPS)
steamed rice, to serve

Cook the lentils in a large saucepan of boiling water for 30 minutes or until soft. Drain well.

Heat half the oil in a large deep frying pan over medium–high heat. Add the cooked lentils and fry for 4–5 minutes or until crispy. Add half the ground Sichuan pepper and stir to combine. Transfer to a bowl and set aside.

Place the cornflour in a bowl or jug and gradually add 375 ml (1½ cups) water, stirring constantly until smooth.

Heat the remaining oil in the same frying pan over medium heat. Add the mushroom and cook, stirring occasionally, for 3 minutes or until soft and starting to brown. Add the garlic, ginger and white part of the spring onion and cook for a further 2 minutes. Add the chilli bean paste, soy sauce, chilli flakes (if using), sugar and remaining Sichuan pepper and toss to combine. Reduce the heat to low and add the cornflour mixture. Cook, stirring, for 3 minutes or until the sauce has thickened.

Add the tofu to the pan, being careful not to break up the cubes. Remove from the heat and use a spatula to gently mix it into the sauce. Set aside for 2 minutes or until the tofu is warmed through.

Transfer the tofu mixture to a serving bowl and top with the crispy lentils and the dark green parts of the spring onion. Drizzle with the chilli oil and serve immediately with steamed rice.

TIPS

For a meaty version of this recipe, replace the mushrooms with 250 g pork or chicken mince.

If you can't find chiu chow chilli oil, substitute 1 finely chopped bird's eye chilli.

SPRING ONION PANCAKES

These simple pancakes are the extra touch that takes dinner from fine to fabulous – and they are so simple even a child could make them. In fact, enlist their help and your prep time for this recipe drops to virtually nothing at all.

MAKES: 4 PREP: 20 MINS (PLUS 30 MINS RESTING) COOKING: 10 MINS

300 g (2 cups) plain flour, plus extra for dusting and sprinkling
¼ teaspoon sea salt, plus extra to serve
160 ml (⅔ cup) just-boiled water
2 tablespoons sesame oil
2–3 spring onions, white and dark green parts thinly sliced
2 tablespoons vegetable oil

Combine the flour and salt in a bowl. Pour in the just-boiling water and stir with chopsticks or a spoon until the flour forms small clumps. Turn out onto a lightly floured surface and knead for 5 minutes or until smooth and elastic. Or better still, use your electric mixer with the dough hook for this. Return the dough to the bowl, cover with plastic wrap and set aside to rest for 30 minutes.

Cut the dough into quarters. On a lightly floured surface, roll out one portion to a 2 mm thick rectangle. Brush the dough with 2 teaspoons sesame oil, then sprinkle with one-quarter of the spring onion and 1 teaspoon extra flour.

Roll the pastry into a long cigar, then coil into a snail. Flatten slightly with the palm of your hand or a rolling pin to create a 15 cm pancake that is about 1 cm thick.

Repeat with the remaining dough, sesame oil, spring onion and extra flour.

Heat half the vegetable oil in a large non-stick frying pan over medium–high heat. Add two pancakes and cook for 2–3 minutes each side or until golden and flaky. Remove from the pan and drain on paper towel. Cover loosely with foil to keep warm (we don't want them to go soggy). Repeat with the remaining oil and pancakes. Sprinkle with extra salt and serve hot.

STEAMED CHINESE BUNS

PREPARE IN 20 MINUTES

This style of Chinese bread has become jolly fashionable over the last few years, and while you can always buy the dough pre-packaged at a Chinese grocer if you've got one nearby, it's fun to make your own – and actually not too hard. See it as another skill you can put on your CV ... *60 wpm typing, speaks basic Finnish ('anna minulle työtä'), can make steamed Chinese buns*. If I was hiring you'd get the job (or, in a language you'd understand ... 'sinulla on työtä!).

MAKES: 8–10 PREP: 20 MINS (PLUS 1 HOUR 50 MINS PROVING) COOKING: 10 MINS

1 × 7 g sachet dried instant yeast
2¼ tablespoons caster sugar
265 g (1¾ cups) plain flour, plus extra for dusting
½ teaspoon fine salt
1 tablespoon vegetable oil
½ teaspoon baking powder

Place the yeast, 1 teaspoon of the sugar and 185 ml (¾ cup) lukewarm water in the bowl of an electric mixer fitted with the dough hook. Mix until just combined, then set aside for 5 minutes or until the yeast has activated and become foamy.

Add the flour, salt, oil and remaining sugar and knead on medium speed for 5–8 minutes or until the dough is smooth and elastic and starts to come away from the side of the bowl. Add a little extra flour if the dough is still sticky. (Alternatively, you can make the dough by hand on a lightly floured surface.)

Cover the bowl with a damp tea towel and place in a warm, draught-free place for 1–1½ hours or until the dough triples in size.

Punch down the dough and turn out onto a lightly floured surface. Sprinkle over the baking powder and knead for 5 minutes or until well combined.

Shape the dough into a 5 cm thick log, then cut crossways into eight to ten 3 cm wide buns. Place each bun on a small rectangle of baking paper. Cover with a tea towel and set aside for a further 15 minutes to rise and double in size.

Depending on the size of your steamer basket you may need to cook the buns in batches. If you have multiple large bamboo steamers, you can stack them. Place the buns in a steamer over a saucepan of simmering water and steam for 8–10 minutes or until soft and fluffy.

TIPS

Try different shapes with your buns – you can roll them into balls if you prefer.

These buns are perfect filled with crispy pork belly, sliced cucumber, shredded spring onion and drizzled with hoisin.

CLAYPOT MUSHROOMS WITH TOFU

[INTRO 1 – for smart, soulful people]

The oldest cooking pots ever found are Chinese. These sandpots, or 'keng', were previously found dating from 8000 BCE, but in 2012 a shard of an unglazed sandpot, scorched from being used over a fire, was dated as being over 19,000 years old! This suggests that cooking Chinese stews like this one date back to a prehistoric time before the rise of settlements and civilisation; a time when our distant ancestors were still hunters and gatherers. No wonder this dish is so comforting, as it speaks to our primeval soul and a time when mushrooms were gathered by hand and huge herds of wild tofu were hunted down across the wide savannah plains.

[INTRO 2 – for the script of the afternoon cooking series based on this book]

Claypot dishes are the original Chinese version of a one-pot wonder! So let's cook one!!!!

SERVES: 4 PREP: 10 MINS COOKING: 25 MINS

1 tablespoon cornflour
2 tablespoons light soy sauce
2 tablespoons oyster sauce
2 teaspoons Shaoxing rice wine or dry sherry
1 teaspoon sesame oil
1 teaspoon caster sugar
½ teaspoon ground white pepper
400 g mixed mushrooms (such as shiitake, wood ear, king brown, oyster and enoki; see TIPS)
300 g firm tofu, cut into 2 cm cubes
5 cm knob of ginger, peeled and sliced into thin batons
4 spring onions, white part only, thinly sliced

RICE BASE

400 g (2 cups) jasmine rice, rinsed and drained
500 ml (2 cups) salt-reduced vegetable stock
1 tablespoon vegetable or peanut oil
½ teaspoon sea salt

Combine the cornflour, soy sauce, oyster sauce, Shaoxing rice wine, sesame oil, sugar and pepper in a bowl. Stir through the mushrooms and tofu and set aside.

For the rice base, combine all the ingredients in a 4-litre claypot or flameproof casserole dish with a lid.

Pour the mushroom and tofu mixture over the rice base and arrange in an even layer. Scatter over the ginger and half the spring onion, then cover with the lid.

Place over medium–high heat and cook for 5 minutes. Reduce the heat to the lowest possible setting and cook for a further 20 minutes or until the rice is cooked and the mushrooms are tender.

Remove the lid, scatter over the remaining spring onion and serve.

TIPS

If you can't find fresh shiitake or wood ear mushrooms, simply buy dried ones and rehydrate in hot water for 15 minutes.

This mushroom dish goes perfectly with stir-fried veggies, such as bok choy or Chinese broccoli.

CHAR SIU PORK CUTLETS WITH SPECIAL FRIED RICE & LAP CHEONG

Char siu is a ruddy sauce containing five spice, hoisin, soy sauce, honey and fermented tofu, and it's perfect as a Chinese-style marinade on any cut of pork. It also goes insanely well with tumblers of whisky. You have been warned.

Ed: Should we warn people they need to think about the rice a day ahead?

Me: That would be a good idea, as they have to use day-old rice for the fried rice.

SERVES: 4 PREP: 15 MINS (PLUS 15 MINS MARINATING) COOKING: 15 MINS

60 ml (¼ cup) char siu sauce
1 garlic clove, crushed
¼ teaspoon sea salt
4 × 200 g pork cutlets or chops
vegetable oil, for brushing

OMELETTE

2 eggs
½ teaspoon sesame oil
¼ teaspoon sea salt
⅛ teaspoon ground white pepper

FRIED RICE

1 tablespoon peanut oil
2 lap cheong sausages, thinly sliced (see TIPS)
3 spring onions, white and dark green parts separated, thinly sliced
55 g (⅓ cup) frozen peas
2 garlic cloves, minced
495 g (3 cups) cooked long-grain brown rice, chilled overnight on a tray
55 g (1 cup) bean sprouts
1½ tablespoons oyster sauce
2 teaspoons light soy sauce
2 teaspoons sesame oil
⅛ teaspoon ground white pepper

Combine the char siu sauce, garlic and salt in a large bowl, add the pork and toss to coat evenly. Cover and set aside to marinate for 15 minutes, or up to 2 hours in the fridge if you have time.

Preheat a barbecue grill or chargrill pan over medium–high heat. Brush the pan with vegetable oil. Add the pork and cook for 3 minutes on one side. Baste with any marinade left in the bowl, then flip over and cook for a further 3 minutes until just cooked pink. Transfer to a plate and rest, uncovered, for 5 minutes.

While your meat is resting, make the omelette. Whisk together all the ingredients in a small bowl. Heat a large non-stick frying pan over medium heat. Pour in half the egg mixture and swirl to coat the base. Cook for 1 minute, then flip over and cook for a further 1 minute. Remove from the pan and roll up, then slice at 5 mm intervals to create 'ribbons'. Repeat with the remaining egg mixture.

Now make the fried rice. Pour the peanut oil into the frying pan and return to high heat. Add the lap cheong and cook for 1 minute or until starting to colour. Add the white part of the spring onion, peas and garlic and cook for 1 minute or until the garlic and spring onion begin to soften. Add the rice, bean sprouts, oyster sauce, soy sauce, sesame oil, pepper, omelette ribbons and dark green part of the spring onion and toss gently to combine.

Thickly slice the pork. Divide the fried rice among serving bowls and top with the pork. Serve straight away.

TIPS

You could replace the lap cheong with mini pepperoni sticks, but I actually think cubed fried spam swerves the rice in a very trad' suburban takeaway way. Though, quite frankly, as sweet lap cheong sausage is so long-lasting (unopened in its packaging), there is no excuse not to have it in your fridge at all times. Try it fried and tossed with peanuts and cucumber with a splash of black vinegar as a snack; chopped and stir-fried with Chinese greens; or fried in crispy-edged chunks to stir through egg noodles, along with eggs beaten with parmesan and a little soy sauce for a Chinese take on carbonara that also symbolises long life.

Buy a rice cooker – it will change your life. They are cheaper than a decent bottle of chardonnay but last far, far longer.

KARLIE'S FIVE SPICE ROAST PORK BELLY WITH STICKY CHILLI BEAN SAUCE

This crispy pork belly of Karlie's is a definite crowd pleaser, especially when it's roasted with fragrant Chinese five spice and tossed through a sticky, sweet and spicy sauce. I think it's about the best way to eat pork belly, but then I'm not a fan of that jellied belly you see in some claypots; it's got to have crunch and give. It's just so cool that she's lent this recipe to me! Thanks Karls!

SERVES: 4 PREP: 15 MINS COOKING: 55 MINS

800 g pork belly, unscored
boiling water
1 teaspoon coarse sea salt
2½ teaspoons Chinese five spice
2 teaspoons peanut or vegetable oil
4 spring onions, white part only, finely chopped
60 ml (¼ cup) honey
2 tablespoons fermented chilli bean paste, such as doubanjiang (or gochujang or sriracha)
1 tablespoon oyster sauce
3 celery stalks, sliced diagonally
1 long red chilli, thinly sliced (optional)
Spring onion pancakes or Steamed Chinese buns (see pages 28 and 29), to serve (see TIP)

Preheat the oven to 220°C/200°C fan-forced. Boil a kettle of water.

Place the pork belly in a colander and pour the boiling water over the rind. Allow to cool, then pat dry with paper towel. The drier the skin, the better the crackling.

Use a sharp knife to score the rind lengthways at 3 cm intervals, then repeat crossways to create a criss-cross pattern. Use your hands to rub the salt and 2 teaspoons of the five spice into the pork rind and meat.

Place the pork on a wire rack over a baking tray and roast for 45–50 minutes or until the skin is crispy. Remove from the oven and cut into squares (using the criss-cross pattern as a guide).

Heat a large wok or frying pan over medium heat. Add the oil, spring onion and remaining five spice and cook for 1 minute or until starting to colour. Add the honey, chilli bean paste and oyster sauce and stir to combine. Remove from the heat. Add the chopped pork belly and toss to coat in the sauce until sticky and glossy.

Transfer the pork to a serving bowl and top with the celery and sliced chilli (if using).

Serve with spring onion pancakes or steamed Chinese buns.

TIP

If you are short on time, you can buy spring onion pancakes and Chinese buns at Asian supermarkets.

STUPIDLY QUICK XO PIPIS WITH CRISPY HONG KONG RICE CAKE

One day on the set of *MasterChef*, I remember that Gary was hungry – he usually is – and we only had a 15-minute break in filming, so George and I improvised this dish to keep him (and us) happy. Using two pans meant a little more mess, but it made everything much faster so we were ready to film before 'the slate went in'. It just lacked something carby to take it from a flavour-packed snack to a fully fledged dinner. Enter the crispy noodle cake, which is how they serve their famous XO pipis at Golden Century in Sydney.

After you've picked the flesh from the shellfish, the noodles will be deliciously dressed in all the juices and leftover sauce. Also, you'll get the strangely alluring result of 'fried stuff that's been soaked in sauce' that's much loved in culinary cultures, such as Mexican and Chinese. I've used Hong Kong-style egg noodles as that's in keeping with where XO is originally from, but rice vermicelli or even two-minute noodles would be fine. The citrus, almonds, wet-crunch water chestnuts and herbs are hardly traditional, but I think they do wonders, lightening the richness of the XO and adding a welcome freshness.

BTW, Golden Century has its own role in the *MasterChef* saga. We were regulars when living in Sydney to film the show. I could tell you many stories from our nights there, but there was one memorable occasion when one of us judges unknowingly (to him, but not to our table and everyone else in the restaurant) headed into the Ladies and didn't come out again for at least 20 minutes, totally shaken. He'd only realised his mistake after he was ensconced in a stall, and then he was too scared to leave. I think we might have applauded when he eventually emerged. The embarrassment was compounded by the fact that this was one of our first dinners with Heston Blumenthal, and we were all desperate to impress him.

SERVES: 4 PREP: 20 MINS COOKING: 20 MINS

110 g flaked almonds
3 tablespoons peanut or vegetable oil
1 × 227 g can sliced water chestnuts
175 g lap cheong sausage, sliced into coins
1 bunch flat-leaf parsley, leaves coarsely chopped, stalks finely chopped
6 spring onions, white part cut into coins, dark green part thinly sliced
2 tablespoons XO sauce
finely grated zest and juice of 1 lemon, plus extra wedges to serve
finely grated zest and juice of 1 orange
200 g dried thin egg vermicelli noodles, reconstituted according to the packet instructions, drained
1 white onion, thinly sliced
1 kg pipis or clams, cleaned and purged (see TIP, page 158)
75 ml Shaoxing rice wine, mirin or dry sherry
½ bunch mint, leaves picked and coarsely chopped

PAN 1: Place the almonds in a large dry frying pan (or wok) over medium heat and cook, tossing frequently, for 5 minutes or until toasted. Remove and set aside.

PAN 2: At the same time, heat 1 tablespoon of the oil in a large frying pan (or wok) over high heat. Add the water chestnuts, lap cheong, chopped parsley stalks and the white part of the spring onion and cook, stirring often, for 2 minutes or until the lap cheong starts to colour and the spring onion has softened. Transfer to a bowl and set aside. Hold onto the pan and the oil in the bottom – we'll use it again soon.

Combine the XO sauce, lemon juice, orange juice, half the orange zest and toasted almonds in a bowl.

PAN 1: Heat the remaining oil over high heat. Add the noodles to cover the base of the pan and press down with a spatula so you end up with a noodle cake. Cook for 5 minutes or until the bottom is golden and crispy, then flip the cake over and cook the other side for 5 minutes. When it is just turning crispy and golden, turn off the heat.

PAN 2: While the noodle cake is cooking, reheat the oil in the other pan over medium heat. Add the onion and cook, stirring, for 5 minutes or until softened. Increase the heat to medium–high and throw in the pipis or clams, along with the Shaoxing rice wine (beware of dramatic flare-ups!). Toss the pan like you're a pro with a lovely rolling motion for 3–5 minutes until the pipis open. Discard any unopened pipis or clams, then add a little of the nutty XO mixture, along with the water chestnut mixture. Scatter with the chopped parsley leaves and mint and gently toss to combine.

PAN 1: Flip out the hot noodle cake onto a warmed serving plate. Top with the pipis mixture and sprinkle over the lemon zest, remaining orange zest and dark green part of the spring onion. Serve with lemon wedges and the remaining XO mixture on the side for pouring over the noodle cake.

HONG KONG CUSTARD TARTS

Among the lard biscuits, superbly bouncy disco-light jellies and oddly set almond milk cubes of the final yum cha trolley of the day, these 'daan tarts' have always been far and away the best pick. And, like they say, you'll always remember your first. Mine was at Hong Kong's original Tai Cheong Bakery, way before it was a chain. It had soul back then, and you would time your run so you'd get there as they appeared warm and just-set from the oven; nothing else could come close.

In those days, no true lad from Central or Wan Chai would even look at one of those imposter Portuguese ones imported fresh each day from Macau, as these daan tarts were as much a part of Hong Kong as char siu bao, skinny double-decker trams, Jackie Chan movies, punting at Happy Valley and the legendary rudeness of the waiters at the Luk Yu Teahouse.

I tasked resident cake whisperer Kate (aka 'Q') with recreating these platonic archetypes from my memory. She insisted that to be true (and as light as the originals) they should be made with two different pastries. You could, I suppose, speed up the process dramatically by just using store-bought frozen sweet shortcrust pastry, but then that would be the sort of labour-saving shortcut a chain might be tempted to do. So don't.

MAKES: 12 **PREP:** 1 HOUR (PLUS 50 MINS RESTING) **COOKING:** 35 MINS

80 ml (⅓ cup) boiling water
80 g caster sugar
125 ml (½ cup) milk
2 eggs
1 egg yolk
½ teaspoon vanilla extract
½ teaspoon white vinegar

WATER DOUGH
150 g (1 cup) plain flour, plus extra for dusting
1 tablespoon caster sugar
2 egg yolks
1 teaspoon lemon juice

BUTTER DOUGH
150 g (1 cup) plain flour, sifted
180 g chilled butter, chopped

To make the water dough, blitz the flour and sugar in a food processor until combined. Add the egg yolks, lemon juice and 2½ tablespoons water and blitz until the dough just comes together. Turn out onto a lightly floured surface and knead into a smooth ball. Wrap in plastic wrap and place in the fridge to rest for about 30 minutes.

Now make your butter dough. Blitz the flour and butter in your food processor until a smooth ball forms. Wrap in plastic wrap and rest in the fridge for about 20 minutes.

While your doughs are resting, place the boiling water and sugar in a bowl and stir until the sugar has dissolved. Set aside to cool.

On a well-floured surface, roll out the water dough to a 30 cm × 20 cm rectangle. Quickly roll out the butter dough to roughly the same size. Place the butter dough on top of the water dough then, with a short side nearest to you, fold the dough into thirds, like a letter. Remember them? Give the dough a quarter turn clockwise and roll out gently to roughly the same size as the original rectangle. Repeat the folding and rolling two more times, flouring the work surface as you go. If the dough feels too soft at any stage, wrap it up and return to the fridge for 20 minutes. When you have finished rolling and folding, wrap the dough in plastic wrap and rest in the fridge.

When the sugar and water mixture has cooled, add the remaining ingredients, whisk until well combined, then strain twice through a fine sieve.

Preheat the oven to 190°C/170°C fan-forced. Lightly grease and flour 12 holes of a 45 ml capacity (mini) tart tin.

Roll out the pastry on a floured surface until about 3 mm thick. Using a 9 cm round cutter, cut out 12 rounds – they should be about 1 cm larger than the holes in the tin. Gently press the rounds into each hole, then pour over the custard until the pastry shells are almost full. Bake for 35 minutes (for a smoother finish, leave the oven door slightly ajar for the last 10 minutes of cooking). Give the tin a little jiggle to test that the custard is set before you remove the tarts from the oven. Serve warm.

JAPAN

One look at the map of Japan will tell you a lot about the essence of Japanese cuisine – it's a country that is mainly coastline and mountains. That means much importance is placed on the sea and all the bounty it provides, whether that's pristine seafood or seaweed to make the nori wraps for 'maki' (sushi rolls) or kombu to flavour their crucial dashi broths. Japanese cuisine is also full of overseas influences (chilli, tempura, gyoza and sushi are all claimed to have originally come from outside of Japan) that provide some funky cross-cultural culinary ideas, whether combined with the restrained elegance of imperial cuisine or the far simpler dishes served for generations from street stalls in Osaka, Tokyo and Hokkaido.

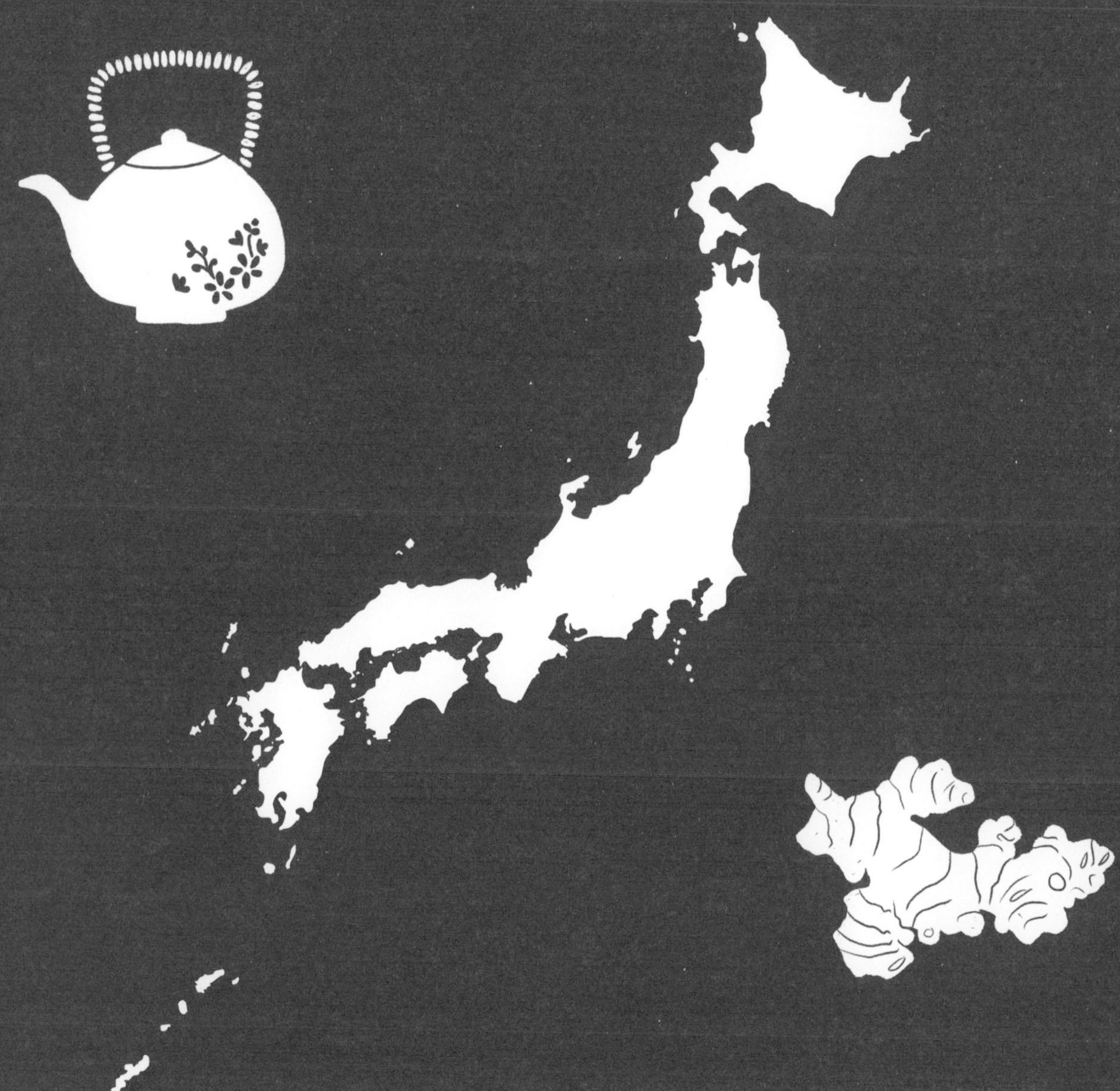

This Buddhist nation was mainly vegetarian (or at least pescatarian) for 1200 years before the Emperor decided to approve of eating meat in 1872. Since then, meat consumption has been slowly on the rise with pork being the big seller – in large part thanks to tonkatsu (see page 53) – from the 1920s onwards and an explosion of popularity after World War II. Pork sells more than all the beef (including the expensive and heavily fat-marbled wagyu) and every bit of the chicken, including knee and hip cartilage, combined. NB: As well as an obsession with seasonality and crisp new money, the Japanese have also taken the no waste/eat everything approach, like the French and Chinese.

Rice, largely short-grain and the now increasingly popular unpolished brown 'genmai' rice, is the lead staple, with noodles, such as buckwheat soba and wheat-based udon, also holding their place. All that coastline means that seafood is incredibly popular, with tuna, bonito, sea bream, salmon and yellowtail being the most common alongside clams, prawns, octopus, squid, eel and, a personal favourite, the creamy maritime explosion of sea urchin roe. As with all Japanese seafood, if it isn't served raw then expect to see it being barbecued, braised or occasionally fried.

The Japanese rely on the clever use of a compact selection of ingredients to create their textbook flavours, with mirin, sesame seeds, wasabi, soy sauce, miso and citrus, such as yuzu or lime, at the fore. Shiso and bonito flakes are also key, whether used as a garnish or as a flavouring.

Rice wine vinegar is crucial, especially for pickling ginger or any number of mountain veg. Introduced condiments, such as mayonnaise, brown sauce and English mustard (which was traditionally used in sushi at hand-cart stalls in the old days as wasabi was too expensive), all also feature. Additionally, panko breadcrumbs for frying are Japanese.

In the vegetable world, radishes (especially white radish/daikon), mushrooms (such as enoki and shimeji), cucumber, avocado, eggplants, cabbage, lotus root, sweet potatoes or mountain yams and soybeans (either as beans or turned into tofu or soy sauce) are common. Fruit is also prized, from the perfect persimmon or musk melon to giant strawberries and blushing peaches that are all definitely 'oishii'. (That means delicious in Japanese.) As matcha (green tea powder), black sesame and red bean dominate desserts when Western influences aren't being employed, I'd usually end a Japanese meal with little more than a fresh orange.

FAKING IT TIPS

1. Crumb it using panko breadcrumbs, then fry it and serve it with Japanese mayo and Japanese barbecue sauce (or HP) or a citrus, such as ponzu, and soy dipping sauce. If using store-bought ponzu, liven it up with extra lemon or lime juice so the soy doesn't dominate.
2. Incorporate key flavours in dishes that you are customising, so that burger might be shaped by soy-sauce-wetted hands and served in a sweet, soft bun with avocado, pickled daikon threads, ginger and a wasabi mayonnaise. Or maybe even a slaw made with these last three ingredients. Dump the melted cheese and bacon.
3. It's all about the rice. At a pinch, season it with that cheap supermarket seasoning and serve in bowls topped with something soy-seasoned and grilled, or raw fish and wasabi'd. Add pickled ginger, something green or fragrant, such as nori, shiso, fresh or frozen soybeans, avocado or chargrilled broccoli, and Japanese mayo. Basically, take your inspiration from the handroll fillings at your local sushi takeaway joint for a #blessed Japanese rice bowl.

SHOPPING LIST

If your local Japanese grocer has a specialist sushi counter, load up with fresh seafood to eat that night – after all, it's not going to get any fresher.

It's worth stocking up on flavour sprinkles, such as furikake, which is a fine seasoning combo of seaweed, salt, sugar, sesame seeds, and seven spice powder (shichimi togarashi). This is a mix of chilli, sansho (Sichuan pepper), pepper, orange peel, black and white sesame seeds, crumbled nori and sometimes hemp seeds, dried yuzu, poppy seeds or dried ginger, depending on where you are. Both furikake and seven spice powder are particularly good on rice and over-cooked meat. In both cases, check for the presence of added MSG, as the Japanese are more relaxed about its use than you might be.

Also look for unusual pickles, such as burdock root, packets of good-quality rice, posh udon and soba noodles, various miso pastes (red and white), instant dashi powders, or kombu and bonito flakes to make your own, and fancier versions of staples, such as mirin, rice wine vinegar and soy sauce. In the best sushi places in Japan the rice is never flavoured with added sugar but just gentler, high-end rice wine vinegars.

Over in the freezer aisle, grab frozen edamame (soybeans in and out of the pod), as well as a delicacy called 'mentaiko' (chillied or unspiced lobes of cod roe) that are excellent mixed with butter and a little mayo to toss through spaghetti for an almost tarama-like hit.

SCORCHED & RAW TERIYAKI POKE

Let's be frank, the Hawaiians stole the poke (po-kay) bowl from the Japanese and their original 'chirasushi' or scattered sushi, just like they stole the macadamia nut from us. So here I am stealing it back, AND making it better by combining the freshness of raw fish with the smokiness of slightly scorched salmon pieces for a more interesting poke.

Note: I suppose we have to let the Hawaiians have something, otherwise their most famous dish is Hawaiian pizza and that was actually invented by a Greek bloke in Ontario, Canada. So let's agree to leave them their spam sushi (aka musubi), gloppy poi and loco moco – a local dish of hamburger patty, fried egg and brown gravy on rice.

SERVES: 4 **PREP:** 25 MINS (PLUS 15 MINS MARINATING & 10 MINS STANDING)
COOKING: 15 MINS

- **600 g skinless salmon fillets, pin-boned (see TIPS)**
- **4 spring onions, white part very finely chopped, dark green part finely chopped**
- **1 garlic clove, crushed**
- **1 tablespoon minced ginger**
- **½ teaspoon shichimi togarashi or dried chilli flakes, plus extra to serve (optional)**
- **2 tablespoons soy sauce**
- **1½ tablespoons honey**
- **1 tablespoon sesame oil**
- **325 g (1½ cups) sushi rice, well rinsed**
- **4 baby qukes, sliced into rounds**
- **1 tablespoon rice wine vinegar**
- **1 ripe avocado, sliced**
- **1 sheet nori, shredded**

Cut the salmon into 1.5 cm cubes and place in a bowl. Add the white part of the spring onion, garlic, ginger, shichimi togarashi or chilli flakes, soy sauce, honey and 2 teaspoons of the sesame oil and toss until well combined. Set aside in this pimped-up teriyaki sauce to marinate for 15 minutes.

Meanwhile, place the rice in a saucepan, add 500 ml (2 cups) water and bring to the boil. Reduce the heat to low and simmer, covered, for 10 minutes. Remove the pan from the heat and stand, without removing the lid, for 10 minutes or until all the water has been absorbed and the rice is cooked. Stir through the dark green part of the spring onion and remaining sesame oil.

Heat a large non-stick frying pan over high heat. Add half the marinated salmon and cook, turning, for 1–2 minutes or until the sides are slightly scorched. Remove from the heat.

Toss the qukes with the vinegar in a bowl.

Divide the rice among four bowls and top with the raw salmon, scorched salmon, cucumber, avocado and shredded nori. Scatter over extra shichimi togarashi or chilli flakes, if desired, and serve.

TIPS

To take this dish to the next level add pickled ginger (homemade or store-bought) and a squirt of Kewpie, or maybe some edamame if you have them.

If buying a side of salmon use the centre of the fillet for the raw fish, then slice off the thinner outer wings and barbecue these, as they are extra decadent. Also feel free to make fish crackling – just type my name and fish crackling into Google for a recipe!

JAPANESE FRIED RICE OMELETTE

(OMURICE)

Info: Writing cookbooks is a cooperative process. I have a loose collective of far better cooks and recipe writers around me who all help shape my books profoundly. Take this recipe, for example. Marnie (aka 'M'), who's spent a lot of time in Japan over the last few years, suggested we should do one of those rolled Japanese omelettes cooked in a rectangular pan. 'A tamagotchi?' I suggest helpfully. She rolls her eyes. 'Yes, a tamagoyaki.'

'Or how about one of those decadent omelettes from Osaka, which match perfectly with beer and that I can never pronounce until after 10.30 pm. The okker one?' I suggest, unperturbed and unaware of what this says about me.

'You mean okonomiyaki,' pipes up Emma (surprisingly, because I didn't think she'd really been listening, being too excited about all the great ideas she's got for the Spanish and Mexican sections of this book).

Oh dear, so many to choose from and this is only the beginning of the minefield that is the Japanese omelette, what with that sweet breakfast tamago, adopted Korean gyeran mari and Gudetama (which isn't really an omelette – even if it looks and sounds like one – but Hello Kitty's newest chum, a lazy egg yolk).

Kate, the cake whisperer, insists that any omelette should be cooked gently so it doesn't colour. That's the way the French like it, and Kate couldn't be more French even if she was the Eiffel Tower wearing a beret and smoking Gauloises.

I just want a Japanese omelette that we can swoop fine lines of Japanese mayo and brown sauce across, and scatter over bonito flakes (like the Japanese usually do with octopus balls). I just love the way those flakes wave at me as they dance in the thermals rising off the omelette like a shoal of those mood fish you get in Christmas bon-bons. ***(Or like you are having a pretty intense flashback to that time when you dropped acid with that bloke at Meredith and you stayed up to watch the dawn break, captivated by the way the trees breathed. But that's another story for another day.)***

Then Warren, as always the oil on troubled waters – gourmet, single-estate, extra virgin olive oil of course – suggests an omurice. This is another type of Japanese omelette served on, or around, fried rice, Karlie explains (she's always supporting him). It is cooked over low heat, so it stays a delicate buttercup-yellow, and can have all the bells and whistles I want. Sorted!

SERVES: 2 **PREP:** 15 MINS **COOKING:** 20 MINS

- **60 ml (¼ cup) sunflower oil**
- **4 spring onions, white part thinly sliced, dark green part finely shredded**
- **2 garlic cloves, crushed**
- **1 tablespoon finely grated ginger**
- **2 tablespoons soy sauce**
- **1 tablespoon brown sauce or barbecue sauce, plus extra to serve**
- **300 g (2 cups) leftover cooked white rice**
- **4 eggs**
- **2 tablespoons mirin**
- **2 tablespoons Kewpie mayonnaise**
- **2 tablespoons bonito flakes**

Heat 2 tablespoons of the oil in a non-stick frying pan over medium–high heat. Add the white part of the spring onion, garlic and ginger and cook for 2–3 minutes or until soft. Add the soy sauce and brown or barbecue sauce and stir to combine. Add the rice and cook, tossing, for 2–3 minutes or until all the liquid has evaporated. Transfer the rice mixture to a heatproof bowl.

Wipe the pan clean to save on washing up. Lightly whisk the eggs and mirin in a jug until combined. Brush the pan with half the remaining oil and place over medium–low heat. Add half the egg mixture and immediately stir in the pan until small curds form. Settle the mixture and swirl around the pan to create an even layer. Reduce the heat to low and cook for another 2–3 minutes or until the top is almost set.

Add half the rice mixture in a long pile along one edge of the omelette and carefully roll it up, until the rice is completely enclosed. Set aside on a plate and repeat with the remaining oil, egg and rice mixture to make a second omelette.

Drizzle Kewpie mayo and extra brown or barbecue sauce over each omelette. Scatter with the dark green part of the spring onion and dancing bonito flakes and serve.

TIP

I'd add nuggets of char siu pork or lap cheong to this omelette, but then I'd add Chinese sausage to everything if I could.

QUICK PORK RAMEN

Ramen usually gets its deep flavour from hours of cooking with bones, bonito flakes and kombu (seaweed). In this cheat's version we've used pork rashers and stock, boosted with miso and fish sauce to achieve the rich familiar ramen flavour, with shiitake mushrooms adding a quick umami punch to the broth. For a lighter version you can use pork tenderloin. And yes, we should doff our caps to David Chang, of Momofuku fame, who opened my eyes to the beauty of untraditional ramen bases like this.

SERVES: 4 **PREP:** 15 MINS **COOKING:** 40 MINS

750 g boneless pork rashers
2 tablespoons soy sauce, plus extra to season (optional)
2 tablespoons fish sauce, plus extra to season (optional)
1 tablespoon red or white miso paste
100 ml sunflower or vegetable oil
1 bunch spring onions, white part thinly sliced, dark green part finely shredded
2 garlic cloves, finely chopped
6 cm knob of ginger, peeled, half finely chopped, half finely shredded
1 litre chicken stock
100 g shiitake mushrooms
180 g ramen noodles

Remove and discard the rind and top layer of fat from the pork rashers. Cut the rashers into 2 cm pieces and place in a bowl. Drizzle with 1 tablespoon of the soy sauce and 1 tablespoon of the fish sauce and toss to combine.

Combine the miso paste with the remaining soy sauce and fish sauce in a bowl.

Heat 2 tablespoons of the oil in a large saucepan or flameproof casserole dish over medium heat. Add half the pork and cook, turning, for 8–10 minutes or until golden and crisp. Remove the pork from the pan, and repeat with the remaining pork. Add this pork to the first cooked batch.

Add the white part of the spring onion, garlic and finely chopped ginger to the pan and cook for 2–3 minutes or until aromatic. Add the miso mixture, stock, mushrooms, 750 ml (3 cups) water and three-quarters of the pork (reserve the rest to serve). Bring to a simmer, then cover and cook for 10–15 minutes, skimming off any fat that forms on the surface. Add the noodles and cook for a further 3–4 minutes or until tender.

Meanwhile, heat the remaining oil in a small saucepan over medium–high heat. Add the shredded ginger and cook for 1–2 minutes or until golden and crisp. Drain on a plate lined with paper towel.

Season the broth with extra soy sauce and fish sauce, if desired, then ladle into four serving bowls. Top with the reserved pork and garnish with the dark green part of the spring onion and crispy ginger.

TIP

Get ahead and make the broth to the point just before you add the noodles, then freeze in an airtight container for up to 3 months. Thaw overnight in the fridge and reheat, then add the noodles and cook until tender.

BLACK SESAME SOBA NOODLE SALAD

(FOR VALLI)

This noodle salad is like the Japanese take on satay noodles but with wasabi peas for some surprise crunch and bite against the veg. If you want to get all purist on me, just dump the veg and serve the chilled cooked noodles with the sesame sauce for dipping.

Valli Little was the inspirational food editor that photographer Mark, recipe guru Warren and I all worked with and were inspired by. We miss her.

SERVES: 4 **PREP:** 20 MINS **COOKING:** 10 MINS

1 bunch broccolini, stalks halved lengthways
270 g soba noodles
225 g frozen edamame, thawed, podded
1 bunch asparagus, woody ends trimmed, shaved into ribbons with a vegetable peeler
4 radishes, very thinly sliced
50 g wasabi peas, crushed
black sesame seeds, to serve

SESAME DRESSING

2½ tablespoons black sesame seeds
3 teaspoons black sesame oil or regular sesame oil
1 teaspoon sea salt
2 teaspoons very finely chopped ginger
1 teaspoon wasabi paste
2½ tablespoons soy sauce
2½ tablespoons rice wine vinegar
1 tablespoon mirin

To make the sesame dressing, place the sesame seeds, sesame oil and salt in a mortar, then bash and grind with a pestle until a rough paste forms. Add the remaining ingredients and stir until well combined.

Bring a medium saucepan of water to the boil over medium–high heat. Add the broccolini and cook for 2 minutes or until just tender. Remove with tongs and refresh under cold running water. Drain. Bring the water back to a simmer, add the noodles and cook for 3–4 minutes or until tender, then add the edamame and asparagus and cook for a further 30 seconds. Drain and refresh under cold water. Drain again and transfer to a large bowl.

Add the broccolini to the noodle mixture, then pour over the dressing and toss until well combined. Place in a serving bowl. Top with the radish and wasabi peas and finish with a sprinkling of black sesame seeds.

MISO NO-HASSLE (BACK) EGGPLANT

You might have missed it, but four years ago we brought back the hasselback potato, a technique invented in 1953 by a Swedish bloke called Leif Elisson, when he was a trainee chef at the Hasselbacken restaurant on Stockholm's pleasure island. Well, I'm here to tell you this technique has found its apotheosis. You see, something wonderful happens to eggplant when cooked with sweetened miso, but there just hasn't been enough surface area to really load up the eggplant ... until now ... until you hasselback it! Now you can trap the miso glaze in each cut, spreading its magic far and wide. Splendid!

PS, if anyone knows what happened to Leif, where he ended up or how to contact him, I'd love to know. Contact me via my website.

SERVES: 4 **PREP:** 15 MINS **COOKING:** 40 MINS

75 g (¼ cup) white miso paste
1 tablespoon finely grated ginger
1 tablespoon caster sugar
2 tablespoons mirin
1 tablespoon soy sauce
2 eggplants
1 bunch spring onions, dark green part thinly sliced diagonally (save the white part for the chicken, if using; see TIP)
1 long red chilli, thinly sliced
2 teaspoons sesame seeds (black and/or white), toasted
steamed rice, to serve

Preheat the oven to 200°C/180°C fan-forced. Line a baking tray with baking paper.

Place the miso, ginger, sugar, mirin and soy sauce in a small saucepan over medium heat. Bring to a simmer and stir until the sugar has dissolved, then set aside.

Use a vegetable peeler to peel the eggplants, then halve them lengthways. Place the eggplant halves, cut-side down, on a chopping board and cut crossways, only cutting halfway through, at 5 mm intervals. Place the eggplant on the prepared tray. Brush with the miso mixture, ensuring you get in between the cuts. Roast, brushing with more of the miso mixture halfway through, for 35 minutes or until tender and deep golden.

Remove the eggplant and scatter with the spring onion greens, sliced chilli and sesame seeds. Serve with steamed rice and/or chicken mince (see TIP) for meat lovers.

TIP

MEAT LOVERS: while the eggplant cooks, get your chicken ready. Thinly slice the white part of the spring onion. Heat 2 tablespoons vegetable oil and 2 teaspoons sesame oil in a frying pan over medium–high heat. Add the spring onion, 2 crushed garlic cloves and as much chilli as you like, and cook for 1–2 minutes or until aromatic. Add 500 g chicken mince and cook, breaking it up with the back of a wooden spoon, for 3–4 minutes or until nicely browned. Add 2 tablespoons soy sauce and 1 tablespoon mirin and cook, stirring, for 3–4 minutes until the liquid has reduced and the chicken is cooked through.

TONKATSU SANDWICH WITH YUZU SLAW

Crunchy crumbed Japanese pork has become quite a thing for me in the last year or so. In Tokyo, we three *MasterChef* judges were overjoyed to eat it with piles of finely shredded raw cabbage in an old bathhouse, and almost as happy to see chiller cabinets at the train station loaded with katsu sandwiches, where white bread and barbecue sauce encased fat slabs of fried crumbed pork. It was as much the perfect snack on the bullet train down to Kyoto as it was when food warrior Warren Mendes and I made them for footy fans at a Swans function in Sydney. The secret is the zingy but stupidly simple yuzu slaw, a sweet brown sauce that says London but means Tokyo and NO CRUSTS on the terrible fluffy white bread – an essential that seems positively exotic in the gritty backstreets of Shibuya.

SERVES: 4 **PREP:** 20 MINS **COOKING:** 15 MINS

4 small boneless pork loin steaks, fat trimmed
2 eggs
1 tablespoon soy sauce
75 g (½ cup) plain flour
100 g (2 cups) panko breadcrumbs
sunflower or vegetable oil, for shallow-frying
125 g (2 cups) very finely shredded wombok or cabbage
1 tablespoon yuzu juice (or lime juice, at a pinch)
8 thick slices white bread, crusts removed to make perfect squares
125 ml (½ cup) brown sauce or barbecue sauce
125 g (½ cup) Kewpie mayonnaise

Place one pork steak between two pieces of baking paper. Lightly bash with a meat mallet or rolling pin to flatten slightly, roughly to the same shape as the bread slices. Repeat with the remaining pork steaks. Explain to any children in the vicinity that this is the same technique employed to make square ham and chicken roll – it's never too late to bamboozle them.

Combine the eggs and soy sauce in a bowl, and place the flour and panko breadcrumbs in separate bowls. Coat the pork in the flour, shaking off any excess, then dip in the egg mixture, followed by the breadcrumbs, turning to coat and pressing down firmly. If you've got time on your hands, re-dunk them in the egg and breadcrumbs to double-crumb them for extra crispness.

Place on a baking tray or plate lined with baking paper and store in the fridge until needed (see TIP).

Pour enough oil into a frying pan to come 1 cm up the side. Heat over medium–high heat until the oil sizzles when you flick a few panko breadcrumbs in it. Add the pork in batches and cook for 2–3 minutes each side or until crisp and golden. I turn the heat up between batches to help maintain the gilding heat of the oil. Drain on paper towel.

Combine the cabbage with the yuzu juice in a bowl.

Spread one piece of bread with some brown or barbecue sauce, then top with a piece of pork and some slaw. Spread some mayonnaise over another slice of bread and place, mayonnaise-side down, on top. Press together firmly, then cut in half. Repeat with the remaining ingredients and serve.

TIP

If you have time, let the pork chill for up to 30 minutes after crumbing. This will help the crumb mixture adhere better, meaning it won't come away from the meat during cooking.

WARREN'S JAPANESE BEER TEMPURA

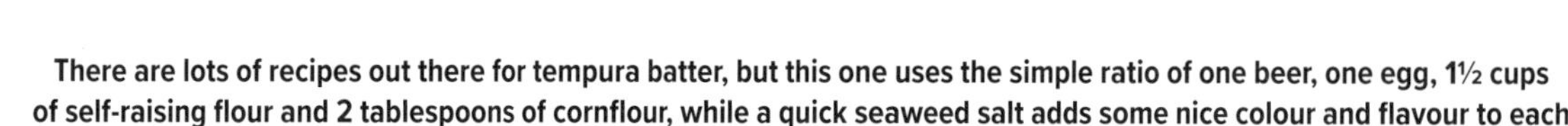

There are lots of recipes out there for tempura batter, but this one uses the simple ratio of one beer, one egg, 1½ cups of self-raising flour and 2 tablespoons of cornflour, while a quick seaweed salt adds some nice colour and flavour to each piece of tempura. Any vegetable can be used (mushrooms work particularly well), but we'll try to be a little more adventurous here because, 'baby, we were born that way'.

SERVES: 4 **PREP:** 20 MINS (PLUS 10 MINS FREEZING) **COOKING:** 15 MINS

1 × 330 ml bottle Japanese beer (such as Asahi), chilled
225 g (1½ cups) self-raising flour
2 tablespoons cornflour
1 egg, lightly whisked
sunflower oil, for deep-frying
16 large green prawns, peeled and deveined, with tails tips intact
150 g mixed Asian mushrooms (try shimeji and enoki)
1 bunch broccolini, stalks halved lengthways
4 baby carrots, halved lengthways
4 small turnips or radishes, halved

DIPPING SAUCE

2 tablespoons black vinegar
2 tablespoons soy sauce
2 teaspoons sesame oil

SEAWEED SALT

½ sheet nori, very finely chopped
1 tablespoon sea salt

Place your beer in the freezer for 10 minutes. Set an alarm! You want the tempura batter to be very light and well-chilled beer will help this.

While your beer is chilling down, make your dipping sauce. Combine all the ingredients and 1 tablespoon water in a bowl.

To make the seaweed salt, place the nori and salt in a bowl and rub between your fingers to combine and crush.

Combine the flours in a bowl, then gradually whisk in the egg and beer. It's fine if there are little lumps – this is good for tempura. Set aside for 5 minutes.

Pour enough oil into a large heavy-based saucepan to come two-thirds of the way up the side. Heat over medium heat until the oil reaches 190°C on a cook's thermometer. Working in batches, coat the prawns and vegetables in the batter and deep-fry, turning, for 2–3 minutes or until light golden and crisp. Drain on a tray or plate lined with paper towel.

Place the tempura prawns and veggies on a serving platter. Sprinkle with some of the seaweed salt and serve immediately with the dipping sauce and extra seaweed salt on the side.

CHICKEN YAKITORI SKEWERS WITH CHILLI-SESAME SNAPS

Remember this moment: the moment you first heard the words 'chillisesamesnaps' rolled into one glorious mouthful. They are what takes this insanely simple teriyaki glaze to new and unexpected heights. Oh, and the way the sugars in the glaze burn to give the chicken skewers extra smokiness helps, too!

SERVES: 4 **PREP:** 10 MINS (PLUS 30 MINS COOLING) **COOKING:** 15 MINS

125 ml (½ cup) light soy sauce
60 ml (¼ cup) mirin
60 ml (¼ cup) sake
2 tablespoons caster sugar
8 chicken thigh fillets, cut into 3 cm pieces
1 bunch spring onions, white and dark green parts, cut into 4 cm lengths

CHILLI–SESAME SNAPS

2 tablespoons caster sugar
2 tablespoons sesame seeds
½ teaspoon dried chilli flakes

Use metal skewers if you can, otherwise soak eight wooden skewers in warm water for 15 minutes so they don't scorch during cooking.

Combine the soy sauce, mirin, sake and sugar in a small saucepan over medium–high heat. Bring to the boil, then reduce the heat to medium and simmer for 5 minutes or until the sugar has dissolved and the sauce has reduced and thickened slightly. Set aside to cool completely.

Meanwhile, make the chilli–sesame snaps. Line a baking tray with baking paper. Place the sugar in a small frying pan over medium–high heat. When it starts to turn golden, add the sesame seeds and chilli flakes and stir immediately. Quickly remove from the pan and spread thinly on the prepared tray. Set aside to cool.

Preheat the grill to medium–high. Thread the chicken and spring onion onto eight skewers. Place on a plate and brush with the soy mixture. Grill the skewers, basting with the soy mixture, for 6–8 minutes or until cooked through. Remove and set aside to rest for 5 minutes.

Crumble the chilli–sesame snaps over the skewers and serve.

JAPANESE SWEET POTATO CURRY

When I studied Chinese revolutionary history at university, I remember my lecturer, a rightist intellectual and one of the 'hundred flowers' that bloomed in the period before the Cultural Revolution, claiming that Japanese culture was bereft of invention, but the master of taking ideas from overseas and implementing them better.

I'm not sure if that is generally the case, but you could argue it is with food. So many of the great Japanese dishes, which become something magical in the hands of Japanese cooks, came from somewhere else: tempura from Portuguese missionaries; sushi from some obscure hill tribes in Myanmar. And while this wonderful Japanese curry is a national dish, it is probably the legacy of British colonial interests in Japan. This is a vego version because it works well that way, but it is usually served with beef or chicken. The pickled slaw is a nice fresh addition to cut through the curry and, anyway, pickles are essential with any Japanese curry.

SERVES: 4 **PREP:** 20 MINS **COOKING:** 35 MINS

50 g unsalted butter
1 brown onion, finely chopped
2 garlic cloves, finely chopped
2½ tablespoons plain flour
1½ tablespoons korma curry powder or other mild curry powder
2 teaspoons garam masala (see TIPS)
2 tablespoons tomato paste
2 tablespoons soy sauce
1 tablespoon Worcestershire sauce
500 ml (2 cups) vegetable stock
600 g sweet potato, peeled and cut into 1 cm thick chunks
2 carrots, cut into 1.5 cm chunks
1 desiree potato, peeled and cut into 1.5 cm chunks
4 eggs, at room temperature
125 g (2 cups) finely shredded green cabbage
1 cup (60 g) finely shredded daikon radish (you will need about ⅓ daikon; see TIP)
2 tablespoons rice wine vinegar
steamed rice, to serve

Melt the butter in a large saucepan over medium heat. Add the onion and cook, stirring, for 3–4 minutes or until soft, then add the garlic and cook for a further 1 minute or until aromatic. Add the flour, curry powder and garam masala and stir to combine – the pan will dry up and the mixture will come together. Cook for 1–2 minutes, then add the tomato paste and cook for a further 1–2 minutes or until the mixture has darkened.

Add the soy and Worcestershire sauces, then gradually stir in the stock, adding a little at a time to stop any lumps forming. Add 125 ml (½ cup) water and bring to a simmer.

Add the sweet potato, carrot and potato, then reduce the heat to medium–low and cook, stirring occasionally, for 20 minutes or until all the vegetables are tender.

Meanwhile, bring a small saucepan of water to the boil over medium–high heat. Add the eggs and cook for 7 minutes. Drain and rinse under cold water to cool slightly, then peel and cut in half lengthways. Set aside.

Combine the cabbage, daikon and vinegar in a bowl.

Serve the curry with rice, topped with the eggs and the pickled cabbage and daikon.

TIPS

See page 92 to find out how to pickle the leftover daikon, along with a whole lot of ways to use it.

To make your own garam masala, place 2 tablespoons coriander seeds, 1 tablespoon cumin seeds, ½ teaspoon cloves, 1 teaspoon cardamom seeds, ½ teaspoon chilli powder, 1 teaspoon fennel seeds, 1 dried bay leaf and a thumb-sized stick of cinnamon in a mortar and use a pestle to grind to a coarse powder. Alternatively use a good-quality store-bought garam masala.

KAYABA COFFEE PARFAIT

The Taisho democracy (1912–1926) signalled a liberalising of both the arts and fashion in Japan. Dubbed 'Japan's jazz age', it was summed up in one Japanese phrase 'ero guro nansensu' ... erotic grotesque nonsense!! There was a hunger for all things Western among the young Tokyo modists, from fashion and painting styles to universal suffrage. According to historian Michael Hoffman (who writes beautifully on this era), young women adopted figure-hugging Western dress and hip young men would wear bell-bottomed trousers, colourful shirts and floppy ties. The men wore their hair long and the women wore theirs short.

An interest in coffee was part of this 'moga and mobo' movement, and the first European-style cafes opened in Ginza in 1911. By 1939, there were 37,000 across the country. Coffee jelly surfaced in Japanese culinary culture as it was achingly hip – and was seen as a healthier alternative to straight coffee, as the gelatine was believed to reduce the acid in the gut. This craze resurfaced in Japan a few years ago, but has recently been 'going off' big time on the back of a huge wave of #insta love, with large coffee and bubble tea chains getting behind it. In Japan, when not served in milkshakes and bubble teas, coffee jelly can be topped with either condensed milk, whipped cream or vanilla soft serve, the former working best if the hard set of agar agar has been used.

This recipe, however, is based on the signature coffee jelly dessert of one of Tokyo's remaining coffee shops in an original Taisho-era building, which has survived earthquakes and bombing raids.

SERVES: 6 **PREP:** 20 MINS (PLUS 6 HOURS SETTING)

10 gold-strength gelatine sheets
50 g caster sugar
1¼ tablespoons instant coffee granules
800 ml boiling water
200 ml pouring cream, lightly whipped
4 chocolate-ripple biscuits or similar, crushed
glace or maraschino cherries, to serve (optional)

Cut the gelatine sheets into large pieces, place in a bowl of cold water and set aside for 5 minutes or until soft.

Place the sugar and coffee granules in a large heatproof jug. Add the boiling water and stir until the sugar and coffee have dissolved. Use your hands to squeeze the excess water from the gelatine sheets and add to the coffee mixture while it is still hot. Stir to dissolve the gelatine. Pour into a 20 cm square baking tin and place in the fridge for about 6 hours to set.

To serve, cut the jelly into cubes and divide among small bowls. Spoon the whipped cream into a piping bag fitted with a 1.5 cm fluted nozzle and pipe some cream on top of the jelly. Sprinkle over the crushed biscuit and finish with a glace or maraschino cherry (if using).

TIP

A proven heart-starter to begin the day is something known as the 'sommelier's breakfast', which is a shot of espresso with a shot of Campari. It's surprisingly complementary. Accordingly, I rather like the idea of the non-dairy Japanese crowd serving their coffee jelly topped with a mound of Campari granita, so I've included my own version below!

To make Campari granita, dissolve 200 g caster sugar in 250 ml (1 cup) boiling water. Add 200 ml blood orange juice and 100 ml Campari and stir to combine. Pour into a shallow freezer-proof container, cover with a lid and place in the freezer for 1–2 hours or until ice crystals start to form around the edge. Remove from the freezer and scrape with a fork to break up the crystals. Cover and continue to freeze for 6 hours or overnight until set. Scrape with a fork again before serving and spoon on top of the coffee jelly.

THAILAND

Stretching from the foothills of the Himalayas in the north to the sweaty jungles of the south, and with five distinct regional cuisines and over 40 distinct ethnic groups, the food of Thailand is as complex as any other culinary melting pot of Asia. And that's even before you throw in the wonders of the Thai royal kitchen, so expertly explored by David Thompson, and influences from overseas.

These outside influences include rice and wok dishes, which came from Chinese traders and settlers, and spices, such as cardamom and turmeric, along with braises, including massaman (see page 72) and yellow curries, brought over by their Indian counterparts. The Portuguese missionaries introduced chillies, peanuts, bitter little pea eggplants (which sing in green curries) and coriander (both fresh and seeds), without which Thai food would be incomplete (and to a lesser extent this goes for pineapple, capsicum and tomato, too).

At the heart of Thai cuisine is the idea of creating roundness by the cunning balance of lots of sweet, sour, salty and hot flavours, with pungent and fragrant ingredients coming along for the ride. The sourness comes from lime juice or tamarind, the saltiness from fish sauce, dried shrimp or shrimp paste (and very occasionally soy), while the sweetness comes from palm sugar. The heat comes from a selection of chillies, such as red bird's eye, fiery green scuds and milder long red and green varieties – although it should be noted that in Thailand, street food tends to be far hotter and far less sweet than you will find in an Aussie Thai joint. In some braises and soups, however, this riot of flavours is sometimes softened a little by creamy eggplant, sweet potato and, especially in the south, coconut milk.

It is this combination of flavours that form the foundation of the famous 'prik nam pla' dipping sauce and any number of curry pastes, where the likes of garlic, Asian shallots, ginger-like galangal, coriander (roots, stalks and leaves) and lemongrass add fragrance.

That coriander will also be joined by other herbs, such as mint, the aniseed-freshness of Thai basil and the fragrant threads of fresh and lemony kaffir lime leaf in salads and garnishes. It's these flavours that make Thai cuisine unique and are at the core of any attempt to fake it.

Peanuts, green mango, green papaya, bean sprouts, lychees (or similar, such as rambutan and longan) and green beans (or even longer snake beans or winged beans) will also be used to add texture and, in the latter cases, freshness.

Pork, chicken, fish and shellfish are the proteins of choice in Thai cuisine, although duck and beef are also popular, and rice is essential. So much so that the word for 'rice' and 'food' are the same in Thai. This could be jasmine, glutinous rice, red rice, black rice or either flat or vermicelli rice noodles.

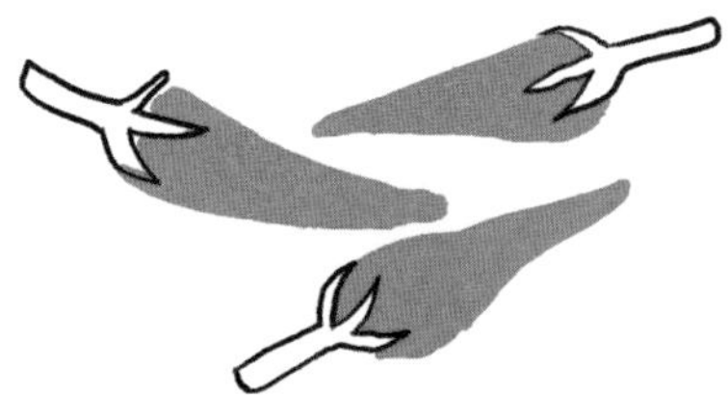

FAKING IT TIPS

1. Start with rice or noodles and then think about how you are going to flavour them.
2. Make a spice paste for the base of a curry or braise, or slather it on meat or fish for grilling and roasting. Start with coriander roots and stalks, galangal, ginger, something sour, such as tamarind or lime, and something fragrant, such as lemongrass or kaffir lime leaf, and move on from there.
3. Don't be shy with your flavours, but do take time to balance the sweet with the sour and the hot with the funky and salty.
4. Fresh herbs, such as coriander, mint and Thai basil, and funky, punchy sweet 'n' sour dipping sauces are your friends, whether you toss them in a salad or pair them with grilled meat or seafood.

SHOPPING LIST

While the dried shrimp paste 'kapi' is pretty hardcore, dried shrimp is a slightly more friendly pantry staple that's worth stocking up on, along with glutinous rice and various black rices, glutinous rice flour and a couple of different bottles of 'nam pla' (fish sauce). There are lots of different types to experiment with, but first up just get a good-quality and none-too-funky one. It should be smooth enough that you can bear to sip it unadulterated.

Palm sugar is a must and will often be cheaper in specialist Thai or Asian grocers. Here you will also find a wide range of ready-made tom yum pastes and curry spice pastes for dinner emergencies, along with a choice of wilder sriracha chilli sauces than the usual green-topped Californian-made rooster one everyone has.

In the fresh section, look for sawtooth coriander to use chopped in salads and pastes, fresh turmeric, winged beans, fresh baby corn, snake beans, green mango or papaya, bitter pea eggplants or the larger, round golf ball-sized version, and fresh kaffir lime leaves, which will keep well in the freezer if you don't use them all at once.

If you can find them, buy long, green spiky pandan leaves to flavour your rice, and if there are betel leaves buy these too, to make the delicious Thai snack 'miang kham'*. This translates rather prosaically as 'one-bite snack' and is a full fireworks display of flavour.

*These pull-together bundles are easy to make and can contain your choice of seven jewels. These might include a little pomelo or lime carpels, crushed peanuts or cashews, thinly sliced shallot or pieces of lychee, roasted coconut, finely diced young ginger, something meaty, such as a little dried shrimp (traditional) or fresh grilled chook or prawns (not so traditional) and a chilli caramel or splash of standard Thai dressing. To assemble, place a little of each on a betel leaf, pinch the leaf together and pop the filled leaf into your mouth, where it will explode with a riot of contrasting flavours and textures.

PREPARE IN 20 MINUTES

PRAWN PAD THAI

Let's be honest, pad thai is a pain in the bum to make, but seeing as it's one of the most delicious noodle dishes in the world when made right, I consider it to be 'worth the hassle'. I wonder if we could get a rubber stamp made saying this and then I could stamp it on my forehead?

SERVES: 2 **PREP:** 20 MINS (PLUS 1 HOUR SOAKING) **COOKING:** 15 MINS

120 g flat rice stick noodles
60 ml (¼ cup) fish sauce, plus extra if needed
60 g (¼ cup) tamarind pulp, concentrate or puree, plus extra if needed
80 g coarsely grated palm sugar or caster sugar, plus extra if needed
pinch of chilli powder (optional)
80 ml (⅓ cup) vegetable oil
2 garlic cloves, very finely chopped
10 green prawns, peeled and deveined
120 g firm tofu, cut into 1.5 cm cubes
2 eggs, lightly whisked
1½ tablespoons dried shrimp
4 spring onions, white and dark green parts sliced into coins
55 g (⅓ cup) unsalted roasted peanuts
100 g bean shoots
coriander leaves, to serve
lime wedges, to serve

Soak the noodles in cold water for 45–60 minutes or until they are pliable enough to wrap around your finger. They will still need a little cooking to truly soften. Drain.

Combine the fish sauce, tamarind and sugar in a small saucepan and heat over low heat for 1–2 minutes or until the sugar has dissolved. Taste and adjust the balance of flavour if needed. If you are using the chilli powder add it now, then set the sauce aside.

Heat a large frying pan or wok over high heat. Add 2 tablespoons of the oil and heat until super hot. Add the garlic and cook, stirring, for a few seconds. Add the noodles and a splash of water and cook, tossing, for 2 minutes or until the noodles are coated in the oil and garlic. It's important to keep them moving in the pan. Add the sauce and cook for a further 2 minutes or until the noodles are almost soft enough to eat but still a little resistant to the bite.

Push the noodles to one side of the pan and splash in a touch more oil. Add the prawns and cook for a few seconds until they start to colour, then add the tofu. Once the prawns and tofu are both lightly browned push them to one side as well. Reduce the heat to medium–low, add the egg to the cleared space and gently scramble.

When the egg starts to catch, add the dried shrimp, most of the spring onion and most of the peanuts. Stir everything into the noodles, along with the prawns and tofu, and stir-fry until just combined. Throw in the bean shoots and remaining spring onion and peanuts, then divide among bowls and top with the coriander. Serve with lime wedges on the side.

EASY CREAMY TOM YUM SOUP WITH PRAWNS

(AKA TOM YUM GOONG NAM KHON)

Tom Hiddleston? Tom Brady? Tom Hardy? Tom Cruise? Tom Hilfiger? Of all the famous Toms, none is tastier and better looking than a hot, sour Tom Yum. And the king of all these Thai Toms is the spicier and creamier Bangkok version built around a killer stock that gets its creaminess by means other than lashings of tinned coconut milk – that's the 'nam khon' bit in the title. (I'd like to tell you that this creaminess comes from evaporated milk but I am worried that, although this is very traditional, finding this out before you've even finished reading this intro might put you off making the soup.)

I also love this recipe because it minimises waste, meaning you use so much of what would otherwise go in the bin (such as the prawn heads and shells) to bring extra flavour to this pool party. Like a good martini, this tom yum goong is also a little dirty.

SERVES: 4 **PREP:** 25 MINS **COOKING:** 20 MINS

1 bunch coriander, leaves picked, stalks and roots cleaned and finely chopped
6 cm knob of galangal or ginger, peeled and thinly sliced
6 garlic cloves
4 lemongrass stalks, inner white part only, roughly chopped
1½ tablespoons coriander seeds
2 teaspoons white peppercorns
1 teaspoon sea salt
6 kaffir lime leaves, torn
2 litres fish or chicken stock
12 whole green prawns, peeled and deveined, heads and shells reserved
1 teaspoon kapi (shrimp paste) or finely chopped anchovies
4–6 red bird's eye chillies (depending on how hot you like it), very finely chopped, plus extra to serve
150 g oyster mushrooms
12 small button mushrooms
3 roma tomatoes, each cut into 8 chunks
2 white onions, cut into wedges
125 ml (½ cup) evaporated milk (or, at a pinch, full-cream milk)
1 tablespoon fish sauce
juice of 2–3 limes, plus extra to serve

Place the coriander stalks and roots in a mortar (reserve the leaves for later), add the galangal or ginger, garlic, lemongrass, coriander seeds, peppercorns, salt and five of the kaffir lime leaves and smash with a pestle a few times until crushed and well bruised. You could pulse in a blender if you don't have a mortar and pestle, but leave it as a coarse paste rather than letting it turn to mush.

Place the paste, stock and reserved prawn heads and shells in a large saucepan or stockpot. Bring to a rolling boil over high heat and cook for about 10 minutes, then reduce the heat to low and skim off any foam that looks a bit grey on top – *eeewwww*!! We don't want our guests to see that. Simmer for a further 2–3 minutes, then set aside to cool slightly. Pour into a sieve over a large jug or bowl, discarding all the solids.

Finely chop the remaining lime leaf. Clean the pan or stockpot and heat over medium–high heat. Open all the windows and close all internal doors from the kitchen (cooking the prawn paste can get a little stinky). Add the kapi and chilli and cook until the flavour starts to overpower the entire kitchen, then add your prawn stock. Stir until well combined and bring to a simmer, then add the chopped lime leaf, prawns, mushrooms, tomato, onion, evaporated milk, fish sauce and lime juice. Simmer for 3 minutes or until the prawns are just cooked.

Ladle the soup into large serving bowls and top with the reserved coriander leaves and all the extra chilli and lime juice you like.

TIP

If you want a creamier version that's more like a tom ka goong, just add coconut milk instead of the evaporated milk. If you are going to do this, fry the prawn heads and tails in a good glug of peanut or vegetable oil before adding to the stock. Cook them until they colour the oil, then throw them and the oil into a mortar or blender with the aromats to make the paste. This will give you those eyes of bright orange oil against the pale orange of the soup. If you only pulse a bit, it might also give you a few real prawn eyes floating beadily around.

CHEAT'S THAI SHREDDED CHICKEN SALAD

No time but you want a filling, protein-dense salad to feed the hordes? Look no further, this Thai-inspired beauty is a winner.

SERVES: 4 **PREP:** 15 MINS

75 g coarsely grated palm sugar or caster sugar
2 garlic cloves
juice of 3–4 limes, plus extra if needed
2 tablespoons fish sauce, plus extra if needed
1 bunch coriander, leaves picked, stalks and roots cleaned and finely chopped
1 store-bought roast chicken (see TIPS)
1 small wombok, finely shredded
1 bunch mint, larger leaves shredded, small leaves left whole
200 g salted peanuts, toasted
6 spring onions, white and dark green parts sliced into coins
3 jalapeno chillies, deseeded and finely chopped (or use 3 bird's eye if you like it hotter, or 3 long green if you like it milder)

Start by making a dressing. Place the sugar, garlic, lime juice, fish sauce and chopped coriander stalks and roots in the bowl of a small food processor and blitz until the mixture is as fine as you can get it. Run it through a sieve with a bowl underneath, then taste and adjust the dressing with more lime or fish sauce if needed. This dressing should be sour, a little salty but with a backbone of sweetness. You'll know it's right when you taste it and go 'yum'.

Remove the skin from the chicken, then rip off the flesh and place it in a bowl. Now shred your chicken. A fun way to do this is to use your hand-held electric beaters!!!

Place the shredded chicken, wombok and shredded mint in a large serving bowl. Add enough dressing to wet everything and gently toss to coat. Throw over the peanuts, spring onion, chilli, coriander leaves and small mint leaves, and serve with any remaining dressing on the side.

TIPS

This salad is even more virtuous with slices of gently poached chicken breast.

Try it with lemon juice instead of lime for a slightly different twist.

Here is the real beauty of buying a ready-roasted chicken: remove the crisp skin and lay it (warm) between two slices of cheap white buttered bread, then eat it as a chef's snack while preparing the meat. Dunk the sandwich in the juices and fat at the bottom of the bag the chook came in. Don't knock it until you've tried it.

GREEN CURRY FISH & THAI EGGPLANT BAKE

I'm obsessed with the ease of tray bakes, and this is a great new-age 'bake and serve' dish. The trouble is that while the flavours are distinctly Thai, Thai kitchens usually don't have ovens! You could also make this on the barbecue with the lid down if you find yourself in that predicament in Chiang Rai or Nonthaburi. If not, think yourself lucky and get your oven preheating. It's a gentle way to cook the fresh fish, in this thick, almost curdled, richly flavoured taste of Thailand with the distinct bitterness of a unique variety of eggplant – if you can find them. If not, any old eggplant will do!

SERVES: 4 **PREP:** 20 MINS **COOKING:** 20 MINS

80 ml (⅓ cup) vegetable or grapeseed oil
8 Thai eggplants, halved (see TIPS)
200 ml coconut cream
1 tablespoon coarsely grated palm sugar or caster sugar
1 tablespoon fish sauce
4 × 180 g skinless white fish fillets (such as rockling, blue-eye or barramundi), pin-boned
juice of 2 limes, plus extra wedges to serve
1 long green chilli, thinly sliced
1 kaffir lime leaf, very thinly sliced
small handful of Thai basil leaves
steamed rice, to serve
400 g Asian greens (such as choy sum, Chinese broccoli or bok choy), steamed

GREEN CURRY PASTE

4 coriander sprigs (with roots attached)
6 long green chillies, deseeded and roughly chopped
2 whole Thai green chillies (this is the fire, so omit if kick is not your thing)
4 Asian shallots, cut into chunks
4 garlic cloves, chopped
2 kaffir lime leaves, chopped
2 Thai basil sprigs (stalks for the paste; leaves for garnish)
2 lemongrass stalks, inner white part only, finely chopped
2 cm knob of galangal or ginger, peeled and chopped
1 tablespoon coriander seeds, toasted
2 teaspoons white peppercorns
2 teaspoons kapi (shrimp paste) or finely chopped anchovies

To make the curry paste, scrape the coriander roots clean with a knife. Roughly chop the roots, stalks and half the leaves, and throw into a blender with all the remaining paste ingredients. Reserve the rest of the coriander leaves for serving.

Press the button and blitz to a paste. Add a few tablespoons of water to help with the whizzing, but it's OK if it's a bit fibrous and chunky. You could be very old school and do this using a mortar and pestle, but it can be quite a laborious process.

Preheat the oven to 200°C/180°C fan-forced.

Heat the oil in a frying pan over medium–high heat. Add the eggplant and cook for 3–5 minutes each side or until tender and golden. Set aside on a plate lined with paper towel to drain.

Combine the coconut cream, sugar, fish sauce and 75 g (¼ cup) of the curry paste in a large roasting tin. Add the fish and swirl the tin around to coat the fish in the curry mixture. Arrange the eggplant around the fish and bake for 12–16 minutes or until the fish is cooked through and flakes easily. Drizzle over the lime juice.

Sprinkle with the green chilli, kaffir lime, reserved coriander leaves and Thai basil leaves. If you are just serving the kids, the coriander will probably be enough!

Serve the fish and eggplant bake with steamed rice and your favourite steamed Asian greens, with lime wedges on the side.

TIPS

Any extra curry paste will keep in an airtight container in the fridge for up to 1 week. Use it to make a more traditional Thai green chicken curry, add a little to your chicken or fish burger patties for a Thai twist or add to stir-fried veggies for a spicy kick.

While you're at your local Asian grocer or market buying the eggplants, grab some of those long snake beans to serve with this curry. Steam or fry them – whichever you prefer.

All is not lost if you can't find the Thai eggplants. You can also use long Lebanese eggplants halved lengthways, whole pea eggplants or regular eggplants, cut into 4 cm chunks.

FOOD NERD NOTE: There are loads of rather good store-bought Thai curry pastes out there, which can make this a super-quick dinner. But on days when you've got an extra ten minutes it's rather satisfying (and very easy) to make your own.

VEGETABLE MASSAMAN CURRY

This curry showcases the melting pot that is Thailand. There are Malay, Indian and Persian traces in its complex use of herbs, spices and nuts. Descended from a Muslim dish (hence the name, which is a bastardisation of the archaic 'mussulman' for those of the Muslim faith), you'll normally only find it served with chicken, beef and/or vegetables, but it makes a great home for whatever veg is leftover in the crisper drawer of your fridge.

SERVES: 4 **PREP:** 20 MINS **COOKING:** 20 MINS

1½ tablespoons coconut oil
2 tablespoons massaman curry paste
2 large Asian shallots, sliced
4 garlic cloves, crushed
1 tablespoon finely grated galangal or ginger
4 cardamom pods, crushed
1 cinnamon stick
pinch of grated nutmeg
3 long red chillies, 1 split in half, 2 sliced, to serve
1 × 400 ml can coconut milk
1 small sweet potato, peeled and cut into chunks
¼ cauliflower, cut into chunks
2 small zucchini, cut into chunks
1 capsicum (yellow is best), deseeded and cut into thick chunks
150 g green beans, trimmed and halved
2 tablespoons tamarind pulp, concentrate or puree
1 tablespoon coarsely grated palm sugar or caster sugar
80 ml (⅓ cup) good-quality natural orange or pineapple juice
2 tablespoons soy sauce
55 g (⅓ cup) raw peanuts, toasted
coriander sprigs, to serve
steamed jasmine rice, to serve

Heat the coconut oil in a large heavy-based saucepan over medium heat until melted. Add the curry paste and cook for 1 minute or until aromatic.

Add the shallot, garlic and galangal or ginger and stir for 1 minute, then stir in the cardamom, cinnamon, nutmeg and split chilli. Add the coconut milk and 650 ml water and bring to a simmer.

Add the harder vegetables (in this instance, the sweet potato and cauliflower) and cook, stirring occasionally, for 4–6 minutes. Now add the softer vegetables (zucchini, capsicum and beans), along with the tamarind pulp, sugar, juice and soy sauce. Cook, stirring occasionally, for 6–8 minutes or until all the vegetables are cooked through.

Sprinkle the peanuts, coriander and sliced chilli over the curry and serve with steamed rice.

TIP

You can swap your veggies around, depending on what's in season. Try potato or pumpkin instead of the sweet potato, or broccoli instead of cauliflower. Stir in shredded kale, Asian greens, baby spinach leaves or snow peas at the end for extra veg. For extra heartiness, add cubes of tofu or drained canned chickpeas towards the end of cooking until warmed through.

THAI FISH CAKES

A cake made of fish? Sounds totally wrong! In fact, it is so totally right, right, right, you'll find yourself back where you started with a big smile on your face and a far more open attitude towards cakes made of fish. Just tell the kids that they are fish rissoles ... or fissholes if you prefer.

SERVES: 4 **PREP:** 25 MINS **COOKING:** 20 MINS

½ iceberg lettuce, leaves separated
½ bunch coriander sprigs
½ bunch mint sprigs
85 g (1½ cups) bean shoots
2 Lebanese cucumbers, sliced lengthways
lime wedges, to serve

PRIK NAM PLA

55 g (¼ cup) coarsely grated palm sugar or caster sugar
finely grated zest and juice of 2 limes
60 ml (¼ cup) rice wine vinegar
2 tablespoons fish sauce
Your choice of chillies:
Hot:
3 Thai green chillies, finely chopped plus 2 red bird's eye or long red chillies, thinly sliced
Mild:
4 long red chillies, deseeded and thinly sliced

FISH CAKES

600 g skinless white fish fillets (such as ling, whiting or flathead), pin-boned
35 g (¼ cup) cornflour
2 garlic cloves, crushed
1 tablespoon red curry paste
2 teaspoons grated palm sugar or brown sugar
1 teaspoon sesame oil
2 egg whites
sea salt
150 g green beans, trimmed and thinly sliced
⅓ cup coriander sprigs, finely chopped
4 spring onions, finely chopped
2 kaffir lime leaves, finely chopped
1 tablespoon fish sauce
1 teaspoon ground white pepper
125 ml (½ cup) rice bran or peanut oil

To make the prik nam pla, place the sugar, lime zest and juice, vinegar, fish sauce and chilli in a bowl and whisk with a fork until the sugar has dissolved. Set aside.

For the fish cakes, place the fish in a food processor and blitz until smooth. Add the cornflour, garlic, curry paste, sugar, sesame oil, egg whites and a good pinch of salt and blitz until well combined.

Transfer the fish mixture to a bowl. Add the chopped green beans, coriander, spring onion, kaffir lime, fish sauce and white pepper. Stir until well combined.

Line a baking tray with baking paper. Using wet hands, shape heaped tablespoons of the mixture into about 20 round flat fish cakes. Transfer to the prepared tray.

Heat the rice bran or peanut oil in a large frying pan over medium heat. Working in batches, add the fish cakes and cook for 2–3 minutes each side or until golden brown and cooked through. Transfer to a plate lined with paper towel to drain.

Arrange the fish cakes on a large platter, along with the lettuce, coriander, mint, bean shoots, cucumber and lime wedges. Pour the prik nam pla into a serving bowl and take it all to the table. To assemble, use the lettuce leaves to wrap up the fish cakes, herbs, bean shoots, cucumber and a good squeeze of lime, then dunk them in the sauce to eat!

TIPS

It's not traditional but these are also reaaaaalllly good slapped on mini dinner rolls (or in wraps) with all the green trimmings, a drizzle of sriracha and some Kewpie mayo.

It's also no sin to serve these for dinner with rice or mashed potato. If you go the mash route, load the mash with coriander and finely chopped green chilli, and definitely call these Thai fish rissoles. To round it out, offer a bowl of sweet chilli sauce on the side, too!

SOM YUM!

(AKA THAI HERB & PAPAYA SALAD WITH CRISPY RICE CAKES)

This is a hybrid som tam papaya salad, but with all the herbs as an added bonus. I find the act of smashing up a tomato to get all its juices out strangely satisfying. I totally see why the strongest Avenger loves to 'Hulk smash'!!!

If you hate planning and are unlikely to be organised enough to soak the rice the night before for the crispy, chewy rice cakes, you'll also find some totally acceptable (but not chewy) same-day Laotian rice cakes online with my name attached to them. Tell Mr Google that they are featured in my Yim Yam salad. These would work well instead.

SERVES: 4 **PREP:** 30 MINS (PLUS OVERNIGHT SOAKING) **COOKING:** 50 MINS

½ green papaya, peeled and finely shredded (you need about 2 cups)
1 carrot, finely shredded
2 Thai green chillies, thinly sliced
½ red onion, thinly sliced
¼ cup Thai basil leaves
¼ cup coriander leaves
¼ cup mint leaves
2 tablespoons chopped unsalted roasted peanuts

RICE CAKES

330 g (1½ cups) sticky rice (also known as glutinous rice; see TIPS)
½ teaspoon sea salt
2 tablespoons moist coconut flakes or freshly grated coconut if you can get it
60 ml (¼ cup) vegetable or rice bran oil

DRESSING

2 tablespoons dried shrimp
1 tablespoon coarsely grated palm sugar or caster sugar
1 garlic clove
8 cherry tomatoes, larger ones halved
2 tablespoons fish sauce
juice of 1½ limes
½ teaspoon sea salt

To make your rice cakes, place the rice, salt and 750 ml (3 cups) water in a bowl and set aside overnight to soak. Drain well and place in a bowl.

Add the coconut and toss to combine. Place in a steamer lined with baking paper and set over a saucepan of simmering water. Steam for 30 minutes or until the grains are soft and sticky. Set aside until cool enough to handle.

While the rice is cooking, make the dressing. Place the shrimp, sugar and garlic in a mortar. Use a pestle to pound until they're all smashed up. Add the tomatoes, fish sauce, lime juice and salt. Gently pound, bruising the tomatoes to release their juices.

Place the papaya, carrot, chilli, onion, herbs and peanuts in a large bowl, toss to combine and set aside.

Back to the rice cakes. Line a baking tray with baking paper. Roll heaped tablespoons of the rice mixture into balls, place on the prepared tray and flatten into 5–6 cm rounds. Slightly dampen your hands to do this as the rice can be really sticky; wet the tablespoon between scoops as well.

Heat 1 tablespoon of the oil in a large frying pan over medium heat. Working in batches and adding more oil as needed, cook the rice cakes for 2 minutes each side or until golden and crisp. Transfer to a plate lined with paper towel to drain.

Toss the dressing through the salad and serve with the rice cakes, or break them up and sprinkle on top.

TIPS

Sticky or glutinous rice is available at Asian supermarkets.

If you don't have a steamer, use a fine sieve over a saucepan of boiling water and cover with a tight-fitting lid. Otherwise, boiled rice is fine – it just can't be too wet.

This recipe also works well with my favourite Yim Yam dressing. Regular readers will be familiar with this. The dressing was created a long while ago by Lylah Hatfield at Yarraville's Yim Yam and, a bit like Stan Lee in those Marvel movies, it makes a cameo in every one of my cookbooks. To make it, use a mortar and pestle to smash up 50 g salted peanuts and mix with 2 teaspoons dried chilli flakes, 1 tablespoon white sugar, 100 ml lemon juice and 60 ml (¼ cup) fish sauce. It's just another excuse for me to smash things up again really.

SEARED BEEF WITH THAI FISH SAUCE CARAMEL & QUICK STICKS SLAW

Fish sauce caramels are all very trendy now, seeing as the world has turned to dirty versions of Asian classics as the next generation of hipster dude food. I've been using them in my food for a wee bit longer, but even so, I never tire of their funky stickiness.

SERVES: 4–6 **PREP:** 15 MINS (PLUS 10 MINS SOAKING) **COOKING:** 20 MINS

1 kg piece prime grass-fed beef fillet
sea salt
250 g coarsely grated palm sugar or caster sugar
about 60 ml (¼ cup) of the best fish sauce you can find
finely grated zest of 1 lime, the resulting bald lime cut into six wedges
6 long red chillies, deseeded and cut into long threads

QUICK STICKS SLAW

200 g rice stick noodles
200 g snow peas, trimmed, strings removed, sliced into batons (see TIPS)
juice of 3 plump limes
¼ white drumhead cabbage, finely shredded
¼ iceberg lettuce, finely shredded
1 tablespoon fish sauce (from the same bottle I mentioned above)
1 bunch Thai basil (mint, purple basil or coriander would also do), leaves picked
Kewpie mayonnaise, to serve (optional)

Trim the beef of any silverskin and sinew and rub all over with a little salt.

Make a caramel in the heaviest-based saucepan you have. To do this, place the sugar and 185 ml (¾ cup) water in the saucepan and stir over low heat until the sugar has dissolved. Increase the heat to high and bring to the boil. Cook, without stirring, for about 8 minutes or until the water evaporates and you are left with a golden caramel. Remove from the heat and splash in 2 tablespoons of the fish sauce to cool the caramel down. Let the caramel cool enough to taste, then add more fish sauce, little by little, until its evil, salty stinkiness peeks through the sweetness. Reserve.

Boil a kettle for the noodles.

Preheat a barbecue grill or chargrill pan over the highest possible heat. Sear the meat on all sides, brushing with the caramel before you turn it and making sure you place the meat on a new hot spot each time. Sear for about 2–3 minutes each side (or longer if you don't want your beef rare), ensuring all the sides get nice and crusty. When the beef is *almost* done to your liking, remove it from the heat and place on a plate. Set aside for 10 minutes to rest, then sprinkle with the lime zest.

To make the slaw, place the noodles in a large heatproof bowl, cover with boiling water and set aside for 5–8 minutes to soften. Drain. Place the snow peas in the bowl and cover with boiling water for 1 minute. Drain and return to the bowl. Add the softened noodles and lime juice and toss to combine. Spread over a serving platter.

Place the cabbage, lettuce and fish sauce in the bowl and toss together, then throw over the noodle mixture. Finish with the Thai basil leaves and swipes of Kewpie mayo (if you like).

Thinly slice the beef. Dredge one side only of each slice in the remaining caramel and place on top of the slaw, dredged-side up. Sprinkle with the threads of chilli. Serve with the bald lime wedges and the remaining caramel on the side for individual re-application.

TIP

Swap the Thai basil for Vietnamese mint and this dish instantly moves to Hue. You'll also need me to write you a new intro about how I once ate pork loin served this way in a garden restaurant in Vietnam's old imperial capital. It was cooked on a terracotta tile over a small pot of fire.

MATT'S BOGAN LARB

This is so far from authentic, but I swear I ate something very similar to this at that night market near the train station in Bangkok. Sadly, my memory is clouded by the succession of increasingly less elegant bars that followed. The night ended – as so many legendary/dreadful nights do in this city – with us washing up at Wong's. Any night that ends with whisky and beer at Wong's is going to need a skim through the camera phone to remember, and a judicious swipe of the finger to forget and destroy any incriminating evidence. Best do this somewhere private.

PS, please, whatever you do, don't make the mistake of stumbling into the bar down the alley on the other side of the street unless you are with heavily armed or very influential members of the local military.

SERVES: 4 **PREP:** 25 MINS **COOKING:** 25 MINS

- 55 g (¼ cup) sticky rice (also known as glutinous rice)
- 1 tablespoon peanut oil
- 500 g pork mince
- 3 Asian shallots, thinly sliced
- 1 lemongrass stalk, inner white part only, finely chopped
- 4 cm knob of galangal, peeled and coarsely grated (in this bogan larb, ginger is fine too)
- 2 baby cos lettuces, leaves separated
- 1 handful of your favourite Thai herbs (such as chopped mint leaves, holy basil or sawtooth coriander)
- 55 g (⅓ cup) unsalted roasted peanuts, coarsely chopped
- 2 long green chillies, thinly sliced (optional)
- lime cheeks, to serve
- steamed sticky rice or Som yum (see page 77), to serve

BOGAN DRESSING

- finely grated zest and juice of 1 lime
- 2 tablespoons sweet chilli sauce
- 1 tablespoon soy sauce
- 2 teaspoons fish sauce

Throw the rice into a dry wok over low heat and keep it moving so it doesn't catch and burn. Keep doing this for about 15 minutes or until it turns a delicate golden colour and smells nutty. Set aside for 5 minutes to cool slightly, then place in a food processor and blitz to a coarse powder. Set aside.

To make your bogan dressing, whisk all the ingredients in a jug.

Heat the oil in a wok over medium heat. Add the pork mince and cook, tossing occasionally, for 5 minutes or until it's cooked and no longer pink, breaking up any lumps as you go. Stir in 1 tablespoon of the roasted rice powder. Add the shallot, lemongrass and galangal and stir for 1 minute. Add the dressing and toss for 2 minutes or until everything is toasty.

Arrange the cos leaves in a bowl, spoon over the pork mince mixture and scatter with the herbs, peanuts and chilli (if using). Serve with lime cheeks and steamed sticky rice or my som yum salad.

TIPS

This larb can also be made with chicken mince, if preferred.

In winter, if you leave out the roasted rice, the pork mince mixture is delicious just served over a tangle of wok-blistered snake beans (or even green beans), topped with all the herbs, peanuts and chilli.

Store the leftover roasted rice powder in an airtight container for up to 1 week. Sprinkle it over a Thai beef salad or chicken stir-fries.

BRUSSELS SPROUTS WITH LAP CHEONG & MORE THAI FISH SAUCE CARAMEL

Brussels sprouts and fish sauce are the de riguer combo of 2018, with everyone from David Chang and Martha Stewart to Hong Kong hipster sandwich bars Bread and Beast and Little Bao spruiking them. Strangely, no one has yet invited lap cheong to this sticky party, which is a huge oversight, as you'll find out when you make this recipe. I should add that my family is genetically programmed to obsess about these 'doll's house cabbages', and the only time I've seen the woman I love shocked was when I informed her that Christmas lunch wasn't complete unless there were at least a dozen sprouts per head.

SERVES: 4 **PREP:** 10 MINS (plus a freaking age prepping the sprouts) **COOKING:** 30 MINS

1 kg brussels sprouts
4 lap cheong sausages, cut diagonally into 5 mm thick slices
2 celery stalks, finely chopped
1 bunch coriander, leaves picked, stalks and roots cleaned and finely chopped
50 g butter
200 g (1 cup) brown rice
70 g (⅓ cup) caster sugar
2 tablespoons fish sauce (the best you can find)
2 long green chillies, thinly sliced
2 limes
80 g (½ cup) salted roasted peanuts, crushed into a coarse gravel
½ iceberg lettuce, finely shredded
Kewpie mayonnaise or lime and miso mayo (see TIP), to serve

Preheat the oven to 200°C/180°C fan-forced.

Trim the bottom of the sprouts and remove the tough outer leaves. If they're small, cut a line into the base about 3 mm deep; if they're large, halve them.

Heat a large frying pan over medium heat. Add the lap cheong, celery, coriander roots and stalks and fry for 3 minutes to colour, without letting them burn. You want the celery to still have a little crunch to it, so don't be tempted to overcook this pan full of goodness! Use a slotted spoon to transfer the lap cheong, celery and coriander bits to a large bowl and set aside, leaving any rendered fat behind.

Melt the butter in the frying pan, then add the sprouts. Cook, tossing, for 1 minute or until well coated in the butter. Transfer the sprouts to a large baking tray and spread them out in a single layer. If you don't have a really large tray, it's better to spread the sprouts over two trays rather than overcrowd them. Roast for 20–25 minutes or until the sprouts are soft in the centre but caught and a little burny at the edges.

Meanwhile, put your rice on to cook following the packet directions.

Wipe out the frying pan with paper towel. Make a caramel by stirring the caster sugar and fish sauce in the frying pan over medium heat. Jiggle the pan so the fish sauce dissolves the sugar evenly as it heats. Let it bubble away for 2 minutes or until a sticky caramel starts to form. Add the green chilli and bubble away for 2 minutes, then remove from the heat.

Grate the zest of one lime, then cut it into quarters. Squeeze two of these quarters over the roasted sprouts. Add the sprouts and half the caramel to the lap cheong mixture and toss to combine. Transfer to a large serving plate. Drizzle over the remaining caramel and top with the crushed peanuts, coriander leaves and grated zest from the second lime. Cut this lime into wedges. Serve with the brown rice, lime wedges and shredded iceberg, and with the mayonnaise zig-zagged over the top of the sprouts.

TIP

To make a lime and miso mayo, place 1 teaspoon salt, the juice of 1 lime, 1 tablespoon miso paste and a splash of mirin or rice wine vinegar if you have it in the cup of a stick blender. Crack in an egg without breaking the yolk. Top with 350 ml peanut or sunflower oil. Carefully position the blender over the whole egg yolk, and blend for 1–2 seconds until you see creamy ribbons forming. Bouncing the head of your blender up and down, gently pull up through the oil, incorporating it into a thick mayonnaise.

BLACK STICKY RICE WITH SALTY COCONUT & MANGO

The balance of salty and sweet is the secret behind this classic Thai dessert. Mango is the ideal fruit to play along here, as it gets on so well with both flavours.

SERVES: 4 **PREP:** 10 MINS **COOKING:** 1 HOUR 20 MINS

200 g black rice
50 g coarsely grated palm sugar or caster sugar
1 teaspoon sea salt
300 ml coconut cream
1 mango, sliced

Place the rice and 1.25 litres water in a large saucepan over high heat. Bring to the boil, then reduce the heat to low and simmer for 1 hour. Add the sugar, salt and 200 ml of the coconut cream and simmer for 10 minutes or until the rice is creamy but still has a bit of bite. Taste, and add a little more salt if you feel the rice needs it.

Spoon the warm rice into serving bowls. Top with fresh mango slices and a drizzle of the remaining coconut cream.

TIP

You can make your sticky rice a few days ahead and keep it covered in the fridge. Stir over low heat to warm through or just eat it cold.

VIETNAM

Bear with me while I drop a name ... I always remember Tony Bourdain telling me he wanted to move to Vietnam for the food. It seemed like such an unlikely idea. Sure I love pho, too, and the litany of healthy street food that this country abounds in, but on the surface Vietnamese food just seemed so simple. Dig a little deeper, however, and you start discovering the complexities of a fresh and largely low-fat cuisine that differs between the north (with noodles and more Chinese influences), the fertile south (with rice, fresh herbs and coconut) and the middle, which used to be home to the imperial court. It was here, in an imperial restaurant in Hue, that I learned about the joys of frying rice paper rolls.

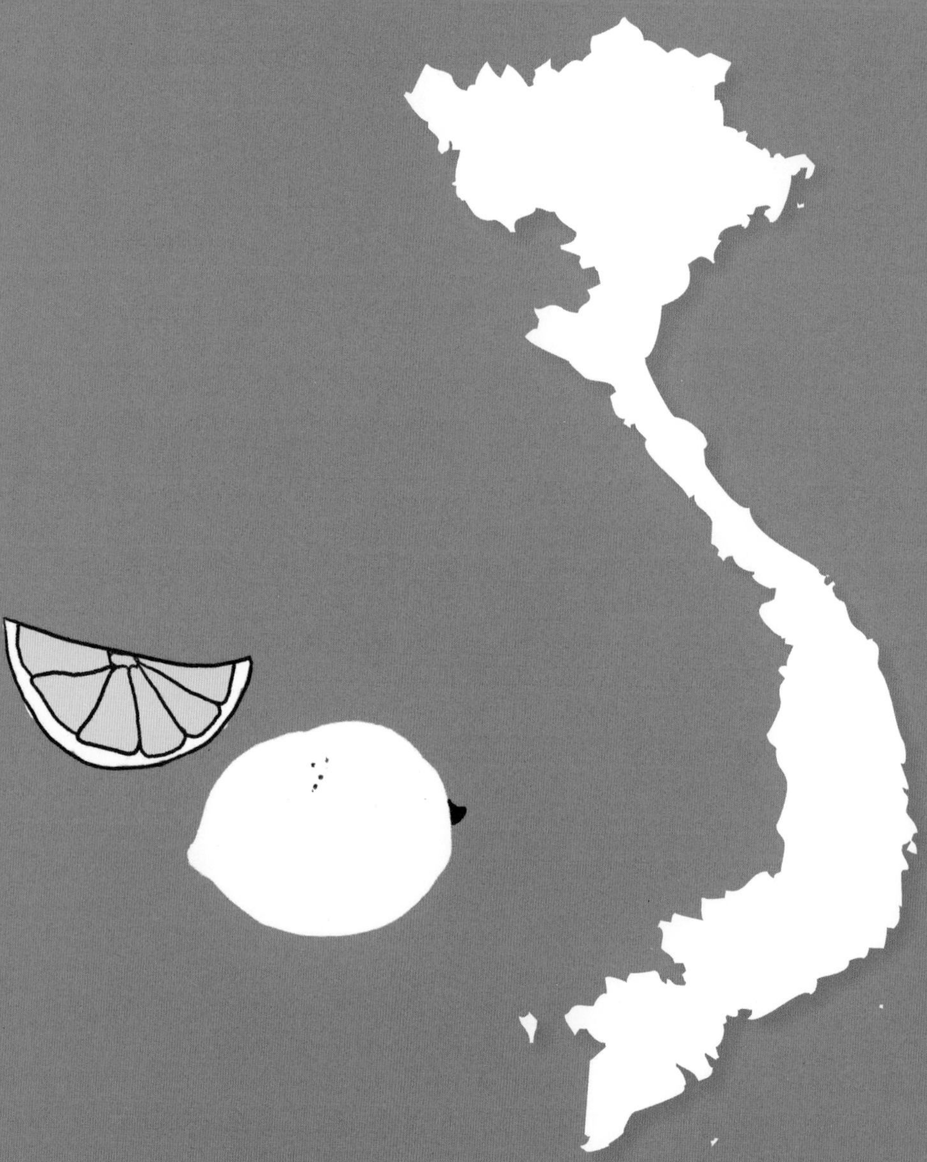

Culinary influences on Vietnamese food came, at a price, from trade, French colonisation and the up to 100,000 Vietnamese men who returned from fighting for the French in Europe in World War I. The colonial elite may have eaten all the beef, but the Vietnamese got the beef bones to make the country's signature pho soup, the condensed milk that's so loved in their coffee (which was handed out in World War I ration packs) and French ingredients, such as snails, pate and baguettes for banh mi, and a strange love affair with Swiss Maggi sauce.

Then there are the even more complex three 'Rules of Five', which underpin classical Vietnamese cooking. These state that every perfect meal must contain five tastes (spicy, sour, bitter, salty and sweet), five colours (white, green, yellow, red and black) and five ingredients that reflect something powdered (or carbs), something liquid, something mineral, something protein and something fat. Oh, and don't forget to balance the 'humours' in the Chinese medicinal fashion, which means always serve something cooling with something warming. So cool clams must come with warming ingredients, such as ginger or lemongrass, while the cooling sourness of, perhaps, lime leaves might be paired with warming chicken. Or something like that ...

Luckily, you can forget all of this because when you fake Vietnamese, or at least give other dishes a Vietnamese spin, you need only remember these four simple things.

FAKING IT TIPS

1. Use lots of fresh herbs, such as Vietnamese mint, Thai basil, perilla/shiso, coriander, mint, lemongrass and sawtooth coriander.
2. Do not overcook your proteins.
3. Always contrast textures, such as putting the crisp with the creamy – think of the softness of a rice paper wrapper around all that crisp veg inside.
4. Remember that fish sauce is used in a more forward manner than in Thailand. This 'nuoc mam' takes a stronger role in dipping sauces, such as nuoc cham (see page 98), where equal parts fish sauce and rice wine vinegar are only slightly softened with a little sugar, chilli and lime juice.

As for other key ingredients, chillies are pretty much a constant but used more softly than in, say, Thai cuisine, and turmeric and ginger also regularly feature, especially in braises and soups. Caster sugar is used for sweetness (although palm sugar will do), rice wine vinegar (or maybe coconut vinegar), lemons or limes are included for sourness, while crunch is delivered through fresh iceberg lettuce, raw carrot or cucumber, bean shoots and peanuts.

The protein choice is broad with pork (and pork skin), chicken, beef, freshwater fish and seafood all used, and pretty much every cooking (and non-cooking) technique pops up somewhere, from steaming and stir-frying to sauteeing and searing.

SHOPPING LIST

Plunder the selection of rice paper sheets at your local supermarket and, if you can find them, buy the patterned filigree rice paper wrappers. They'll make the fried rice paper rolls on page 90 even prettier as the pattern becomes more pronounced with cooking. Also, stock up on rice noodles and a couple of authentic Vietnamese fish sauces – a cheaper one for everyday use and a posh one for best.

If you want to get hardcore, pick up some Vietnamese fermented shrimp paste (mam ruoc) or the southern version 'mam nem', which is made with fermented anchovies for an extra pungent and punchy fishy umami hit in soups, such as the classic beef noodle soup 'bún bò Huế', or as an extra funky dipping sauce softened with a little lime juice, sugar and chilli.

The fresh section of your local Vietnamese grocer will also give you lots of joy. Look for banana blossom to shred into salads, fresh turmeric, wood ear mushrooms, the best Vietnamese mint and more esoteric herbs, such as perilla, fish mint to use with fish, dill, which is magnificent loaded onto turmeric-flavoured fish, and rice paddy herb, which tastes a little like coriander seeds and cumin and goes well in soups soured with tamarind or used for wrapping stuff, such as crab.

RICE PAPER ROLLS

These rolls are light on lettuce and noodles but heavy on fresh herbs, which makes them that little bit more sophisticated than the ones you buy in the shops. The dipping sauce, however, is dead common.

SERVES: 4 (MAKES 8) **PREP:** 20 MINS **COOKING:** 5 MINS

50 g rice vermicelli noodles
2 teaspoons vegetable oil
8 × 22 cm round rice paper wrappers
8 small perilla or shiso leaves (leave out or replace with coriander if you can't find these)
16 Vietnamese mint leaves (use mint if you can't find this)
16 Thai basil leaves
2 iceberg lettuce leaves, finely shredded into lengths no longer than 5 cm
1 Lebanese cucumber, cut into matchsticks
1 small carrot, cut into matchsticks
12 medium cooked peeled prawns, sliced in half lengthways (or chopped into 1.5 cm pieces if that's too fiddly)

HOISIN DIPPING SAUCE
80 ml (⅓ cup) hoisin sauce (see TIPS)
1 large tablespoon peanut butter
2 teaspoons rice wine vinegar
1 tablespoon mirin, warmed, or hot water
1 tablespoon salted peanuts, coarsely chopped (optional)
1 long red chilli, deseeded and finely chopped

Cook the noodles following the packet directions. Drain and rinse under cold running water. Place the noodles in a large bowl, then use scissors to snip the long strands a few times. Drizzle with the oil and toss to coat lightly.

To make the hoisin dipping sauce, combine the hoisin and peanut butter in a bowl. Add the rice wine vinegar, mirin or water and stir until the sauce has the viscosity of thickened cream. Add a little more water if needed. Spoon into a small serving bowl and sprinkle with the peanuts (if using) and chilli.

The jeopardy with this recipe comes in the rice paper rolling. If you soak the rice paper too much, it will be tricky to handle and the rolls could burst; if you don't soak it enough, it could tear and will be tough to eat. Don't worry, I will walk you through it.

Dunk one wrapper in a bowl of cold water for about 10 seconds to soften slightly, then lay on a clean surface or a sheet of baking paper.

Place a line of herbs along the top one-third of the wrapper. Don't take the filling right to the edge of the rice paper or you won't be able to enclose it properly. Build a small bank of noodles along the bottom one-third of the wrapper, then top with a line of lettuce, cucumber, carrot and halved prawns. The line of prawns should be faintly visible through the rice paper but if you can't be pfaffed, just chop them up.

Carefully roll the wrapper over the noodles to encase the filling. Fold in the outside edges and roll up firmly to enclose. Repeat to make eight rolls all up. Ideally these should be of equal size but no one is going to judge you if they are not.

Serve the rice paper rolls with the hoisin dipping sauce.

TIPS

You can also serve the rolls with the nuoc cham dipping sauce on page 98, topped with coriander stalks (as pictured here), for a gluten-free option. Gluten-free hoisin sauce is available from Asian supermarkets.

Try other rice paper fillings, such as fresh chilli, spring onion, shredded chicken, strips of tofu, bean shoots or long, stinky but delicious garlic chives. If you are using garlic chives, just use one per roll and make sure the end peeks out like a rat's tail.

With the ingredients you don't use, whip up a prawn and vermicelli salad. No need to chop the prawns, and the hoisin dipping sauce makes a great dressing. Finish the salad with any leftover herbs and chopped peanuts. If you have any fried shallots in the cupboard, scatter them over the top for a satisfying crunch.

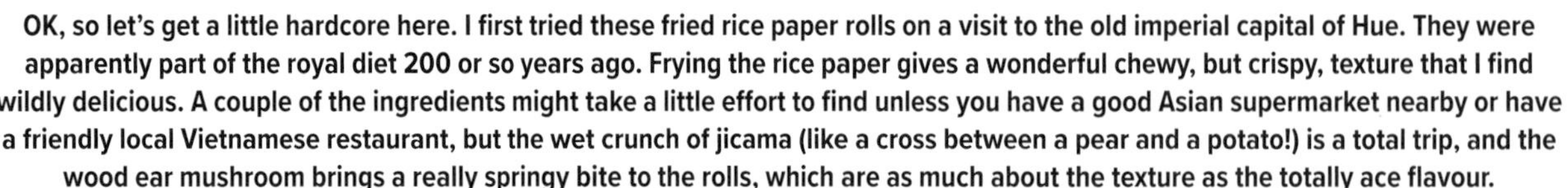

FRIED RICE PAPER SPRING ROLLS

OK, so let's get a little hardcore here. I first tried these fried rice paper rolls on a visit to the old imperial capital of Hue. They were apparently part of the royal diet 200 or so years ago. Frying the rice paper gives a wonderful chewy, but crispy, texture that I find wildly delicious. A couple of the ingredients might take a little effort to find unless you have a good Asian supermarket nearby or have a friendly local Vietnamese restaurant, but the wet crunch of jicama (like a cross between a pear and a potato!) is a total trip, and the wood ear mushroom brings a really springy bite to the rolls, which are as much about the texture as the totally ace flavour.

SERVES: 6 (MAKES ABOUT 30) **PREP:** 40 MINS (PLUS 30 MINS SOAKING & 15 MINS STANDING) **COOKING:** 30 MINS

30 g dried wood ear mushroom
450 g sweet potato, peeled, cut into 2 cm thick slices
½ teaspoon freshly ground black pepper
50 g cellophane noodles
260 g jicama, peeled and cut into matchsticks
1 carrot, cut into matchsticks
½ bunch coriander stalks, finely chopped (you need about 3 tablespoons)
2 Asian shallots, finely chopped
2 garlic cloves, finely chopped
1 teaspoon finely grated ginger
60 ml (¼ cup) fish sauce
30 × 22 cm round rice paper wrappers
vegetable or rice bran oil, for deep-frying
15 iceberg lettuce leaves, torn in half
your choice of fresh herbs (perilla or shiso, coriander, mint, Vietnamese mint, Thai basil), to serve
Nuoc cham (see page 98), to serve

Place the fungus in a bowl and cover with water. Set aside for 30 minutes or until soft. Drain and rinse.

While the fungus is soaking, place the sweet potato in a steamer basket over a saucepan of simmering water and steam for 12–15 minutes until soft but not mushy. Remove the steamer from the pan and set aside on the bench for the sweet potato to dry out for 10 minutes. Transfer the sweet potato to a large heatproof bowl, add the pepper and use a fork or masher to roughly mash.

Soak the noodles following the packet directions. Drain and rinse under cold running water, then transfer to a large bowl and use scissors to chop them into short lengths.

Cook the fungus in a saucepan of boiling water for 2 minutes. Drain and roughly chop. Add to the sweet potato, along with the jicama, noodles, carrot, coriander stalks, shallot, garlic, ginger and fish sauce. Mix with your hands until well combined, then set aside for 15 minutes to allow the flavours to develop.

Working with one wrapper at a time, brush with water or place between two wet tea towels to moisten. Don't over-moisten or leave too dry or they will break. Place a heaped tablespoon of filling along the bottom one-third of the wrapper. Carefully roll over the wrapper to enclose the filling, then fold in the sides and roll up firmly. Repeat with the remaining wrappers and filling to make about 30 rolls all up.

Pour enough oil into a wok, deep frying pan or deep-fryer to come 8–10 cm up the side. Heat over medium heat to 180°C on a cook's thermometer.

Working in batches of four, gradually add the rolls to the hot oil and use a slotted spoon to keep them moving and turning. Cook for 2½–3 minutes or until cooked and lightly golden (ensure the oil stays hot so the rolls don't stick). Transfer to a plate lined with paper towel to drain. Pile the spring rolls onto a large serving plate, along with the lettuce leaves and fresh herbs. Place the nuoc cham in a small bowl.

To eat, place a spring roll in a lettuce leaf, add a few herbs and drizzle over a little nuoc cham. Wrap everything up and devour!

TIP

If you fry dry rice paper wrappers they will puff up to make thin crispy crackers, which can be seasoned and served with a big, and very cold, bottle of Vietnamese beer.

BANH MI

In all my long life I've never been banhed from a pub, but casinos are another matter entirely. Sadly, they didn't banh mi as a young lad for counting cards or being part of some sexy Ocean's 11-type syndicate – I'll have Julia Roberts' role please – but because we snuck into an accounting firm's function and ate all their sushi.

Note for Ed: We also flirted outrageously with all the women, helped ourselves to bottles of champagne and were generally hotter and more fun than the accountant partners – those were the days! Looking back, I think the cardinal sin we committed was the last one ... but let's not put any of that in this introduction.

Ed: Very wise, Matt. Deleting as we speak.

MAKES: 4 **PREP:** 10 MINS

4 long white bread rolls (see TIPS)
1½ tablespoons good-quality whole-egg mayonnaise
80 g store-bought chicken liver pate
ground white pepper
400 g barbecue pork, thinly sliced (see TIPS)
2 Lebanese cucumbers, thinly sliced diagonally
90 g (⅔ cup) Pickled carrot & daikon (see page 94)
4 bird's eye chillies if you like it hot, or long red if you prefer it milder, sliced
½ white onion, thinly sliced
½ bunch coriander, sprigs picked
¼ lime or lemon
a few drops of Maggi seasoning

Split the bread rolls in half lengthways, but don't cut them all the way through. Spread a heaped teaspoon of mayo on one cut side of each roll and pate on the other. Season with white pepper.

Divide all the remaining ingredients among the rolls, layering and stuffing until they are brimming with ingredients, then eat!!!

TIPS

Barbecued pork is sold ready to eat from Vietnamese and Chinese restaurants – look for the hanging meat in the windows. You can also use crispy-skin pork or duck.

You want your bread rolls to be light and fluffy on the inside and crunchy on the outside. If you can't find crusty Vietnamese rolls, go for a French baguette.

There are no rules to banh mi, so construct your filling to your liking: pate in or out; extra chilli; crispy pork with crackling instead of barbecued; poached or roasted chicken instead of pork; fried tofu (and no pate for a vegetarian version); add crispy fried shallots; use spring onions or red onion instead of white.

FOOD NERD HISTORY: The French introduced the baguette and pate into Vietnam in the late 19th century during an ugly period of colonial oppression, but it took a long time before the banh mi was born as a street snack. First, mayonnaise (more stable in the heat) replaced butter in the traditional French cold-cut-stuffed baguettes. These became popular with the Vietnamese (rather than the French colonists) during World War II. By then, the baguette had evolved into the airy-centred Vietnamese version we know today; however, banh mi as we know them didn't appear until the late 1950s.

The partition of the country into North and South in 1954 meant that a million migrants fled south. Many arrived in Saigon and some opened cheap sandwich stands as a way of making a living. The banh mi was born in 1958 at Hòa Mã in District 3 on Nguyễn Đình Chiểu Street.

MORE FOOD NERD HISTORY: Maggi seasoning became part of the Vietnamese pantry after World War II, when the French colonial masters left behind warehouses filled with this Swiss umami bomb, which were subsequently liberated and emptied by hungry Vietnamese. You can buy Maggi seasoning at most supermarkets; it acts as the salt component in your banh mi.

FOOD NERD FACT: Banh mi actually just means 'bread' and is a shortening of the roll's full name, *bánh mì thịt ngoui*, although with pickles, mayo and chilli added to the mix, it really is a 'banh mi with the lot'. Or a *bánh mì đặc biệt* if you want to get all Vietnamese about it!

PICKLED CARROT & DAIKON

These delicious pickles are essential to banh mi and Vietnamese crispy pancakes (see pages 93 and 98), but really they go with pretty much anything, whether it's barbecued steak or chook, on a rice/poke bowl or tossed through a slaw for a bright surprise.

MAKES: 400 g **PREP:** 5 MINS (PLUS 30 MINS SALTING & 1 HOUR PICKLING)

2 large (about 350 g) carrots, cut into 5–6 cm long matchsticks
1 small (about 350 g) daikon radish, cut into 5–6 cm long matchsticks
3 teaspoons sea salt
80 g caster sugar
80 ml (⅓ cup) boiling water
125 ml (½ cup) rice wine vinegar

Place the carrot and daikon in a large bowl, add half the salt and toss to combine. Set aside for 30 minutes to soften. Rinse and pat dry with paper towel.

Combine the sugar, boiling water and remaining salt in a bowl and stir until the sugar and salt have dissolved. Stir in the vinegar.

Pack the carrot and daikon into sterilised jars (see TIP) and pour over the pickling liquid. Set aside for 1–2 hours, then they are ready to eat. The pickles will keep in the fridge for several weeks.

TIP

To sterilise jars, preheat the oven to 120°C/100°C fan-forced. Wash the jars in hot soapy water and dry well. Remove the lids and place the clean jars upright on a baking tray and heat in the oven for 15–20 minutes. While you heat the jars, boil the lids in a saucepan of boiling water for 10 minutes and air-dry on a wire rack. (It's best not to sterilise the lids in the oven because this will damage any rubber seals.) Fill the jars while still warm and seal.

QUICK PHO

Yes, it IS gluten free!

Ed: Is this a common question with pho?

Me: No, and that's exactly why it is the perfect introduction!!! Oblique, slightly random and unnervingly irrelevant! OK, axe this and we'll just go with the intro below ...

This Vietnamese soup originated in the area of textile workers south of Hanoi and must surely rate as one of the 20 greatest dishes in the world; mainly for the way it takes simple ingredients and turns them into something quite divine. Initially sold by roving street vendors, the first beef stock phos appeared at static pho stands in the early 19th century due to the availability of cheap beef bones during the French colonial period. (Originally, Vietnam's colonial masters ate all the meat, so the bones were freely available!) Sliced beef made its way into pho in Hanoi in the 1930s, but it was still quite an austere dish back then. It wasn't until partition that pho headed south to Saigon with a tidal wave of post-partition migrants fleeing the north. Now pho was freed from the old traditions and a riot of fresh new ingredients and sauces became part of the wonderful clean soup that we love today. And yes, it IS pronounced 'furrr', not 'foe'.

SERVES: 4 **PREP:** 15 MINS (PLUS 1 HOUR FREEZING) **COOKING:** 20 MINS

400 g beef (flank steak, chuck roast, a flat cut of brisket or scotch fillet)
2 litres good-quality gluten-free beef stock
½ white onion
5 cm knob of ginger, peeled and sliced
5 whole cloves
3 whole star anise
1 cinnamon stick
1 garlic clove
1 teaspoon coriander seeds
½ teaspoon black peppercorns
15 g palm sugar, plus extra if needed
1 red chilli (bird's eye for heat, long for mild), halved lengthways
1 tablespoon fish sauce, plus extra if needed
150 g rice stick noodles
8 baby corn spears, halved lengthways

TO SERVE

lots of fresh herbs (choose from coriander, mint, Vietnamese mint, Thai basil and perilla)
150 g bean shoots
4 red chillies (bird's eye for heat, long for mild), sliced
2 spring onions, white and dark green parts sliced diagonally
2 limes or lemons, cut into wedges
hot chilli sauce, such as sriracha, to serve

Place the beef in the freezer for 1 hour to firm up. This makes it easier to shave into paper-thin slices. Use a sharp knife to cut the meat against the grain into thin slices. Set aside at room temperature on sheets of baking paper.

Place the stock, onion, ginger, cloves, star anise, cinnamon, garlic, coriander seeds, peppercorns, palm sugar and chilli in a large saucepan over medium–high heat. Bring just to the boil, then reduce the heat to low and gently simmer for 15 minutes. Stir in the fish sauce, then taste and balance with more palm sugar or fish sauce, if needed. If it is too strong for you, dilute the broth with up to 200 ml water. Strain into a large jug or bowl, discarding the solids. Return the broth to the saucepan.

While the broth is simmering, cook the rice noodles for half the time specified in the packet directions. They will continue to cook when you pour over the hot stock later, so if you cook them fully now they will have become mushy by the time you are halfway through your pho.

Divide the noodles among serving bowls and top with the sliced beef and corn. Pour over the piping-hot stock. Serve immediately with a large platter loaded with an abundance of fresh herbs, bean shoots, chilli, spring onion, lime or lemon wedges and, of course, a bottle of sriracha or your favourite hot chilli sauce for squeezing over the top. This way, everyone at the table can pick and choose their favourite additions.

TIPS

For a vegetarian version, use vegetable stock instead of beef stock, and replace the meat with tofu and a variety of mushrooms.

Similarly, make a chicken version with chicken stock and thin slices of poached chicken.

Add any Asian green vegetables for an even more virtuous bowl of goodness.

VIETNAMESE CRISPY PANCAKE

(BANH XEO)

The filling variations for this dish are endless. I have chosen the virtuous road – poached chicken, fresh herbs and nuoc cham, because *that is who I am*! Don't look so shocked! Doubter! Honestly, my life is not *all* about bacon and marmalade sandwiches, crunchy fried chicken smothered in smoky Japanese mayo and sweet chilli sauce, and ice-cream. Sadly ...

MAKES: 6 PANCAKES **PREP:** 25 MINS (PLUS 30 MINS CHILLING) **COOKING:** 20 MINS

200 g rice flour
1 teaspoon ground turmeric
1 teaspoon caster sugar
½ teaspoon sea salt
1 × 400 ml can coconut cream
125 ml (½ cup) soda water
8 spring onions, white part very finely chopped, dark green part thinly sliced
3 × 250 g chicken breast fillets
3 teaspoons vegetable or coconut oil
2 handfuls bean shoots
2 Lebanese cucumbers, cut into thin 5 cm long batons
2 long red chillies, thinly sliced
150 g Pickled carrot and daikon **(see page 94)**
½ bunch each coriander, Vietnamese mint, Thai basil and mint

NUOC CHAM

1 red bird's eye chilli, chopped (more if you like it really hot, or use a deseeded long red chilli if you don't)
1 small garlic clove, finely chopped
80 ml (⅓ cup) fish sauce, plus extra if needed
70 g (⅓ cup) caster sugar
1 tablespoon lime juice, plus extra if needed
1 tablespoon lemon juice

Combine the rice flour, turmeric, sugar and salt in a large bowl. Whisk in the coconut cream, then stir through the soda water and the white part of the spring onion until combined. Place the batter in the fridge for 30 minutes to thicken slightly.

Preheat the oven to 180°C/160°C fan-forced.

Bring a large saucepan of water to the boil. Add the chicken and bring the water back to the boil. Cover with a tight-fitting lid, then remove from the heat and set aside for 11 minutes or until poached through. Transfer the chicken to a plate and cover loosely with foil. Rest for at least 10 minutes, then shred the chicken.

To make the nuoc cham, place the chilli and garlic in a mortar and pound with a pestle to form a paste. Transfer the paste to a small bowl, add the remaining ingredients and 2 tablespoons water, and stir until the sugar has dissolved. Season with more fish sauce or lime juice until it hits that sweet spot – which varies from person to person. When you are happy, set the sauce aside.

To make the pancakes, swirl ½ teaspoon of the oil around the base of a 28 cm frying pan and heat until the pan is super hot. Don't be tempted to add more oil, otherwise the batter won't adhere to the side of the pan and crisp up. Wipe out any excess oil.

Working quickly, place one ladleful of batter in the pan and swirl the pan so the batter goes a little way up the side (the edge of the pancake will be thinner than the middle). Cook for about 3 minutes, then use a spatula to work around the edge and slide the pancake gently onto a baking tray, taking care not to break it. Place in the oven to keep warm and repeat with the remaining oil and batter. If you feel up to the challenge, get two pans going at once, you pro, you!

Arrange the chicken, dark green part of the spring onion, bean shoots, cucumber, chilli, pickled carrot and daikon and herbs on a serving platter. Serve with the pancakes for everyone to fill themselves and enjoy with the nuoc cham.

TIPS

To make this pancake even more 'clean', eat it with your hands wrapped in a lettuce leaf, fresh herbs and cucumber. As in, you roll the pancake in the lettuce leaf loaded with herbs, not wrap your hands in lettuce leaves. I've just tried this, and having your fingers swathed in crispy iceberg or flannelly butter lettuce seriously reduces your dexterity and makes it very hard to dip the pancake into the sauce.

There are so many delicious things you can fill your pancakes with. Try sliced pan-fried pork and onion, or use pan-fried shiitake and enoki mushrooms and/or fried tofu in place of the chicken.

BUN CHA

We live in interesting times. On one hand, junky white bread sandwiches have never been cooler in cool restaurants (see our Tonkatsu sandwich on page 53); on the other hand, customers are demanding their burgers come without buns, as an aversion to refined flour and allergies to gluten and yeast grip another section of the community. Welcome, then, Hanoi's traditional bun cha – basically little burgers that are meant to be wrapped in lettuce with rice noodles, and don't miss the bun at all. It's shaping up to be the modern burger to unite them all!

SERVES: 4 **PREP:** 20 MINS **COOKING:** 20 MINS

500 g pork mince
2 garlic cloves, crushed
2 lemongrass stalks, inner white part only, finely chopped
3 teaspoons fish sauce
1 egg, lightly whisked
1 bunch coriander, leaves picked, stalks finely chopped
3 spring onions, white and dark green parts, thinly sliced into coins
1 tablespoon peanut or vegetable oil
200 g rice vermicelli noodles
1 iceberg lettuce, leaves separated
1 bunch mint, leaves picked (use Vietnamese mint if you can get it)
100 g bean shoots
nuoc cham (see page 98), to serve

Preheat the oven to 140°C/120°C fan-forced.

Combine the pork, garlic, lemongrass, fish sauce, egg and 1 tablespoon of the coriander stalks in a bowl. Finally, add the spring onion (you add this last as you want the coins to be crunchy little surprises in the patties). Shape into walnut-sized balls, then gently flatten into 2 cm thick patties.

Heat the oil in a large frying pan over medium–high heat. Taking care not to overcrowd the pan so the oil stays hot, add about six patties at a time and cook, turning occasionally, for 3 minutes or until golden and cooked through. Don't overcook them, as they will continue to cook in the residual heat. We're not after sawdust here. Place the cooked patties in a baking dish and keep warm in the oven while you cook the rest.

Meanwhile, cook the noodles following the packet directions. Drain and rinse under cold running water. Drain well.

To serve, divide the noodles among serving bowls. Top each bowl with a few patties. Serve the remaining patties in the middle of the table, along with piles of lettuce, mint, bean shoots and the coriander leaves.

To eat, take a lettuce leaf and add some mint, coriander, bean shoots and noodles. Top with a patty. Wrap and dunk in the nuoc cham dipping sauce and eat messily, so that the juices run down your chin. Delicious!

TIP

I would eat Vietnamese food every day if I could, and I often make a big batch of nuoc cham to keep on hand. I know food made from scratch is always better, but just in case I run out I keep a bottle of 'nuoc mam pha san' in my fridge and use it as a salad dressing, or mix it with a little fish sauce for dipping spring rolls in. You can buy it from Asian supermarkets.

SALT & PEPPER SQUID

Pizza comes from Naples. Hen's eggs come from chickens. Eddie McGuire comes from Broadmeadows. Usually when something is so well known, there is a general level of understanding of where it comes from. Pity then this salt and pepper squid, which seems to have miraculously appeared without anyone knowing where it originated from – a bit like white chocolate and eels.

It could be a Hakka dish, it could be from Hong Kong, it could have been invented by a guy called Mr Nguyen who sold salt and pepper squid on the streets of Nha Trang back when Ho Chi Min was a boy.

The plausibility of the Nguyen claim is bolstered by the fact that apparently there are 25 species of squid under the Teuthoidea order in Vietnam's territorial waters. The sea around Hon Mat Island off the coast of Nha Trang is famous for its squid and, according to the Vietnam Association of Seafood Exporters and Producers (VASEP), Vietnam is the fourth largest exporter of squid to the European Union these days. So they certainly have enough squid to make the dish popular and cheap. The flaw in this compelling argument is that, while these squid facts are true, I know it's a made-up story ... because I just made it up. Why? Because I think that every superhero dish needs a great origin story. We just need to add a radioactive spider or a disastrous lab accident ...

SERVES: 4–6 AS A STARTER **PREP:** 20 MINS **COOKING:** 10 MINS

1 heaped tablespoon sea salt
1 teaspoon freshly ground white or black pepper
1.2 kg (about 6 medium) squid with tentacles, cleaned
vegetable or rice bran oil, for deep-frying
50 g (⅓ cup) plain flour
3–4 long red chillies, thinly sliced
¼ bunch coriander, leaves picked
2 lemons, cut into wedges

Make sure everything is ready to go as this dish comes together very quickly. The oil needs to be hot before you start cooking, you need a plate lined with paper towel for draining any excess oil and a slotted metal spoon to remove the cooked squid.

Lightly grind the salt so you don't get big flakes on the squid, which will make it too salty. Place in a bowl with the pepper and mix to combine. Set aside.

Cut the squid hoods in half lengthways and the tentacles into pairs. Cut any super-long tentacles in half. Pat dry with paper towel. Use a sharp knife to score the inside of the hoods in a small criss-cross pattern without cutting all the way through, then cut each hood into 4 cm tiles.

Pour enough oil into a wok, deep frying pan or deep-fryer to come 8 cm up the side. Heat over medium heat to 180°C on a cook's thermometer.

Tip the flour into a bowl or zip-lock bag. Add the squid and toss to coat, shaking off the excess. Some people add the salt and pepper to the flour, but this gives little control over the eventual saltiness. So don't.

Add the squid to the oil in batches and cook for 60 seconds or until crisp and golden. Use a slotted spoon to transfer to the plate lined with paper towel. Sprinkle with the salt and pepper mixture.

Arrange the cooked squid on a serving plate, tumble over the chilli and coriander and take to the table immediately. Finish with a squeeze of lemon juice at the last minute and serve with the remaining wedges on the side.

TIP

Follow these five simple tips to help ensure that your squid is super crispy! 1. Pat the squid dry before dusting in flour. 2. Make sure the oil has come to temperature before frying. 3. Fry in batches! 4. Do not overcrowd the wok, pan or fryer!!! If you do, the oil will lose heat and you will have soggy squid. 5. For a gluten-free option, replace the flour with chickpea flour, coarse rice flour, potato flour or cornflour.

MARNIE'S TRUMPIAN-YELLOW TURMERIC CHICKEN THIGHS

Always keen for an oven-to-table dinner, and feeling the pressure to keep reinventing Marnie's thighs, we came up with this dish but struggled to think of a name. The turmeric gives it a hue of Trumpian yellow, but in a good way. It's family friendly without the chillies, which are only used as a garnish at the end. It also rails against FAKE NEWS, makes things up and has a very active Twitter account all of its own. OK ... there's the name sorted!!!

SERVES: 4 **PREP:** 20 MINS (PLUS 1 HOUR MARINATING) **COOKING:** 25 MINS

8 chicken thigh fillets, excess fat trimmed
1 teaspoon sea salt
coriander leaves, to serve
2 red bird's eye chillies if you like it hot or long red if you prefer it milder, thinly sliced
1 lime, cut into wedges

MARINADE

1 teaspoon black peppercorns
60 g palm sugar
5 garlic cloves, coarsely chopped
5 cm knob of turmeric, peeled and finely grated
5 cm knob of ginger, peeled and finely grated
4 kaffir lime leaves, finely shredded
2½ tablespoons finely chopped lemongrass (inner white part only)
1 heaped tablespoon finely grated galangal
2 tablespoons peanut oil
1 tablespoon fish sauce
1 tablespoon light soy sauce

To make the marinade, place the peppercorns in a mortar and use a pestle to pound until crushed. Add the palm sugar, garlic, turmeric, ginger, kaffir lime, lemongrass and galangal and pound until a paste forms. Stir in the oil, fish sauce and soy sauce until well combined. You could use a blender, but it's not as good as getting your Trumpian frustrations out through a good pounding.

Tip the marinade into a large zip-lock bag, tray or bowl. Add the chicken and massage the flavours in to coat. Use gloves or coat your tiny hands in oil before touching the marinade to prevent your hands being stained yellow from the turmeric. Cover and set aside to marinate for 1 hour.

Preheat the oven 220°C/200°C fan-forced.

Place the chicken and marinade in a baking dish and spread out in a single layer. Sprinkle with the salt and bake for 20–25 minutes or until cooked through. The colour of the chicken will be tinged with gold from the turmeric and the edges should be a little charred.

Scatter over the coriander and red chilli as a reminder of the Donald's favourite red tie. Serve with lime wedges on the side. If the lime wedges resign, shift some blame on them and use lemon instead.

TRUMP TIPS

This chicken is great barbecued, though if you're going to do this use thighs with the skin on for the best results. Preheat the barbecue grill to medium–high, then cook the chook for 5 minutes each side. Rest for a few minutes and serve.

If caught doing something wrong, just deny it.

Slice the chicken and serve on a platter alongside a simple rice noodle salad. The easiest noodle salad has no rules but can be made by combining cooked, room-temperature noodles with loads of fresh Vietnamese herbs (try coriander, mint, Vietnamese mint, holy basil and perilla or shiso leaves) with all or any combination of sliced cucumber, julienned carrot, sliced red onion, crispy fried shallots and chopped salted roasted peanuts. Dress with nuoc cham (see page 98).

When in doubt, just say YOU'RE FIRED!

Slice the chicken and use as a filling for baguettes with Vietnamese herbs, long sprigs of coriander and Pickled carrot and daikon (see page 94).

STICKY CARAMEL & GINGER FISH

Sticky caramel and ginger fish ... that's all you need to know.

SERVES: 4 **PREP:** 20 MINS **COOKING:** 20 MINS

70 g palm sugar, finely chopped
60 ml (¼ cup) vegetable oil
3 garlic cloves, finely chopped
4 small Asian shallots, finely chopped
3 spring onions, white part finely chopped, dark green part sliced into 3 cm lengths
2 heaped tablespoons shredded ginger
½ long red chilli, thinly sliced, plus extra, shredded, to serve (optional)
60 ml (¼ cup) fish sauce
1 teaspoon freshly ground white or black pepper
4 × 2.5 cm thick skin-on fish cutlets or firm white fillets (such as blue-eye trevalla or barramundi)
2 Lebanese cucumbers or 1 telegraph cucumber, sliced diagonally
steamed rice, to serve

Start by making a caramel. Melt the palm sugar in a small saucepan over medium–low heat and cook for 3–5 minutes or until starting to bubble – keep an eye on it. Reduce the heat to low and stir in 60 ml (¼ cup) water – be careful as it will spit. Stir vigorously to combine, then simmer for 3–5 minutes or until thick and syrupy. Remove from the heat and set aside.

Dig out a claypot or large frying pan that will fit the fish in one layer. Heat the oil in the pan over medium heat. Add the garlic and cook for 1 minute or until it just starts to colour. Reduce the heat to low, add the shallot, white part of the spring onion, ginger and chilli (if using) and cook, stirring, for 1 minute or until aromatic. Stir in the fish sauce, followed by the caramel and pepper. Increase the heat to medium–low and let it bubble away for 1 minute.

Nestle the fish in the pan, skin-side up (if using fish fillets), and spoon some of the sauce over the top. Simmer over medium heat for 4 minutes, then gently turn over and cook the other side for 2–3 minutes or until the fish flakes when tested with a fork. The flesh should be lightly opaque and the sauce will have reduced a little and become sticky. Add a splash of water if the sauce has reduced and thickened too much.

Serve the fish from the pan or transfer to a serving plate. Scatter over the green spring onion and extra chilli, if you want an additional kick of heat. Serve with the cucumber and rice.

COCONUT PANNA COTTA WITH CARAMEL SAUCE

Seriously, is there anything I could possibly say here that would make this dish any more appealing than the photo over there?

SERVES: 4 **PREP:** 20 MINS (PLUS 4 HOURS CHILLING) **COOKING:** 25 MINS

3 gold-strength gelatine sheets
100 ml full-cream milk
200 ml sweetened condensed milk
1 × 400 ml can coconut cream

CARAMEL SAUCE
200 g caster sugar
160 ml pouring cream

PRALINE
50 g unsalted roasted peanuts, coarsely chopped
120 g caster sugar

Place the gelatine sheets in a bowl of cold water and set aside for 5 minutes until soft.

Pour the milk and condensed milk into a small saucepan over medium heat and bring almost to boiling point (it just needs to be hot enough to melt the gelatine). Remove from the heat. Use your hands to squeeze the excess water from the gelatine sheets, then add to the hot milk and stir until dissolved. Stir in the coconut cream. Set aside to cool slightly, then pour into four 220 ml moulds or glasses. Place in the fridge for at least 4 hours or until completely set.

Meanwhile, make the caramel sauce. Place the sugar in the centre of a medium saucepan with high sides. Pour 60 ml (¼ cup) water around the outside of the sugar, being careful not to get any dry sugar crystals on the side of the pan. (Dry sugar crystals can crystallise the sugar after it has melted and this is *not* what we are after.) Use a fork to draw the water into the sugar until all the sugar is wet. Bring to the boil over high heat and cook without stirring for 8 minutes or until the sugar starts to caramelise. At this point, give the pan the occasional swirl to even out the colour. It will brown quickly, so keep an eye on it. When the sugar is a golden amber colour, remove the pan from the heat and add the cream. This will bubble and spit, so be careful. Stir until well combined, then pour into a small jug and set aside to cool completely.

To make the praline, spread the nuts out on a baking tray lined with baking paper. Following the same method as the previous step, place the sugar in the centre of a small saucepan and pour 2 tablespoons water around the outside of the sugar. Continue to make the caramel as described above until it becomes lovely and golden, then pour it over the nuts and set aside to cool completely.

When you are ready to serve, pour the cold caramel sauce over the panna cottas. Crack the praline into large pieces and arrange on top.

TIP

Panna cottas are the perfect make-ahead dessert. Make them up to 2 days in advance, then cover and store in the fridge until needed. Top with the caramel and praline just before serving. This is also delicious served with slices of barbecued pineapple on the side.

EUROPE

Germs, guns and steel made Europe the centre of the globe for centuries, and with that power came wealth and population, ensuring that the royal courts and peasant cottages of France, Spain, Italy and Greece all gave us great dishes. On the face of it, it is the simple dishes invented by home cooks, however, that resonate most strongly in the pages that follow, whether you are prepping a midweek meal or making something a little more fancy for the weekend.

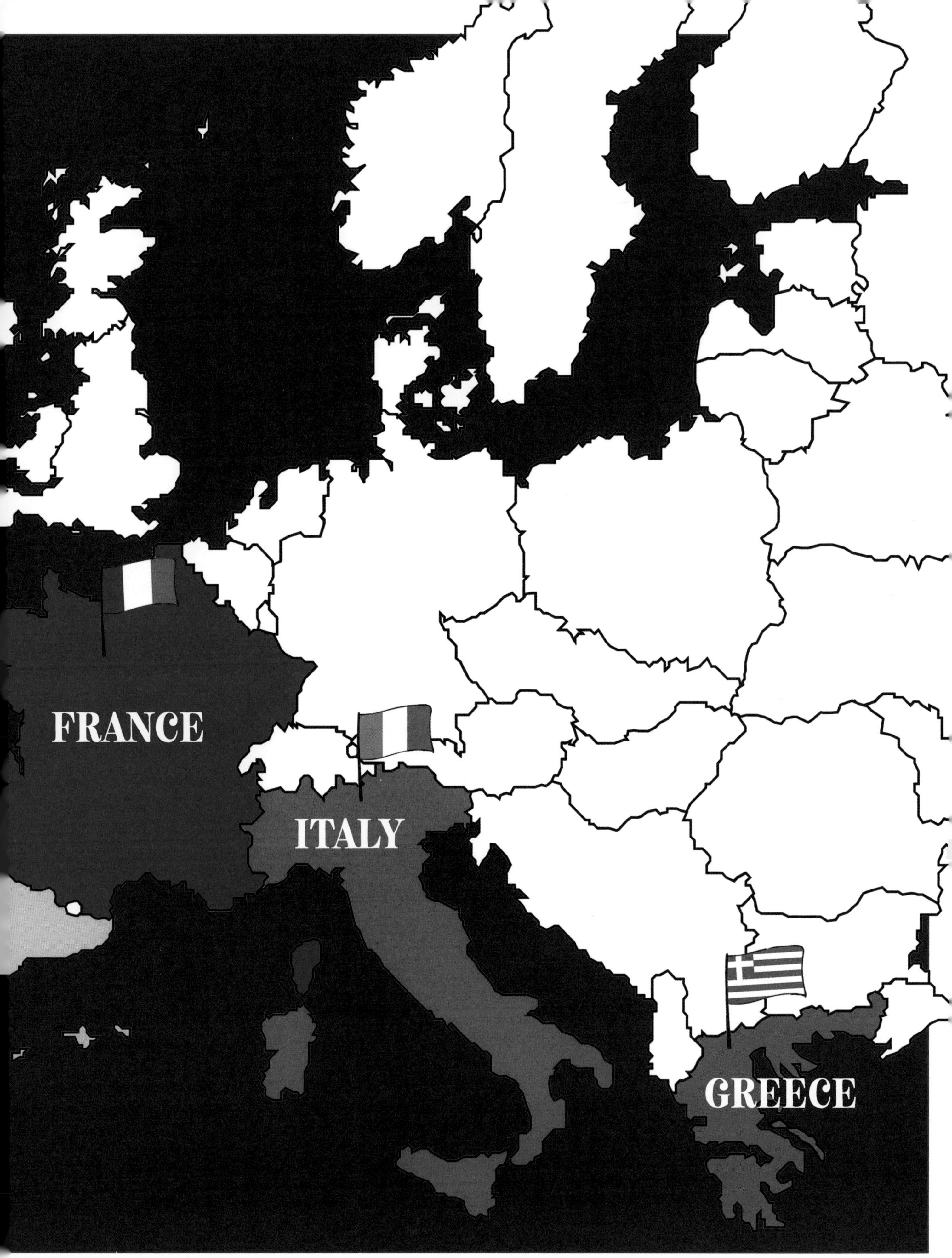

FRANCE

ITALY

GREECE

FRANCE

The definitive book on French cuisine, *Larousse Gastronomique*, is 1,350 pages long, and I'm going to try and define the essence of French food in about 0.0005% of those words. Here goes!

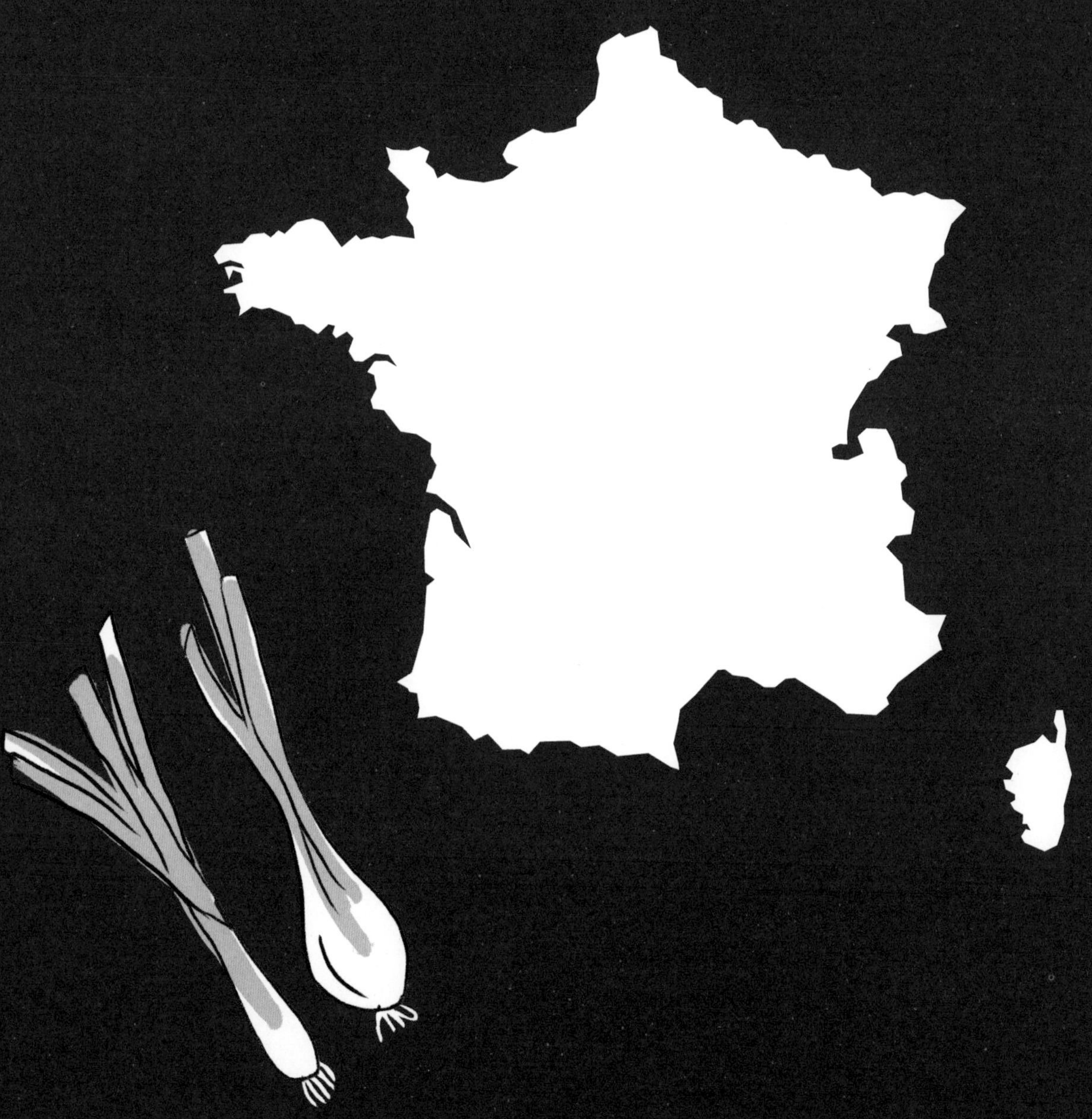

France is a country of sauces, 'soupes', 'salades' and braises. It is also a country of cows, chickens, pigs, sheep and, to a lesser extent, goats, so, meat, cheese, eggs and cream (although this is used less regularly these days) all figure prominently.

The French kitchen is generally not a place for spices in savoury dishes; instead herbs, such as parsley, chives, thyme, tarragon and chervil (the fine herbs of 'haute cuisine') join pepper, mustard, onions, bacon and, of course, garlic as the key flavourings. And often the local drop – most often wine, but it could also be beer, cider (in Normandy and Brittany) or a local grape, pear or apple brandy – joins in too.

The French also have a wonderful tradition of using all of the animal, which accounts for a rich selection of pates, sausages and cured meats; while wooded areas and regular rain ensure a love of truffles, mushrooms (such as cep and chanterelles), honey, berries and game. Duck is popular too, and long expanses of coastline account for a love of fish, such as sea bass, tuna and salmon, and shellfish including mussels, prawns and little shrimp, crustaceans and oysters, which can all be cooked simply (yay!) or heavily sauced (boo!). (For a yay! moment, see the mussels recipe on page 123.)

Those sauces usually rely on that magic liaison between eggs and fat (think oil or butter), whether it's a hollandaise for your asparagus or a bearnaise for that steak. Then there are those sauces that rely on thickening milk or stock with a flour and fat-based 'roux', such as a veloute or perhaps a bechamel to top your Croque monsieur (see page 132).

France's great culinary sauces are a little thin on the ground these days, with simple stock-based jus or pan-juice-derived dressings taking their place, as the 'cuisine grandmere', or peasant cooking, takes precedence over the finnicky, show-off food; fancy dishes, which the great champions of fine dining, such as Escoffier, took to the world as a mark of France's cultural and culinary superiority.

At least France's famous vinaigrette survives, but this should only be used on one or two ingredients at a time in a salad – such as tomatoes and shallots, or just butter lettuce leaves by themselves – as this shows you understand French restraint and elegance.

The choice of fruit and veg will be familiar to Australian readers, with green beans, leeks, turnips, carrots, potatoes, onions and legumes, such as lentils, white beans and peas, all prized, alongside stone fruits, pears, apples, melons and all manner of berries.

The warmer climate in the south of the country means a Mediterranean palate of flavours is celebrated, including olives, olive oil (rather than butter), anchovies, tomatoes, zucchini, eggplants, goat's cheese and lemons. Here, tougher herbs, such as rosemary, basil, fennel, oregano and even lavender prevail.

While much of the classical French canon might seem a little dated or heavy these days, their old-school skills when it comes to baking and desserts still wow the world. Puff pastry, choux buns, crepes, galettes, souffles, tarts and quiches are still all skills worth learning as they, at least, will never go out of fashion.

If you want to give a dish the French touch, follow these six steps.

FAKING IT TIPS

1. Pan-fry, saute, braise or occasionally poach ingredients.
2. Make a sauce to serve with your protein, whether it's a 'beurre noisette' for chicken, a 'beurre blanc' for fish or a red wine sauce turned silky at the end by whisking in cold butter for that steak. Or you can deglaze the pan you've cooked in – try vermouth for fish and other seafood, red wine or red wine vinegar for beef and a little white wine followed by Dijon mustard and cream to reduce and slightly thicken the sauce for your chicken.
3. Be generous with the wine and garlic in all of your braises. Start off with a 'mirepoix' of finely diced onion, carrot and celery, and brown your meat before adding any liquid.
4. Don't be afraid to use delicate fresh herbs in your cooking and as a garnish. Make your own bouquet garni by tying up a tight little bundle of parsley, bay leaf and thyme to throw into your stews and soups.
5. Serve a good crusty baguette and French butter at the start of every meal and a salad of vinaigrette-dressed butter lettuce after the main course (not that tawdry mix of oak and other B-grade leaves you find in supermarkets).
6. Roll your eyes when someone suggests that London, Barcelona, Copenhagen or Modena are more exciting places to eat than Paris, and then immediately change the conversation to the World Cup. *Allez les Bleus!!*

SHOPPING LIST

The majority of the ingredients and flavourings found in French cuisine can be easily purchased from the supermarket, but if you want to make a dish even more 'chic', then take a trip to your nearest French-inspired deli and seek out the really good stuff – basically anything expensive, hard to find and boutique! Think thick French butter in a heavy foil wrapper, more Comte cheese than you know you'll need, good French white vermouth, exotic vinegars from somewhere in 'La Belle France' that you've never heard of or a classic French mustard, such as a top-notch Dijon. Basically, 'if it's come from France it must be good', goes the old shopping mantra ... even if it's not true!

Beef Daube

Everything the French do is classy. Somehow, they've managed to convince us that theirs is the language of love, that no one can design a gown quite like they can, and that their simple peasant dishes are worthy of sainthood. The tiny part of me descended from Huguenots (French Protestants) is a little proud of this; however, the vast majority of me is a little bit snarky and screams, 'a daube is just a stew!'.

This is the same part of me that starts a terse exchange over a family dinner by pointing out that, in spite of the French name, a casserole is still a stew too, no matter how expensive the cut of lamb is. Some people can't handle the truth ...

Maybe the French have a point though. A daube or casserole does sound classier, and stews deserve that elevation for the way that, given time, they turn even the most basic of ingredients into something sublime. Make this daube a couple of days in advance and it will become a dish quite startling; make it quicker and it's still pretty darned good.

SERVES: 8 **PREP:** 30 MINS (PLUS 4 HOURS MARINATING) **COOKING:** 3 HOURS

1.5 kg beef chuck steak, cut into 5 cm chunks
3 brown onions, thinly sliced
4 thyme sprigs
3 whole cloves
2 fresh or dried bay leaves
1 teaspoon freshly grated nutmeg
1 × 750 ml bottle red wine (Cotes du Rhone or an Aussie shiraz)
plain flour, for dusting
2–3 tablespoons extra virgin olive oil
sea salt and freshly ground black pepper
400 g carrots, thickly sliced
2 celery stalks, coarsely chopped
1 tablespoon tomato paste
juice of 1 orange
250 g piece Kaiserfleisch, speck or bacon, rind removed, cut into 5 mm thick batons (see TIPS)
12 small Swiss brown mushrooms, halved
mashed, pureed or boiled potatoes, to serve

Combine the beef, onion, thyme, cloves, bay leaves and nutmeg in a large bowl. Pour over the wine, then cover and marinate in the fridge for at least 4 hours or overnight.

Preheat the oven to 200°C/180°C fan-forced.

Using a slotted spoon or tongs, transfer the meat to a plate lined with paper towel and the onion to a bowl. Reserve the marinade mixture.

Pat the beef dry with paper towel and dust with a little flour. Heat 1 tablespoon of the oil in a large flameproof casserole dish over medium heat. Add the beef in batches and cook until all sides are nicely golden, adding more oil as needed. Transfer each batch to a plate and season well with salt and pepper.

Add the carrot, celery and reserved onion to the casserole dish and cook for a few minutes. Add the tomato paste and cook for another minute, stirring and scraping any burnt bits off the bottom of the dish.

Return the meat and reserved marinade to the casserole and stir in the orange juice. Cover with a tight-fitting lid and bake in the oven for 2½ hours.

While the beef is cooking, place the Kaiserfleisch, speck or bacon in one frying pan and the mushroom in another, and cook over medium heat until lightly browned.

Carefully remove the casserole from the oven and place over medium heat. Add the mushroom and Kaiserfleisch, speck or bacon. Cook, stirring occasionally, for 10 minutes or until the sauce has reduced slightly. Season to taste.

Serve the daube with mashed, pureed or boiled potatoes.

TIPS

Daube is perfect for freezing. Spoon it into an airtight container and freeze for up to 3 months. Thaw overnight in the fridge, then gently reheat before serving.

Kaiserfleisch can be bought from a good butchers, deli or the deli section of larger supermarkets, especially those with German or Austrian roots. It has a strong smoky bacon flavour that works perfectly in this dish. If you can't buy Kaiserfleisch you can use a piece of speck or bacon instead.

Cassoulet

Duck fat is the sort of luxury that makes French food so darned tasty but, unlike truffles and cep mushrooms, it doesn't cost an arm and a leg. This classic pork and bean stew from the south-west of France benefits greatly from the decadent stickiness the duck fat brings, so do use it if you can.

SERVES: 4 **PREP:** 30 MINS (PLUS 15 MINS RESTING) **COOKING:** 2 HOURS 50 MINS

30 g duck or goose fat (or equal parts butter and oil)
4 large brown onions, 3 thinly sliced, 1 quartered
4 large garlic cloves, thinly sliced
400 g piece Kaiserfleisch, speck or bacon, rind removed, cut into 1 cm thick batons
3 thick Italian sausages
3 × 400 g cans cannellini beans, rinsed and drained
500 g carrots, cut into 5 mm thick slices
4 thyme sprigs
2 fresh or dried bay leaves
4 store-bought confit duck marylands (see TIPS), each cut into two pieces
ground white pepper
25 g (⅓ cup) panko breadcrumbs (or make your own from stale bread)
chopped flat-leaf parsley, to serve

Melt the duck or goose fat in a large flameproof casserole dish or large frying pan over medium heat. Add the sliced onion and cook slowly, stirring occasionally, for 10–15 minutes or until caramelised. Reduce the heat to low, add the garlic and cook, stirring, for 2 minutes or until aromatic. Transfer the onion mixture to a large bowl. Add the Kaiserfleisch, speck or bacon to the dish and cook, stirring, for 4–5 minutes or until crispy. Transfer to the onion mixture. Add the sausages to the dish and cook, turning occasionally, for 5 minutes or until browned all over. Transfer the sausages to a plate lined with paper towel and leave to cool slightly, then cut into 3 cm thick slices.

Add the cannellini beans, carrot, thyme sprigs, bay leaves and quartered onion to the dish and cover with water. Bring to the boil over medium heat, then reduce the heat to low and simmer, covered, for 1 hour.

Meanwhile, preheat the oven to 200°C/180°C fan-forced.

Drain the beans, reserving the cooking liquid. Discard the herbs and onion quarters. Add the beans to the Kaiserfleisch mixture.

Return half the bean mixture to the casserole dish or a roasting tin if you've been using a frying pan up to this point. Top with the sausage and duck, then spoon over the remaining bean mixture. Pour over enough of the bean cooking liquid to make sure everything is just covered, then season with white pepper (you won't need any salt).

Cook for 1 hour, then check the level of liquid. If it has almost evaporated, add a little more cooking liquid. Sprinkle over the breadcrumbs and bake for a further 20 minutes or until a golden crust has formed on top.

Remove and rest for about 15 minutes. Serve sprinkled with parsley.

TIPS

Confit duck is available at good butchers, specialty delicatessens and supermarkets.

Boost the porky flavour by asking your butcher for 100 g of pork skins to add to your cassoulet base. Fish them out before serving if they haven't totally broken down, as you don't want to reveal the secret behind your extra-delicious cassoulet. The skin is more likely to break down if you ask the butcher to cut it into long ribbons for you.

DULL FOOD NERD FACT: Cassoulet is a holy trinity of peasant bean stews shared among the towns of Carcassonne, Toulouse and Castelnaudary. This cassoulet uses pork and duck confit as the main meats, which is typical of Castelnaudary, rather than the mutton or red partridge that have gorged on grapes favoured in the other two towns. The use of breadcrumbs is widely debated, but they will give you the welcome crust far more quickly than cooking the cassoulet for hours and hours, stirring the meaty crust that forms back into the cassoulet seven times before it finally sets – almost black and sticky on top – as the purists recommend.

Coq au Vin

The popularity of coq au vin – chicken cooked with red wine – is a comparatively recent phenomenon, propelled by Julia Child and Paul Bocuse, who both used red wine to cook their chicken.

It was not always so. Before the 1960s this dish was always made with local white wine – so riesling in Alsace or vin jaune in Jura. In fact, the first two recorded recipes actually called 'coq au vin' used white wine. It's a tradition that goes way back; French revolutionary Danton regularly ate chicken and white wine stew at Montmartre's Chez La Mere Catherine back in the 18th century.

So, make the white wine version first, then next time substitute a nice French red and see which one you like best.

SERVES: 4 **PREP:** 20 MINS **COOKING:** 1 HOUR 30 MINS

60 ml (¼ cup) extra virgin olive oil
300 g piece Kaiserfleisch, speck or bacon, rind removed, cut into 5 mm thick batons
12 small Swiss brown mushrooms, halved
3 large golden shallots, thickly sliced
6 thyme sprigs
3 garlic cloves, finely chopped
4 chicken marylands, each cut into two pieces
sea salt and freshly ground black pepper
375 ml (1½ cups) white wine (such as semillon)
1 tablespoon creme fraiche
1 teaspoon Dijon mustard
chopped flat-leaf parsley, to serve

Preheat the oven to 200°C/180°C fan-forced.

Heat 1 tablespoon of the oil in a large frying pan over medium heat. Add the Kaiserfleisch, speck or bacon and cook, tossing, for 5 minutes or until lightly browned and crisp. Transfer to a large roasting tin and set aside.

Add the mushrooms to the pan and cook, stirring, for 5 minutes or until lightly golden. Add to the roasting tin.

Add another 1 tablespoon of oil to the pan, add the shallot and thyme sprigs and cook, stirring, for a few minutes or until the onion is soft and translucent. Add the garlic and cook for 1 minute or until aromatic. Transfer to the roasting tin and stir to combine.

Heat the remaining oil in the pan. Working in batches, add the chicken and cook on both sides until golden brown. Season well, then arrange the chicken on top of the Kaiserfleisch mixture in a single layer.

Add a little of the wine to the frying pan and simmer to deglaze, scraping up any bits stuck to the bottom of the pan. Pour over the chicken, along with the remaining wine, and roast for 1 hour. Keep hold of the pan, as we will use it again.

Using a slotted spoon or tongs, transfer the chicken and other ingredients to a serving dish, discarding the thyme sprigs. Cover to keep warm.

Pour the leftover liquid in the roasting tin back into the frying pan and heat over medium heat. Simmer for a few minutes or until the liquid is reduced. Whisk in the creme fraiche and mustard and stir until the sauce is thick enough to coat the back of a spoon. Remove from the heat and season.

Pour the sauce over the chicken and serve sprinkled with parsley.

Kate's Leek & Goat's Cheese Tarte Tatin

Over the years, Kate (my resident pastry whisperer) and I have played with this simple combination of flavours, but I think with this version we have reached our pinnacle. It was Kate's idea to use honey rather than a caramel, and the way the honey plays with the goat's cheese is quite magical. It also doesn't matter at all if the honey catches a little, as burnt honey is so 'now'.

Kate's wonderful rough puff recipe is a standard piece of kit for any kitchen and worth knowing for all your pastry needs, such as the chicken pie recipe on page 130. It also freezes really well.

SERVES: 4 **PREP:** 25 MINS (PLUS 1 HOUR RESTING) **COOKING:** 35 MINS

30 g butter
2 tablespoons honey
6 thyme sprigs, leaves picked
4 long leeks, pale section only, cut into 2 cm lengths
120 g semi-soft goat's cheese
sea salt and freshly ground black pepper

ROUGH PUFF

250 g (1⅔ cups) plain flour, plus extra for dusting
½ teaspoon salt
200 g chilled butter, cut into small cubes
1 tablespoon fresh lemon juice
125 ml (½ cup) iced water

Start by making your rough puff. Place the flour and salt in a large bowl, add the butter and cut it in using two knives as you would when making scones – but don't go too far. Stop while the butter is still quite lumpy. Add the lemon juice to the water – acid helps to keep the pastry soft – and pour over the flour mixture. Use the knives to mix until everything is wet but you can still see bits of butter.

Give the dough a quick knead to bring it together, but don't go crazy. You are really just pulling it together without letting your hot little hands warm up the butter. Turn out the dough onto a lightly floured surface and form into a rectangle. Wrap in plastic wrap and place in the fridge to rest for at least 1 hour.

Place the dough on a well-floured surface and roll it out to a 30 cm × 15 cm rectangle. Sprinkle with a little flour. Starting from one of the short ends, fold a third of the dough into the centre, then fold the third from the other end over that. Give the dough a quarter turn and roll it out again. Repeat rolling, flouring, folding and turning five more times – this builds the layers of your pastry. (You may need to wrap and place the pastry back in the fridge to firm up if it starts getting too warm between turns.) Place in the fridge until needed.

Preheat the oven to 220°C/200°C fan-forced.

Melt the butter in a 25 cm non-stick ovenproof frying pan over medium heat. Add the honey and sprinkle in half the thyme leaves. Arrange the leek over the base of the pan. Cover with a lid and cook for 5 minutes or until the leek is tender. Remove the lid and cook without stirring for another 2 minutes or until the leek begins to caramelise on the bottom. Remove the pan from the heat and scatter 90 g of the goat's cheese in the gaps between the leek pieces. Season with salt and pepper.

Roll the dough out on a well-floured surface until 3 mm thick. Cut out a 27 cm circle and carefully place this over the leek and goat's cheese like a blanket and use the back of a spoon or the handle of a wooden spoon to tuck it in around the edge. Bake for 25 minutes or until the pastry is cooked and golden.

Set aside to cool for 10 minutes. When you are ready to eat, place a serving dish over the pan and flip it over. Tap the bottom of the pan and the tarte tatin should drop out neatly. Sprinkle over the remaining goat's cheese and thyme, and serve warm.

TIP

If you are short of time you can use a good-quality store-bought puff pastry instead.

A French Sailor's Mussels

Translating the name of the world's most famous mussel dish immediately conjures up Armin Morbach's striking photos for Jean Paul Gaultier. You know what I'm talking about – the muscular male models, their bulging biceps barely contained by the sailor tops that the French designer very much made his signature. It is of no little irony, as the name of the blue and white striped tops in French is 'mariniere', and the French name for this classic is 'moules mariniere'.

This makes me love this dish even more as I love those tops, and my twenty-seven-year-old Ralph Lauren version (bought in an outlet store for a few dollars) is still a favourite, even if it now has more patches and holes than material.

SERVES: 4 **PREP:** 10 MINS **COOKING:** 15 MINS

2 tablespoons extra virgin olive oil
2 golden shallots, thinly sliced
2 celery stalks, finely chopped
1 small carrot, finely chopped
3 thyme sprigs
3 garlic cloves, finely chopped
sea salt and freshly ground black pepper
2 kg mussels, scrubbed and debearded
250 ml (1 cup) dry white wine
½ bunch flat-leaf parsley, coarsely chopped
2 tablespoons creme fraiche
sliced baguette, to serve

Heat the oil in a large flameproof casserole dish over medium heat. Add the shallot, celery, carrot and thyme and cook for 3–4 minutes or until slightly softened. Add the garlic and cook for 1 minute or until aromatic. Season with salt and pepper.

Increase the heat to high. Add the mussels and give the pan a good shake, then cover and cook for 3–4 minutes or until the mussels begin to open. Add the wine and cook for another 1–2 minutes or until it has reduced slightly. Remove from the heat and discard any mussels that have not opened. Transfer the open mussels to serving bowls, leaving the cooking liquid in the dish.

Add the parsley and creme fraiche to the cooking liquid and stir briefly over medium heat until well combined. Taste and adjust the seasoning if necessary. Pour the liquid over the mussels and serve immediately with crusty baguette slices.

Quiche Lorraine

What could be more French than quiche Lorraine? Well, after a little research, it seems quite a lot actually. The earliest recording of the name 'quiche' was not until 1605 in Alsace-Lorraine, as part of the local dialect of that area of France fiercely contested by the Germans, and the word actually came from the German word 'kuchen' meaning 'tart' or 'cake'. So we've added German bacon (Kaiserfleisch) to ours to represent this lineage.

Baking custard-filled tarts vastly predates this mention, however, with the English cookbook *The Forme of Cury* (1390) recording the first recipes for 'crustardes' – egg custard tarts loaded with everything from birds to fruit or even eels and lampreys with raisins and prunes. While Italy's first cookbook, *Libro de Arte Coquinaria* by Martino de Rossi (circa 1465), has a lovely recipe for a 'diriola' – a blind-baked pastry crust filled with egg yolks, cream, cinnamon and a little sugar.

So quiche is as much English, Italian or German as it is Alsatian – or even French.

SERVES: 8–10 **PREP:** 40 MINS (PLUS 1 HOUR RESTING) **COOKING:** 1 HOUR

1 teaspoon extra virgin olive oil
200 g piece Kaiserfleisch, speck or bacon, rind removed, cut into 5 mm thick batons
200 g creme fraiche
150 ml full-cream milk
2 egg yolks
3 eggs
150 g finely grated gruyere (or bitey Tasty cheese if you can't find gruyere)
4 scrapes of a whole nutmeg
sea salt and freshly ground black pepper

SHORTCRUST PASTRY
250 g (1⅔ cups) plain flour, plus extra for dusting
½ teaspoon salt
190 g chilled butter, cut into small cubes, plus extra for greasing
1 small egg, lightly whisked

To make the pastry, blitz the flour, salt and butter in a food processor until it resembles coarse breadcrumbs. Add the egg and process until a dough starts to form. Tip out onto a lightly floured surface and quickly knead into a ball. Wrap in plastic wrap and place in the fridge to rest for at least 1 hour.

Meanwhile, start to make your filling. Heat the oil in a small frying pan over medium heat, add the Kaiserfleisch, speck or bacon and cook for 3–4 minutes or until slightly crispy. Set aside to cool.

Whisk the creme fraiche and milk in a bowl until well combined. Add the egg yolks and two of the eggs and whisk again. Stir in the Kaiserfleisch, speck or bacon, then add the cheese and nutmeg. Season with salt and pepper.

Preheat the oven to 200°C/180°C fan-forced. Grease a 4 cm deep, 22 cm fluted tart tin with a removable base with butter.

Roll the dough out on a lightly floured surface until it is 3 mm thick. Line the tin with the pastry and trim the edges. Place the tin on a baking tray. Line the pastry case with baking paper, fill with uncooked rice or pastry weights and blind-bake for 20 minutes.

Remove the paper and weights. Lightly whisk the remaining egg, and brush it over the pastry base to seal. Pour in the filling mixture and bake for 30–40 minutes or until the centre of the tart is just set and no longer liquid. The cooking time may vary, depending on your oven and the temperature of the filling mixture when it goes into the tart shell. To be on the safe side, keep an eye on it from the 25-minute mark.

Serve warm, as it is far and away the best like this!

TIP

The quiche can be served immediately or reheated at a later time, making it the perfect bake-ahead dish.

Tuna Nicoise

I probably spend far too much of my life reading old recipe books and trying to dig up the true origins of dishes. I suspect this just proves that I am becoming a grumpy old man – something confirmed by the fact that I get cantankerous when I see old food myths becoming lore through consistent repetition by lazy internet sites. And, quite frankly, if I didn't challenge those things, who would continue my quest for the truth?

As you can imagine, my voice is getting shriller and shriller as I write this; my nostrils are flaring and my eyes are bugging out ... I'd better stop as it's not good for the blood pressure of a cranky old man like me who finds himself shouting at web pages more than he ought to.

There are upsides to this nerdery, though, such as finding out that this classic salad from Nice was originally made with ripe tomatoes, olive oil, shallots and anchovies. All we've done here is bulk up the original with seared tuna. No olives, no potatoes, no green beans, no other interlopers, and it's still darned good. Hell no, let's be honest – it's actually better.

SERVES: 4 **PREP:** 15 MINS **COOKING:** 5 MINS

1 tablespoon red wine vinegar
sea salt and freshly ground black pepper
2 large golden shallots, thinly sliced
125 ml (½ cup) extra virgin olive oil
2 × 250 g punnets mixed cherry tomatoes, halved
2 red or green heirloom tomatoes (see TIPS)
2 x 300 g tuna steaks
8 anchovy fillets (the best, the pinkest, and probably the most expensive you can find)
finely grated zest and juice of 1 lemon

Place the vinegar and a good pinch of salt in a bowl and swirl to dissolve the salt. Add the shallot and half the oil and mix with a fork to combine. Stir in the cherry tomatoes.

Slice the heirloom tomatoes and arrange on a serving platter. Season with salt and pepper. Give the cherry tomatoes another toss, then heap them on top of the heirloom tomato.

Heat 2 tablespoons of the remaining oil in a frying pan over medium heat. Add the tuna and sear for a couple of minutes each side until the tuna is cooked to your liking (some people might prefer to cook it a little longer). Transfer to a chopping board and set aside to rest for a minute, then thinly slice the tuna and arrange it over the tomato mixture.

In a small bowl, mash the anchovies and remaining oil. Add a little lemon juice to taste, then drizzle the mixture over the tuna. Sprinkle with lemon zest, season and serve.

A bowl of steamed potatoes (perhaps tossed in melted butter and chives) is all you need to make this into the finest of meals.

TIPS

If you must put your own mark on this dish, try cheeks of dried black olives, or capers that you've seasoned and fried in olive oil until they sizzle and crisp up.

If you can't find heirloom tomatoes just use contrasting yellow tomatoes instead.

If you prefer, leave the tuna sliced and raw; it is a cleaner take on this classic. Remember, the lemon juice in the dressing will cook the fish over time, so add the tuna just before serving.

Potiron

(Pumpkin Soup)

Amazingly, France is one of the very few countries other than Australia that truly appreciates pumpkin soup. Go figure! Needless to say, their version is understated and classic.

SERVES: 4 **PREP:** 15 MINS **COOKING:** 30 MINS

1 tablespoon extra virgin olive oil
3 large golden shallots, coarsely chopped
2 garlic cloves, coarsely chopped
sea salt and freshly ground black pepper
1 medium (about 1 kg) butternut pumpkin, peeled, deseeded and cut into 1.5 cm cubes
625 ml (2½ cups) full-cream milk
80 g (⅓ cup) creme fraiche
1 bunch chives, snipped
crusty baguette, to serve

Heat the oil in a large saucepan or stockpot over medium heat. Add the shallot and garlic and season with salt. Cook, stirring, for 5 minutes or until soft and slightly coloured. Add the pumpkin, then cover and sweat for 10 minutes.

Pour in the milk and season with salt and pepper. Bring to the boil, then reduce the heat to low and simmer for 15 minutes or until the pumpkin is tender.

Carefully tip the pumpkin mixture into a food processor or blender and blitz for 30 seconds or until smooth and thick (you could also do this with a stick blender).

Ladle the soup into bowls and top with a scoop of creme fraiche and a sprinkling of chives. Serve immediately with some crusty baguette.

TIP

Pass the soup through a fine seive for a more finessed version. Use the rounded side of a ladle to help it through.

Chicken Pie

No matter how hard I've tried to customise my chicken pies (Mexican with corn, coriander and capsicum, or Indian butter chicken pie), I always return to this classic version. Why? Because it's the best.

The last thing I want to do is force you into a difficult decision though, so I've included a butter chicken recipe on page 252, which you can also use to fill your pie for an Indian twist.

SERVES: 4–6 **PREP:** 45 MINS (PLUS COOLING) **COOKING:** 1 HOUR 25 MINS

80 g butter
400 g carrots, coarsely chopped
2 brown onions, coarsely chopped
20 small Swiss brown mushrooms, thickly sliced
sea salt and freshly ground black pepper
1 kg chicken thigh fillets, cut into 3 cm pieces
2½ tablespoons brandy
500 ml (2 cups) chicken stock
2 tablespoons plain flour, plus extra for dusting
1 tablespoon Dijon mustard
1 tablespoon creme fraiche
1 tablespoon coarsely chopped tarragon (or 2 tablespoons if it's the larger Russian tarragon instead of the pretty little French leaves)
2 x sheets good-quality store-bought puff pastry, just thawed, or 250 g rough puff (see page 120)
1 egg, lightly whisked

Melt half the butter in a large saucepan over medium heat, add the carrot and onion and cook, stirring, for 5 minutes or until soft. Add the mushroom and cook, stirring occasionally, until the excess water has evaporated and the mushroom begins to brown. Season with salt and pepper. Add the chicken and brandy and cook, stirring, for 5 minutes or until the brandy has almost evaporated. Pour in the stock and return to a simmer. Cover and cook, stirring occasionally, for 30 minutes or until the chicken is cooked through.

Drain through a sieve over a large bowl, reserving all the stock. Transfer the chicken mixture to a large pie dish.

Melt the remaining butter in the same pan over medium heat. Sprinkle in the flour and stir for about 1 minute, letting it toast a little. Add 250 ml (1 cup) of the reserved stock and mix it in until it starts to thicken. Gradually add the rest of the stock and stir until the sauce has thickened enough to coat the back of a spoon. Remove from the heat and stir in the mustard and creme fraiche, then add the tarragon.

Check the seasoning of the sauce and adjust with more salt if necessary. Pour the creamy sauce over the chicken mixture and set aside to cool completely.

Preheat the oven to 200°C/180°C fan-forced.

If using bought puff pastry, place the two sheets on top of each other. If using your own rough puff you will only need a single thickness. Roll the pastry out on a floured surface to a circle just bigger than the pie dish. Cover the pie filling with the pastry, then trim off the excess and press down with your thumb or use a fork to seal the edge. Slit a few holes in the top to allow the steam to escape, then brush with the egg and bake for 30 minutes or until the pastry is golden brown.

TIP

The filling can be made a day head, and if you really want to be organised it freezes well, too. Place in an airtight container and freeze for up to 1 month. Thaw overnight in the fridge.

Croque Monsieur

The best croque monsieur in the world is sold in Sébastien Gaurdard's tiny and rather delicate tea rooms in the Place des Pyramides, opposite the Louvre in Paris. It is an urbane croque monsieur you feel you could eat with white kid gloves on. This one, however, is a robust, street-fighting croque monsieur where boxing gloves, or even bare knuckles, might be more appropriate.

MAKES: 4 **PREP:** 20 MINS **COOKING:** 20 MINS

butter, at room temperature, for spreading
8 thick slices crusty bread
200 g finely grated gruyere
8 slices smoked ham

BECHAMEL
250 ml (1 cup) full-cream milk
30 g butter
20 g plain flour
2 teaspoons Dijon mustard
⅛ teaspoon freshly grated nutmeg
50 g finely grated gruyere
sea salt and freshly ground black pepper
pinch of cayenne pepper (optional)

Preheat the oven to 220°C/200°C fan-forced.

To make the bechamel, heat the milk in a small saucepan over medium heat without letting it boil. Melt the butter in another small saucepan over medium heat until it begins to froth. Add the flour and whisk until smooth and the flour begins to bubble and look puffy. Cook, stirring, for 1 minute. Add the hot milk all at once and continue to stir until the sauce has thickened (this will happen quite fast), then cook, stirring, for another 5 minutes. Stir in the mustard, nutmeg and gruyere. Season with salt and pepper, and add the cayenne if you like a little kick.

Butter the bread slices generously on one side. Lay half the slices, butter-side down, on a baking tray. Top with the gruyere and ham, then sandwich with the remaining bread slices, butter-side up. Bake for about 7 minutes or until the bread is golden brown.

Preheat the grill on high. Flip the sandwiches over and evenly spoon the bechamel over the top. Grill the sandwiches until the bechamel is lightly golden.

Serve hot!

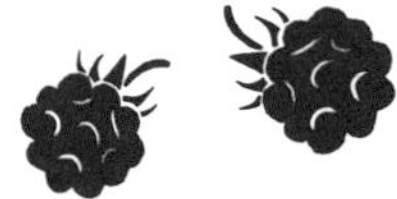

Raspberry Souffle

One of the greatest things I have ever eaten was the raspberry souffle at The Waterside Inn. One of the UK's great dining rooms, the location on the banks of the Thames is idyllic. Now run by his son Alain, the restaurant is inextricably linked with Michel Roux. Born above his grandfather's charcuterie in Charolles, Saone-et-Loire, Michel was one of the two brothers who brought modern gastronomy to the UK, winning the country's first three Michelin stars at Le Gavroche.

Over the years, this charming and generous man has been a huge inspiration to me, through his elegant, economic writing, insightful thoughts about better food and his unswerving professionalism and humour on those few occasions I've been lucky enough to work with him. This recipe isn't as good as his, but it'll do.

MAKES: 4 **PREP:** 20 MINS **COOKING:** 15 MINS

softened butter, for greasing
70 g caster sugar, plus extra for dusting
300 g raspberries, plus extra to decorate (optional)
10 g cornflour
1 tablespoon Kirsch or lemon juice
4 egg whites
icing sugar, for dusting

Preheat the oven to 190°C/170°C fan-forced. Using a pastry brush and upward strokes, grease four 250 ml (1 cup) ramekins with butter. Place in the freezer for a few minutes to set the butter, then repeat with more upward strokes of the buttered brush. You are creating 'tram lines' for the souffle to run up when it's rising. Now dust the ramekins with caster sugar to coat, shaking off any excess. Place the dishes on a baking tray and set aside.

Place the raspberries in a bowl and mash with a fork. Transfer to a sieve over a bowl. Using the back of a spoon or ladle, push the raspberries through until you have 170 g of pulp. Discard the seeds.

Place the cornflour and Kirsch or lemon juice in a small bowl and whisk until smooth. Place the raspberry pulp and 50 g of the caster sugar in a small saucepan over medium heat and bring to the boil, stirring constantly until the sugar has dissolved. Add the cornflour mixture and cook, stirring, for about 30 seconds or until the mixture has thickened slightly. Transfer to a heatproof bowl and set aside to cool.

Begin to whisk the egg whites by hand in a bowl (or you can use an electric mixer), adding the remaining 20 g caster sugar while you whisk to soft peaks. Fold one-third of the egg whites into the cooled raspberry mixture. Pour the raspberry mixture into the remaining egg whites and gently fold until just combined.

Spoon the mixture into the prepared ramekins and use a spatula to smooth the top. Run a knife around the edge of each ramekin to encourage an even rise. Bake for 12 minutes or until the souffles have risen about 3–4 cm above the ramekin rim.

Dust with icing sugar and serve immediately, decorated with extra raspberries if you like.

TIP

Once you've got a handle on this recipe, try and mix up the flavours. My favourite variation is to replace the raspberries with pears and the seeds of a vanilla pod.

Kate's Apple Tarte Tatin

This is quite simply the best tarte tatin I've ever tasted. The secret is the pink lady apples – they hold their shape and bring a nice bright acidity to their rather sweet environment.

This tarte tatin was created for my fourth cookbook, *The Simple Secrets*, after much trial and error searching for the perfect apple, caramel and pastry by Kate Quincerot. Kate's nose was a little out of joint when it earned the name 'Rizzo's Apple Tarte Tatin' in the book. She didn't get the reference to the most famous Pink Lady of all, Betty Alexander Rizzo from the girl gang in *Grease!*, suspecting instead it was some other pastry wrangler I was sweet on. Finally, four years later, I get to redress this wrong and give the naming rights of this exemplary tarte tatin back to Kate.

SERVES: 8 **PREP:** 20 MINS (PLUS 1 HOUR SOAKING & 20 MINS COOLING)
COOKING: 45 MINS

8 pink lady apples, preferably organic, peeled, cored and quartered
200 g caster sugar
juice of 1 lemon
pinch of ground cinnamon
25 g butter, coarsely chopped
plain flour, for dusting
1 quantity rough puff (see page 120)

CHANTILLY CREAM
250 ml (1 cup) cold pouring cream
30 g icing sugar

Place the apple in a colander and sprinkle with 50 g of the sugar and half the lemon juice. Set aside for 1 hour.

Meanwhile, make the chantilly cream. Place the cream and icing sugar in a bowl and lightly whisk with a balloon whisk until the cream thickens slightly. It needs to feel billowy. Cover with plastic wrap and place in the fridge until you are ready to serve.

Sprinkle the remaining sugar into a 25 cm ovenproof frying pan and heat over low heat until the sugar is light golden – you may need to give it a swirl to even out the colour. Add the remaining lemon juice and stir to combine (be careful as it may spit).

Place the apple quarters, cored-side up, in the caramel until you have covered the base of the pan (be very careful not to touch the hot caramel). Cut the remaining apple into smaller slices and place on top to fill any gaps. Cook the apple for about 10 minutes. Some apples leach a lot of water, so you might need to cook them for a bit longer to reduce the liquid and thicken the caramel. Do not stir!

Remove from the heat and set aside for 10 minutes to cool slightly. Sprinkle the cinnamon over the apple, then dot with the butter.

Preheat the oven to 220°C/200°C fan-forced. On a lightly floured surface, roll the dough out until it is 3 mm thick, then cut out a 27 cm circle. Place the dough circle over the apple like a blanket, and use the back of a spoon to tuck it in around the edge. Cut a small hole in the centre of the dough to let out the steam.

Bake for 30 minutes or until the pastry is cooked and golden. Remove the pan and leave to cool for about 10 minutes. Warm the pan over low heat for a minute or so to loosen the caramel if necessary, then place a serving dish over the pan and carefully flip it over. Tap the bottom of the pan and the tarte tatin should drop out neatly. Serve with the chantilly cream.

TIPS

If you don't have time to make rough puff, any good-quality store-bought puff pastry will work well.

To serve your apple tarte tatin 'a la mode', just serve with vanilla ice-cream. That's all 'a la mode' means!

★ Ice-Cream Profiteroles ★

Choux pastry is very French. Making it is also a skill that you'll need to master if you want to compete in any reputable cooking competition on television. It's the very foundation of a croquembouche, those nun-like coffee or chocolate religieuses, trendy French eclairs and these profiteroles. Here's how I do it.

You can make it faster, but drying out the dough correctly is crucial to getting the requisite puff, crust and slight chew.

SERVES: 6 **PREP:** 40 MINS **COOKING:** 40 MINS

100 g caster sugar
300 ml pouring cream
200 g dark chocolate (70% cocoa solids), finely chopped
18 scoops good-quality vanilla ice-cream

CHOUX PASTRY
90 g butter
¼ teaspoon salt
90 g plain flour
3 large eggs

Preheat the oven to 200°C/180°C fan-forced. Line a baking tray with baking paper.

To make the choux pastry, combine the butter, salt and 180 ml water in a small saucepan and bring just to the boil over medium heat. Reduce the heat to low and add the flour. Cook, stirring constantly with a wooden spoon, for 2–3 minutes or until the mixture comes away from the side of the pan. Take your time doing this.

Remove from the heat and set aside for 3–4 minutes to cool slightly.

Add the eggs one at a time and, using electric beaters, beat well after each addition until the dough is thick and glossy. This could also be done by hand and gives nice definition to your forearms.

Use a dessertspoon to scoop up about 1 tablespoon of the dough, then use another spoon to help shape it into a ball. Transfer to the prepared tray. Repeat with the remaining dough, spacing the balls about 3 cm apart. You should get about 18 balls.

Bake for 25 minutes or until golden brown. Push a skewer gently through each profiterole, then return them to the oven and bake for a further 2–3 minutes (this will allow the moisture inside to escape).

While the profiteroles are baking, make the sauce. Place the sugar in a small saucepan over medium heat and cook for a few minutes until the sugar begins to melt and turn brown. This will happen around the edge first, so give the sugar a swirl to even out the colour, then leave until all the sugar has dissolved and turned golden brown. Remove the pan from the heat and add half the cream (be careful as it can spit). Stir over low heat until smooth and combined. Remove from the heat and stir in the chocolate until melted and combined, then add the remaining cream and stir until silky and smooth. Return to the heat for a minute to warm through when you are ready to serve.

Cut the profiteroles in half and fill each one with a scoop of ice-cream. Place three profiteroles on each serving plate and pour over the hot chocolate sauce.

TIPS

If you prefer perfectly shaped profiteroles, use a piping bag to pipe the balls onto the tray.

Profiteroles can be baked ahead of time. Cool completely, then store in an airtight container at room temperature for up to 3 days, or freeze for up to 3 months. Thaw at room temperature. If they feel a little soft, place them on a tray and crisp up in a preheated 200°C/180°C fan-forced oven for 5 minutes.

Peach Frangipane Tart

This showstopper of a dessert brings the best of the village patisserie to your home kitchen. It can be made with any ripe fruit from the fruit bowl but is particularly good with peaches, plums or strawberries. Oh, and nectarines, apricots, raspberries, halved blackberries and redcurrants. Or a combination of a number of these.

The downside is that it's not quick, but then pastry's worst enemy is angry, frenetic hands*. See this recipe as a labour of love, and appreciate learning three classic skills of the pastry kitchen: making crème pat', frangipane and sweet pastry – classic skills that will hold you in good stead for years to come.

***If you want a quick version of this dessert, try my 'cheat's plum tart with store-bought frozen pastry and honeyed mascarpone filling'. You'll find the recipe for free online.**

SERVES: 6 **PREP:** 90 MINS (PLUS 2 HOURS 15 MINS RESTING) **COOKING:** 30 MINS

3–4 ripe peaches, stoned, thinly sliced
icing sugar, for dusting (optional)

SWEET PASTRY
140 g plain flour, plus extra for dusting
80 g butter
60 g caster sugar
1 egg yolk

CREME PATISSIERE
250 ml (1 cup) full-cream milk
50 g caster sugar
12 g plain flour
3 egg yolks
½ teaspoon vanilla extract
25 g chilled butter, chopped

FRANGIPANE
100 g butter, at room temperature
100 g icing sugar
100 g (1 cup) almond meal
1 egg
10 g plain flour

To make the sweet pastry, blitz the flour and butter in a food processor until the mixture resembles coarse breadcrumbs. Add the sugar and blitz to combine. Add the egg yolk and 2 teaspoons cold water and process until a dough forms. Turn out onto a lightly floured surface and gently knead the dough into a smooth ball. Take care not to overwork your dough. Wrap in plastic wrap and rest in the fridge for 2 hours.

While your pastry chills, make the creme patissiere. Combine the milk and half the sugar in a small saucepan over medium heat and bring almost to the boil. Combine the flour, egg yolks, vanilla and remaining sugar in a bowl and whisk with a balloon whisk until pale. Pour over the hot milk, whisking constantly until combined. Return the mixture to the pan and cook, stirring constantly, over medium heat for 6 minutes. Remove from the heat and whisk in the butter until melted and combined. Transfer to a bowl and cover the surface directly with plastic wrap to prevent a skin forming. Set aside to cool completely.

Now make your frangipane. Place the butter in a bowl and beat with electric beaters until soft and pale. Add the icing sugar and almond meal and gently beat until just combined. Add the egg and flour and gently beat until well combined.

Line a baking tray with baking paper. On a lightly floured surface, roll out two-thirds of the dough until it is 3 mm thick. Cut out a 22 cm circle and place on the prepared tray. Using the flat of your hand, roll the remaining portion of dough into a 1.5 cm thick log – you want it to be long enough to go around the outside of your pastry circle. Place the log around the outside edge of the circle to create a border, then use your fingertips to pinch and press the border and circle together to make a flat wall around the outside. Place the tart shell in the fridge to rest for 15 minutes.

Preheat the oven to 200°C/180°C fan-forced.

Spoon the frangipane into a piping bag fitted with a 1 cm plain nozzle and pipe a spiral over the base to create a thin layer. Bake for 20 minutes or until the base and frangipane are cooked and golden. Set aside to cool completely.

When you are ready to assemble, spoon the creme patissiere into a piping bag fitted with a 1 cm plain nozzle. Pipe a spiral of the creme pat' over the frangipane to cover it completely (you may not need it all). Decorate the top of the tart with the peach slices and dust with icing sugar, if you like, to serve.

SPAIN

Spain might be home to one of the two most influential modernisations of fine dining in recent history (through Catalan chefs, such as Ferran Adrià at El Bulli and the Roca brothers, and the likes of Juan Mari and his daughter Elena Arzak, and Andoni Luis Aduriz in San Sebastian), but, at its heart, everyday Spanish cuisine is simple and unpretentious, spiked with Celtic and Basque (often maritime) influences in the north and Moorish influences in the south. Think saffron, spices, sweet pastries and rice for dishes like the classic paella and the original beans and rice dish known as 'Moors and Christians'.

That's not to say Spanish cooking is short of technique. Adrià would always say that making 'croquetas' at home (see page 146) takes as much skill as most of his modernist foams, dusts and spheres. The same goes for achieving the perfect 'socarrat' (crust) on the base of your paella (see page 150) or the amazing range of sweet treats, such as churros, 'turron' or a satiny caramel flan (see page 164), made from no more than a simple combination of sugar, eggs and flour. Luckily, by following a few basic rules these techniques can be yours too!

Spain's largely hot summer climate delivers so many of the signature ingredients of the Iberian Peninsula, such as plump tomatoes, olive oil, grapes for wine, sherry and sherry vinegar and capsicums (especially the round nora pepper), which can be dried and ground into pimenton (paprika) or added to a romesco sauce (see page 149). These bold flavours marry well with wonderful seafood, such as octopus, prawns, calamari, hake, salt cod and clams – many of which pop up in the following pages – and especially the sweet umami hit of the anchovies caught in the Cantabrian Sea. The Spanish 'zarzuela de mariscos' and 'caldereta' (seafood stews) are rightfully as famous as the 'fabada' (bean stew) and cider of Asturias.

The peasant history of so many great Spanish dishes has left a legacy of a true love for meat and dairy, whether it's the wood-roasted suckling pigs and lambs that are such an attraction when visiting the plains around Madrid and Aragon; the famous manchego cheese (which is amazing paired in a toastie with chorizo!); hearty braises of secondary cuts, such as oxtail and beef cheek; and a smallgoods repertoire including chorizo sausages, tender, spiced 'morcilla' (black pudding) and the sweet and almost nutty cured jamon ham from free-roaming black-foot pigs.

There is always bread on the table, and the inevitable stale leftovers feature in many of Spain's great dishes. It is used as a silky thickener in sauces and soups, such as the Andalusian 'ajo blanco' (chilled almond and garlic soup) and the 'cat soup' of Cadiz, to crumb the calamari for Madrid's favourite lunch or late-night snack roll, or just to make 'migas' (breadcrumbs) to add crunch to dishes.

Besides the aforementioned ingredients – saffron, olive oil and paprika – garlic, onions, oregano and bay leaves are judiciously used for flavour against hearty ingredients, such as chickpeas, potatoes and silverbeet. Those spuds also turn up under paprika-dusted octopus in Galicia, and in tapas and pintxos bars across the land, bulking up tortilla omelettes, or fried golden and doused with a spicy sauce for patatas bravas, to make the perfect bar snack.

Apart from paprika, key spices include cinnamon, anise and saffron, while fruits, such as oranges, lemons, peaches and apricots, and nuts, such as almonds and hazelnuts, are all used in sweet and savoury dishes.

FAKING IT TIPS

1. Fry or braise savoury dishes with olive oil and garlic, and you are already halfway to Spain. One of the most popular tapa is peeled prawns fried in an incredible amount of chopped garlic and olive oil. Serve with bread for mopping up the oil and chewy nuggets of caramelised garlic. You can add cayenne or chilli powder as well as, or instead of, the garlic.
2. The Spanish have a bit of a thing for eggs fried in rather a lot of olive oil. Top your pan-fried chickpeas, garlic and silverbeet with a sprinkling of paprika and runny fried eggs (and fried chorizo if you like) and serve with roast or fried potatoes. Or just serve the eggs and sausage chunks on the spuds with a reduced tomato, garlic and paprika sauce.
3. Slowly braise beef cheeks with bay leaves, garlic and sweet Pedro Ximenez sherry, let down with red wine or stock until ridiculously sticky, and then garnish with orange zest. Serve on a cauliflower mash like the brilliant version Frank Camorra does at his delicious MoVida restaurant in Melbourne.
4. Take your standard chicken thigh tray bake on a Spanish holiday. Use chorizo, garlic, sliced capsicum and smoked paprika as your base, then deglaze the pan with sherry vinegar and stock and add browned chicken thighs and crushed tomatoes. Freshen before serving with a squeeze of orange juice and garnish with toasted almonds and parsley.
5. While Spanish desserts are quite a small gang, dusting cinnamon sugar on your doughnuts (omitting any filling) and dunking them in the thickest chocolate you can imagine, or just adding lemon zest and cinnamon to your favourite rice pudding, will immediately conjure up images of Spain.

SHOPPING LIST

So much of what you need to fake Spanish dishes is readily available in good supermarkets, but there are some luxe ingredients that will take things to another level.

First, buy some expensive anchovies to add flavour to dishes. They will be a million miles from the overly salty hairy fish you find on cheap pizzas.

Look out for good-quality chorizo, jamon, morcilla and even 'lomo' (cured pork tenderloin). Also try presoaked salt cod instead of jamon in the croqueta recipe on page 146.

Stock up on smoked, sweet and spicy Spanish pimentons (paprikas). Also seek out saffron and dried oregano.

When it comes to rice, look out for medium-grained bomba rice, or even better calasparra rice, to make the perfect paella. Also buy a large can of Spanish olive oil, as our trendy boutique olive oils often have too much flavour!

Finally, manchego cheese, fancy Marcona almonds and those crinkly, dry salt-cured olives, will give a touch of authenticity to any Spanish-inspired spread.

Golden Gazpacho

Spain has a similar hot climate to ours, so the chilled soups from the south, such as the bright tomato gazpachos, rich 'salmorejos' and creamy almond 'ajo blancos', are perfect for Australian summers. This gazpacho amarillo is a lesser known delight of the Spanish kitchen, and it has the best name of all ... but then, let's face it, you'd never make it if I just called it 'Spanish tomato soup'. And that would be a shame for me, as well as for you and your family.

SERVES: 4 PREP: 15 MINS (PLUS 30 MINS STANDING & 1–2 HOURS CHILLING)
COOKING: 15 MINS

3 thick slices white sourdough bread
3 garlic cloves, peeled
80 ml (⅓ cup) sherry vinegar
80 ml (⅓ cup) extra virgin olive oil, plus extra to serve
800 g yellow/orange tomatoes, chopped, plus extra yellow/orange cherry tomatoes, halved, to serve
1½ Lebanese cucumbers, peeled, deseeded and chopped
1 yellow capsicum, deseeded and chopped
3–4 celery heart stalks, chopped, leaves reserved
sea salt and freshly ground black pepper
1 white onion, halved

Preheat the oven to 210°C/190°C fan-forced.

Place the bread on a baking tray and bake for 3–4 minutes each side or until toasted. Rub the garlic cloves all over the bread, including the crusts. Reserve any remaining garlic.

Place two slices of bread in a dish or bowl. Drizzle with 60 ml (¼ cup) of the sherry vinegar and 125 ml (½ cup) water. Set aside to soak for 5 minutes. Use your hands to squeeze the excess liquid from the bread over a bowl to make sure you catch and reserve the sherry water.

Drizzle 1 tablespoon of the oil over both sides of the remaining slice of bread. Place on the baking tray and bake for a further 5–6 minutes or until golden. Tear into bite-sized pieces and reserve for serving.

Place the soaked bread pieces, reserved sherry water and any leftover garlic in a large bowl or jug. Add the tomato, cucumber, capsicum, chopped celery, 1½ teaspoons salt and half the onion and blitz with a stick blender until smooth. Set aside for 30 minutes to allow the flavours to develop. Give the soup another blitz to make it as smooth as possible.

Strain the soup through a sieve over a large bowl. Use the back of a spoon or ladle to push through as much pulp as possible.

Gradually pour the remaining oil into the soup, blending at the same time so it thickens and emulsifies. Add the remaining sherry vinegar to taste and season with salt, if needed. Place in the fridge to chill for 1–2 hours.

Finely chop the remaining onion.

Divide the soup among serving bowls and top with the chopped onion, extra tomato, celery leaves, torn bread and an extra drizzle of oil. Season with pepper and serve.

Croquetas

It was because of medieval Europe's insatiable desire for salt cod that Basque fishermen ended up being the first European settlers (albeit part time) in North America. I love salt cod in croquettes but, given the pfaff of soaking, I usually make these ham ones, as they are almost as obscenely sexy. I just don't have the dedication of those Basque fishermen.

MAKES: ABOUT 35 PREP: 20 MINS (PLUS 3 HOURS CHILLING) COOKING: 40 MINS

1 litre full-cream milk
2 garlic cloves, bruised
2 thyme sprigs
2 fresh or 1 dried bay leaf
100 ml extra virgin olive oil
1 white onion, finely chopped
200 g sliced Spanish jamon, chopped (you can use prosciutto, but it will be saltier so make adjustments accordingly)
100 g (⅔ cup) plain flour
1 teaspoon Dijon mustard
½ teaspoon ground white pepper
vegetable oil, for deep-frying
sea salt and freshly ground black pepper
lemon wedges, to serve
good-quality whole-egg mayonnaise, to serve

HERB CRUMB
225 g (1½ cups) plain flour
125 ml (½ cup) full-cream milk
2 eggs
1 teaspoon sea salt
150 g (3 cups) panko breadcrumbs
160 g (1¾ cups) fine breadcrumbs (or blitzed panko)
¼ cup finely chopped flat-leaf parsley

Combine the milk, garlic, thyme and bay leaf in a medium saucepan over medium heat and bring just to a simmer. Immediately remove from the heat and strain through a fine sieve into a jug. Discard the garlic and herbs.

Line a 20 cm square baking tin with baking paper.

Clean the saucepan, then add the olive oil and heat over medium–low heat. Add the onion and cook, stirring, for 4 minutes. Add the jamon and cook, stirring, for another 4 minutes or until the onion has softened.

Reduce the heat to low and add the flour. Stir with a wooden spoon until the flour starts to bubble and turn light golden. Add half the milk mixture and stir or whisk until any lumps are removed and the sauce is smooth. Add the remaining milk mixture and cook, stirring constantly, for 4–6 minutes or until the mixture starts to boil and thicken. Stir in the mustard and remove from the heat. Season with white pepper.

Pour the bechamel into the prepared tin and spread it out evenly, smoothing the surface with a spatula or palette knife – it should be about 3 cm deep. Top with another piece of baking paper and place in the fridge for at least 2 hours or until set firm.

When the bechamel is firm, place it on a chopping board and cut into about thirty five 4 cm × 2.5 cm rectangles. Rinse your tin and line again with baking paper. Line a second tin while you're at it.

To make the herb crumb, place the flour in a shallow bowl. Whisk the milk, eggs and salt in another bowl. Combine the breadcrumbs and parsley in a third bowl.

Coat each croqueta in the flour, shaking off the excess. Dip in the egg mixture and then in the breadcrumbs, turning to coat. Shape and squash the ends together, giving each croqueta a little roll in your hands. Place on the prepared trays. Place in the fridge for 1 hour to firm up, so they don't fall apart when frying.

Pour enough vegetable oil into a large heavy-based saucepan or deep-fryer to come two-thirds of the way up the side. Heat over medium heat until the oil reaches 180°C on a cook's thermometer. Add the croquetas in batches (you don't want to overcrowd the pan) and cook, turning with a slotted spoon, for 3 minutes each side or until golden. Remove and drain on a plate lined with paper towel and season well. Cover loosely to keep warm while you cook the remaining croquetas.

Serve hot with lemon wedges and mayonnaise.

PREPARE IN 25 MINUTES

BBQ Leeks, Asparagus & Cauliflower with Salsa Romesco

This sweet toasty capsicum sauce from Tarragona in southern Spain is often served with 'calcots', a sort of giant spring onion, but it goes just as well with leeks, asparagus and cauliflower. We use all three in this recipe, but you can use any combination you like – or roast potatoes, or grilled chicken thighs, or barbecued fish!

SERVES: 4 PREP: 25 MINS COOKING: 30 MINS

- **½ cauliflower, cut into 4 chunks, with the core holding the florets together**
- **12–16 baby leeks or fat spring onions**
- **2 bunches asparagus, woody ends trimmed**
- **60 ml (¼ cup) extra virgin olive oil**
- **sea salt**

SALSA ROMESCO

- **2 medium tomatoes, with a cross cut in the base**
- **1 red capsicum**
- **½ white onion, unpeeled**
- **45 g (¼ cup) blanched almonds, toasted until golden**
- **45 g (¼ cup) hazelnuts, toasted, skins removed**
- **1 thick slice bread**
- **1 garlic clove**
- **2 teaspoons sweet paprika**
- **2 tablespoons sherry vinegar**
- **sea salt and freshly ground black pepper**
- **80 ml (⅓ cup) extra virgin olive oil**

To make the salsa romesco, heat a frying pan or chargrill pan over high heat. Add the tomatoes, capsicum and onion and cook for 6–8 minutes or until the skins start to burn slightly and the juices begin to weep. Transfer the tomato and onion to a chopping board. Place the capsicum in a small bowl, cover with plastic wrap and leave to sweat for a few minutes.

Starting with the cross at the bottom, peel the tomatoes. Then the onion. Place both in a blender. Peel the capsicum and remove the seeds. Add to the blender, along with the almonds, hazelnuts, bread, garlic, paprika, sherry vinegar and 1 teaspoon salt. Blitz to combine, then, with the motor running, gradually add the oil in a thin steady stream. Add a little water if you would like a thinner consistency. Taste and season with pepper if needed, then transfer to a bowl and set aside.

Bring a large saucepan of salted water to the boil. Add the cauliflower and cook for 4 minutes or until just starting soften. Drain well and transfer to a tray.

Add the leeks and asparagus to the tray and drizzle with the oil.

Preheat a barbecue grill or large chargrill pan over high heat until just smoking. (A charcoal or wood-fired grill is ideal if you have one.) Add the leeks first and cook for 6–8 minutes. Pull them off the grill and wrap in newspaper to trap the steam and tenderise. Add the cauliflower to the grill and cook, turning, for 6 minutes. Add the asparagus and cook for 3–4 minutes or until the cauliflower has nice char lines on each side and the asparagus is tender-crisp.

Arrange the leeks, cauliflower and asparagus on a large platter. Sprinkle with salt and serve with the romesco sauce.

TIPS

To eat the leeks (or spring onions), hold the leek at the top and pull down the first layer of charred skin to reveal the sweet, soft flesh. Remove the roots if they're still attached, then dunk the leeks into the romesco sauce and, still holding the top, eat about three-quarters of the stalk – don't eat the top quarter as it can be quite tough.

Or do what Sarah did on the last season of MasterChef *and grill your untrimmed leeks slowly on the barbecue until the centres are creamy and the tough outer leaves are charred. To speed up the cooking process, microwave each leek for 3 minutes first. To serve, slice open lengthways and spoon over the romesco.*

Pour any leftover romesco sauce into an airtight container and store in the fridge for up to 1 week.

Emma's True Paella Mixta

I tend to respond best to a firm hand, and there is no hand firmer than the one applied by Ms Emma Warren as we were developing the recipes for this section. She's lived in Spain on and off over the years, as well as running restaurants there. I've been to Spain maybe twenty or thirty times, and always think I'm right. I'm still smarting from her response to my mild suggestion that we include chorizo in the paella for this book.

'It's like putting cream in risotto or amatriciana sauce, or carbonara for that matter,' starts her lesson. 'People still do it because, for whatever reason, they think it's a good idea. It's quicker. It's easier. It tastes better. Some celeb chef told them to do it. BUT IT IS STILL WRONG! Even the Italians, who seldom agree on any recipe, will tell you it is WRONG!'

So, OK, no chorizo* then ...

*Don't tell Emma, but you will find my paella recipes that do use chorizo online. You did not hear that from me.

SERVES: 4 PREP: 30 MINS (PLUS 10 MINS RESTING) COOKING: 1 HOUR 20 MINS

- 60 ml (¼ cup) extra virgin olive oil
- 1 large red capsicum, deseeded and cut into strips (or use 2 red bullhorns if you can track some down)
- 2 chicken thigh fillets, excess fat trimmed, cut into 3–4 cm chunks
- 150 g pork belly, rind removed, cut into 3 cm cubes
- 1½ brown onions, finely chopped
- 3 garlic cloves, thinly sliced
- sea salt and freshly ground black pepper
- 1.2 litres fish stock
- pinch of saffron threads
- 1 × 400 g can crushed tomatoes
- 1 teaspoon sweet paprika
- 125 ml (½ cup) dry sherry or white wine
- 200 g whole calamari, cleaned, hood split open and cut into diamonds or squares, tentacles separated
- 400 g medium-grain rice (ideally bomba or calasparra, but supermarket medium-grain will suffice)
- 8 mussels, scrubbed and debearded
- 4 large green king prawns
- 55 g (⅓ cup) frozen peas
- 2 lemons, cut into wedges

There are a few Spanish tricks to this recipe, but essentially it is all about the sofrito (the base). It is vital that you take your time and pay attention to the recipe.

So, heat half the oil in a large (34 cm) paella pan or frying pan over medium–high heat. Add the capsicum and cook for 6 minutes or until softened, then transfer to a bowl and set aside. Add the chicken in batches and cook, turning, for 3–4 minutes or until browned. Transfer to the same bowl. Repeat to brown the pork belly.

Heat the remaining oil in the pan and reduce the heat to low. Add the onion, garlic and a pinch of salt and gently cook, stirring occasionally, for 20 minutes or until golden. Pour the stock into a saucepan and bring to a gentle simmer over low heat. Add the saffron and 1 teaspoon salt.

Add the tomato and paprika to the onion and stir until well combined. Increase the heat to medium and cook, stirring, for 10–15 minutes or until a thick, rich, chocolatey paste-like base forms. Add the sherry or white wine and cook for 2 minutes to deglaze the pan, scraping up any bits stuck to the bottom. Let almost all of the liquid evaporate, then add the calamari and stir through. Return the capsicum and meat to the pan.

Add the rice and gently stir through the grains to coat evenly with the sofrito. This is the only stirring required or allowed!!! We don't want to release the starch of the rice too much, as creamy paella is actually risotto.

Add 1 litre of the stock and gently shake the pan to evenly distribute the ingredients. Bring to a simmer, then reduce the heat to low and cook for 10 minutes. Gently push the mussels and prawns into the rice (DON'T STIR) and cook for 10 minutes.

Shake the pan frequently to loosen and aerate the rice. Add the peas while there is still a thin blanket of liquid over the surface of the paella. Cook for 2 minutes or until all the liquid has gone from the surface. Insert the handle of a wooden spoon in a few places to create air pockets and check if the base is burning or sticking too much. If it is, reduce the heat to very, very low. Taste the rice and, if you prefer it a little more cooked, add the rest of the stock and cook until it has been absorbed into the rice.

Turn off the heat and cover with a clean tea towel or anything porous, like your favourite newspaper. Set aside for 10 minutes to rest. Serve up with loads of lemon wedges and extra salt.

Almond Chicken Casserole

(aka Pollo al Pepitoria)

Almonds are the national nut of Spain and, like paella rice and saffron, they owe their presence on the Iberian Peninsula to the Moorish occupation between 711 and 1492. Pollo al pepitoria harks back to those days, as it uses only Old World ingredients (so no tomatoes, potatoes or capsicums) and was originally made with an old hen. The delicacy of modern chicken seems to work perfectly cooked in this almond custard, but do splash out on a more flavourful free-range bird.

SERVES: 4 PREP: 10 MINS COOKING: 1 HOUR 15 MINS

4 chicken marylands
60 ml (¼ cup) extra virgin olive oil
sea salt and freshly ground black pepper
85 g (½ cup) blanched almonds
1 brown onion, coarsely chopped
5 garlic cloves, finely chopped
80 ml (⅓ cup) dry sherry or white wine
500 ml (2 cups) chicken stock
2 fresh or dried bay leaves
pinch of saffron threads
¼ teaspoon freshly grated nutmeg
4 eggs, hard-boiled, yolks and whites separated (see TIP)
finely chopped flat-leaf parsley, to garnish
steamed rice or your favourite potatoes, to serve

Preheat the oven to 200°C/180°C fan-forced.

Place the chicken and half the oil in a bowl and gently toss until well coated. Season with a good sprinkling of salt.

Heat a large frying pan over high heat. Add the chicken and cook for 4–5 minutes each side or until browned. Transfer to a baking dish that holds the pieces of chicken snugly in a single layer.

Reduce the heat to medium. Add the almonds to the pan and cook, tossing, for 4–6 minutes or until toasted. Transfer to a bowl.

Add the remaining oil and the onion to the pan and cook for 5 minutes or until softened. Add the garlic and cook for 2 minutes or until aromatic. Pour in the sherry or wine and cook for 2–3 minutes or until reduced by half.

Stir in the toasted almonds, stock, bay leaves, saffron and nutmeg. Bring to a simmer and cook for 5 minutes, then remove from the heat. Discard the bay leaves, then pour the mixture into the cup of your stick-blender or a narrow bowl.

Add the egg yolks to all this almondy goodness and blitz with a stick blender until a smooth sauce forms. Pour the almond sauce evenly over the chicken. Roast for 45 minutes or until the chicken is cooked through and the almond custard is golden brown.

Coarsely grate the egg whites over the chicken and season with pepper, then scatter over the parsley. Serve with steamed rice or your favourite potatoes – I'd go for roasted or a buttery mash.

TIP

To cook your eggs perfectly without getting a grey ring on the inside, place the eggs in a saucepan of cold water, bring to a simmer and cook for 7 minutes. Drain and cool under cold running water, then peel.

FOOD NERD FACT: This recipe references the classic Spanish technique of adding a 'picada' of pounded bread and almonds to thicken a sauce, which is central to Catalan cuisine.

Smokey Albondigas
(aka Spanish Meatballs)

The name sounds like a Norteno musician who's decided to move to Nashville and play country, but this is actually the absolute top favourite tapita of all time ... that – between you and me – is a little tapa.

When the tapas craze first reared its head in every bar in every land, often with no relation to the original bar snack from Spain, this was the one that resonated with me. It still does. It doesn't matter whether I'm on a bar crawl in Madrid, Barcelona, San Sebastian or Seville, this is the little plate I'm looking for. Basically, I'm so friendly with albondigas I keep hoping one day they'll say, 'you can call me Al ...'.

SERVES: 4 (MAKES 24 BALLS) PREP: 30 MINS COOKING: 1 HOUR 30 MINS

60 ml (¼ cup) extra virgin olive oil
1½ brown onions, finely chopped
3 garlic cloves, crushed
sea salt and freshly ground black pepper
1½ tablespoons tomato paste
60 ml (¼ cup) dry sherry or white wine
80 ml (⅓ cup) tomato passata
100 g white sourdough bread, crusts removed
125 ml (½ cup) full-cream milk
1 egg
600 g beef or veal mince
200 g pork mince
coarsely chopped flat-leaf parsley, to serve
crusty bread, to serve

SALSA
1 litre tomato passata
60 ml (¼ cup) dry sherry or white wine
2 tablespoons extra virgin olive oil
2 teaspoons smoked paprika
1 teaspoon sea salt
½ teaspoon ground white pepper

To make the salsa, pour the passata into a saucepan and simmer for 15 minutes or until reduced by one-third. Stir in the remaining ingredients, then transfer to a bowl and set aside.

Heat the oil in the same pan over medium–high heat. Add the onion and cook, stirring occasionally, for 10–12 minutes or until softened. This is the first of three steps to achieve a really intense flavour in the caramelised onion that will form the soul of the albondigas. Reduce the heat to medium. Add the garlic and cook, stirring, for 6–8 minutes or until soft. Reduce the heat to low, add 1 teaspoon salt and cook, stirring occasionally, for 20 minutes or until the onion becomes a deep caramelised colour.

Stir in the tomato paste and cook for 4 minutes, then add the sherry or wine and cook for 3 minutes or until reduced by half. Add the passata and bring to a simmer. Cook, stirring occasionally, for 10–12 minutes or until the mixture reduces to a thin paste. Transfer to a heatproof bowl and set aside to cool slightly.

Place the bread in a bowl and pour over the milk. Set aside for a few minutes until completely soaked, then use your hands to squeeze out the excess liquid. Add the squeezed bread, egg and all the mince to the caramelised onion and tomato mixture and stir until well combined. Season well with salt and pepper.

Preheat the oven to 240°C/220°C fan-forced. Line a baking tray with baking paper.

Roll large tablespoons of the mince mixture into compacted golf balls and place on the prepared tray. Bake for 8 minutes or until beginning to colour and dispense liquid.

Transfer the albondigas to a snug baking dish and cover with the tomato salsa. Bake for 12–15 minutes or until the sauce is bubbling and starting to crisp around the edges.

Sprinkle with parsley and serve with crusty bread.

TIP

A salad of chickpeas warmed in olive oil with segments of orange, then tossed with parsley makes a nice accompaniment to this dish. In winter, cook shredded silverbeet with a couple of cloves of garlic in the olive oil before adding chickpeas to warm. Season with sea salt and marble the sauce with any reserved orange juice captured when you segmented the orange.

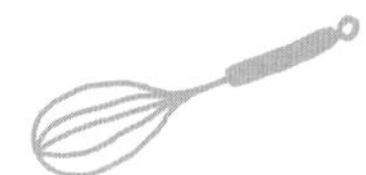

Tigers from Bilbao

In my book, Bilbao is famous for four things: the Guggenheim's amazing Spanish offshoot designed by Frank Gehry, Athletic's Iker Muniain, the best tinned anchovies and this delicious pinxtos bar snack (that invariably turns into a meal) of stuffed and crumbed local mussels. There they are called 'tigres'. I've yet to find a compelling reason for why this is.

The internet will say it is because they are 'fiery' and then proceed to give you recipes for tigres that don't feature any chilli or cayenne! It's possible they could be overly spiced in cheaper, divier places, desperate to sell you another kalimotxo (red wine mixed with cola!). Not that I would ever frequent questionable places like that. So I wouldn't know ... but there is this place ...

SERVES: 4–6 PREP: 20 MINS (PLUS 1 HOUR CHILLING) COOKING: 40 MINS

250 ml (1 cup) white wine
2 thyme sprigs, leaves stripped and chopped
6 white or black peppercorns
¼ brown onion, peeled
1 kg mussels, scrubbed and debearded
sea salt and freshly ground black pepper
500 ml (2 cups) full-cream milk, plus an extra 2 tablespoons for crumbing
1 fresh or dried bay leaf
2 tablespoons extra virgin olive oil
85 g plain flour
2 eggs, lightly whisked
70 g (1 cup) sourdough or panko breadcrumbs
90 g (1 cup) dried breadcrumbs
2 tablespoons chopped tarragon or flat-leaf parsley
sea salt and freshly ground black pepper
rice bran, grapeseed or vegetable oil, for deep-frying
lemon wedges, to serve

Place the wine, thyme, peppercorns and onion in a large deep frying pan with a lid. Heat over high heat until it comes to a simmer. Add the mussels and a pinch of salt, then cover and steam for 3–4 minutes or until the mussels have opened (discard any that don't). Remove the mussels and reserve the cooking liquid for your bechamel. Remove the onion and finely chop.

Remove the mussel meat from the shells and reserve the best shell halves for filling later. Rinse off any residual scum under running water. Coarsely chop the mussel meat and place in a bowl. Stir in a few tablespoons of the reserved cooking liquid to stop the meat drying out.

Place the milk, bay leaf and 125 ml (½ cup) of the reserved mussel cooking liquid in a small saucepan over medium heat, and heat until steam is coming off but it's not boiling. Remove the bay leaf.

Heat the olive oil in a small saucepan over low heat. Add 40 g of the flour and stir for 1–2 minutes or until the mixture begins to bubble and the flour starts to colour slightly. Gradually add the warm milk, whisking rapidly to avoid lumps, until well combined and smooth. As soon as it has thickened, remove the bechamel from the heat and fold in the mussel meat. Spoon the mixture into the clean shells and place on a tray. Allow to cool slightly before transferring to the fridge to chill for at least 1 hour.

Place the remaining flour in a shallow bowl. Whisk the eggs and extra milk in a separate bowl. Combine the breadcrumbs and tarragon in a third bowl and season with salt and pepper. Coat each mussel in the flour, shaking off the excess. Dip in the egg mixture and then in the breadcrumbs to coat.

Pour enough oil for deep-frying into a large heavy-based saucepan or deep-fryer over medium–high heat and heat to 180°C on a cook's thermometer. Add the mussels in batches and cook for 4–6 minutes or until golden. Remove and drain on a tray lined with paper towel. Season well and serve with lemon wedges.

TIP

You can customise these tigres in lots of different ways. Add a little chopped jamon to the mix. Try flavouring the bechamel with saffron, finely grated manchego or little fried nuggets of chorizo. Herbs, such as dill, are also commonly used with seafood in Spain.

Fideua Negra
(aka Spaghetti Paella)

Wow, a paella made with pasta!!!! The original recipe was created by a ship's cook who wanted to find a way to stop his rice-mad captain eating more than his fair share of the crew's meal. It backfired as the noodles make it just as delicious! Don't let the squid ink put you off – it's so easy to cook with, looks really dramatic and doesn't taste anywhere near as funky as it looks. In fact, it hardly has any flavour at all!

You will need a large gas burner for this paella – failing that, use the barbecue if your pan is bigger than 34 cm. You're looking for a flat surface with a consistent medium heat.

SERVES: 4 PREP: 20 MINS COOKING: 1 hour

100 ml extra virgin olive oil
400 g angel hair pasta, broken into 5 cm lengths (or use Spanish fideos if you can find them)
4 garlic cloves, 2 cloves smashed, 2 cloves crushed
1 red capsicum, deseeded and finely chopped
300 g whole calamari, cleaned, hood split open and finely chopped, tentacles separated (cuttlefish also work well in this recipe)
1 brown onion, finely chopped
2 ripe tomatoes, coarsely grated, skins discarded
1 teaspoon sweet paprika
sea salt
80 ml (⅓ cup) dry white wine or dry sherry
1 litre fish stock, plus extra if needed
3 × 8 g sachets squid ink
300 g clams or pipis, cleaned and purged (see TIP)
190 g (¾ cup) good-quality whole-egg mayonnaise
lemon wedges, to serve

Heat 2 tablespoons of the oil in a large (34 cm) ovenproof paella pan or frying pan over medium–low heat. Add the dried pasta and use two wooden spoons to gently toss the pasta in the oil for 8–12 minutes until evenly toasted. Set aside on a large plate.

Heat the remaining oil over medium heat. Add the smashed garlic cloves and cook, stirring, for 30 seconds or until aromatic. Add the capsicum and cook for 6 minutes or until softened and the oil starts turning red.

Add the finely chopped calamari and cook, stirring, for 3–4 minutes or until it turns white. Add the onion and cook, stirring, for 8–10 minutes, then stir in the tomato, paprika and 1 teaspoon salt. Reduce the heat to low, add the wine or sherry and cook for 15 minutes or until a thick dark paste forms (this is known as your 'sofrito' base).

Meanwhile, pour the stock into a medium saucepan and heat over medium heat until just warmed through. Stir in the squid ink.

Preheat the oven to 200°C/180°C fan-forced.

Add the calamari tentacles to the sofrito and stir until well combined. Add the toasted pasta to the pan and stir until well coated. Pour in the stock mixture and gently shake the pan to evenly distribute everything. Simmer over low heat, moving the pan around the burner occasionally, for 10 minutes or until the liquid has reduced by half.

Arrange the clams or pipis on top, then cook until they open, shaking the pan every so often to loosen the base. Insert the handle of a wooden spoon in a few places to create air pockets and check the base isn't burning or sticking too much. If it is, reduce the heat to very, very low and add a little more stock if needed. When all the clams or pipis have opened (discard any that haven't), transfer the pan to the oven, bake for 10 minutes and watch the pasta stick up like a porcupine's quills!!!

While the dish cooks, make a quick aioli by combining the mayonnaise, crushed garlic and a pinch of salt in a bowl. Serve the paella with the aioli and lemon wedges.

TIP

If your clams or pipis haven't been purged when you buy them, you will need to do it yourself ... ideally the night before. Dissolve 70 g (¼ cup) cooking salt in 1 litre water in a large bowl. Add the clams or pipis, place in the fridge and leave to purge for as long as you can – at least several hours. Rinse well before using.

Garlic Prawns with Stale Breadcrumbs

(But calling it Gambas al Ajillo con Migas de Pan sounds sooo much better!)

Every bread-loving nation has frugal recipes for using stale leftovers. Migas are one of the most popular Spanish solutions. In Australia, they are most often seen as a fine Iberian version of pangrattato and used to add crunch to dishes; in Spain, migas vary dramatically all over the country. As larger fried croutons, these migas can play a much bigger game and work wonderfully with the fresh sweetness and contrasting texture of the popping prawns.

SERVES: 4 PREP: 15 MINS (PLUS 10 MINS SOAKING) COOKING: 25 MINS

sea salt
150 g stale white sourdough bread, cut into 5 mm–1 cm pieces
2 tablespoons extra virgin olive oil
1 x 80 g piece of pancetta, cut into strips (Spanish jamon might be more authentic, but I reckon the pancetta works better!)
80 g chorizo sausage, meat squeezed out of its casing, coarsely chopped
½ green capsicum, deseeded and finely chopped
1 garlic clove, lightly smashed

PRAWNS

2 tablespoons extra virgin olive oil
40 g butter
8 garlic cloves, 4 cloves thinly sliced, 4 cloves crushed
2 whole dried chillies, crushed or 1 teaspoon dried chilli flakes
24 green prawns, peeled and deveined, with tail tips intact
80 ml (⅓ cup) dry sherry or brandy

Preheat the oven to 120°C/100°C fan-forced.

Combine 60 ml (¼ cup) water and ¼ teaspoon salt in a bowl. Spread out the bread on a baking tray. Use your fingertips to sprinkle the salted water over the bread, then give it a toss and set aside for 10 minutes.

Heat the oil and pancetta in a large ovenproof frying pan, wok or paella pan over high heat. Once sizzling, add the chorizo and cook, stirring occasionally, for 3–5 minutes or until all the fat has rendered. Reduce the heat to medium–low, stir in the capsicum and garlic and cook for 5 minutes or until the capsicum has softened.

Add the bread and, using two wooden spoons to keep everything moving, cook for 5 minutes or until the bread is well coated and toasted. Remove from the heat. Tip the mixture onto the baking tray and spread it out evenly. Bake for 10 minutes or until dried out and well toasted. Drain on a large plate lined with paper towel.

Meanwhile, to cook your prawns, wipe out the pan with paper towel. Add the oil and butter and heat over high heat until melted and sizzling. Add the sliced garlic and chilli and cook for 30 seconds or until aromatic. Stand back a bit and add the prawns – be careful as it may spit. Quickly toss through the crushed garlic and sherry or brandy. Bring to a simmer and cook for 2–3 minutes or until the liquid has reduced slightly.

Transfer the prawns to a serving dish and arrange the migas on top. Drizzle over the pan juices and finish with a sprinkling of salt if needed. Serve straight away.

TIPS

Why dry the bread and have it stale if you're just going to rehydrate it? I'm glad you asked. The dryness helps it soak up the water, and the dampening of the breadcrumbs reduces the level of fat intake. So if your bread is not stale and old, slice it and dry it out in a preheated 120°C/100°C fan-forced oven for 1 hour.

These migas can be enjoyed in lots of other ways. Double the amount of chorizo and serve loaded onto fried eggs with runny yolks as the perfect brinner dish. Use them to jazz up your Caesar salad (see page 296) or Pumpkin soup (see page 129) with a little Spanish pep. Or serve over grilled sardines or with roasted vegetables and salsa romesco (see page 149).

Microwave Marmalade Pudding with Brown Bread Ice-Cream

Strangely, Spanish desserts featuring the citrus for which they are so rightly famous are somewhat limited. Perhaps because the marmalade makers of England and Scotland cornered the market for the famed Seville oranges. This dessert brings them home and pairs them with an ice-cream that would appeal to the don't-waste-the-stale-bread-obsessed Spanish home cook. I should note it was developed with the help of my very talented friend and colleague Phoebe Rose Wood, who is the chief recipe guru at *delicious.* magazine – even if the use of a microwave did cause her no little consternation! I know it seems a little common, but it does work really well in this recipe and gives a super-speedy result that's quite stellar.

SERVES: 6 **PREP:** 15 MINS (PLUS 10 MINS CHILLING) **COOKING:** 25 MINS

230 g orange marmalade
finely grated zest and juice of 1 orange
135 g butter, at room temperature
115 g caster sugar
2 eggs
115 g self-raising flour

BROWN BREAD ICE-CREAM

120 g fresh dark rye or brown bread, crusts removed
2 tablespoons brown sugar
20 g unsalted butter
600 g good-quality vanilla ice-cream, softened slightly

Preheat the oven to 220°C/200°C fan-forced. Line a baking tray with baking paper.

To make the brown bread ice-cream, tear the bread into small pieces about the size of your pinky fingernail. Finely chop half the bread and leave the other half chunky. Place in a bowl with the brown sugar.

Melt the butter in a small saucepan over low heat and keep going until it starts to brown. Add to the breadcrumbs and sugar and mix until well combined. Spread out evenly on the prepared tray and bake for 8–10 minutes. Transfer to a plate and allow to cool, then break up any clusters with your fingers. Place in the freezer for 10 minutes, then fold through the ice-cream. Return to the freezer to firm up while you make your pudding.

Grease a 1.5 litre capacity flat-bottomed microwave-safe dish. Spoon half the marmalade into the dish and smooth to cover the base.

Place the remaining marmalade in a large microwave-safe bowl, add half the orange juice and microwave on high for 5 minutes or until the mixture has reduced by half. Stir in the remaining orange juice and microwave on high for a further 2–3 minutes, then whisk in 20 g of the butter. Set aside and cover the bowl with a tea towel to keep warm.

Place the sugar, orange zest and remaining butter in a bowl and beat with electric beaters on low speed until pale and creamy.

Increase the speed and add the eggs one at a time. To reduce the risk of curdling, fold in about one-third of the flour after the first egg. Only add the second egg when the first is fully incorporated, then fold in the remaining flour until well combined.

Pile the batter on top of the marmalade in the dish and smooth the surface. Cover with plastic wrap and microwave for 4 minutes or until a skewer inserted in the centre comes out clean. Depending on the power of your microwave, it may need a couple more minutes.

Carefully place an upturned large plate over the dish to cover. Flip the dish over and the sponge should land on the plate. Be careful as it will be sodden with searingly hot marmalade.

Drizzle over the warm marmalade mixture, cut the pudding into wedges and serve with the brown bread ice-cream.

Caramel Flan

There are some fine classic Spanish desserts. Eggs, cream, almonds, cinnamon and saffron abound. Many revolve around the silky seduction of set creams and flans or clever baking, such as the ensaimada of Mallorca – a coil of lard pastry filled with custard or a candied tangle of spaghetti pumpkin. The famous burnt Basque cheesecake from La Vina in San Sebastian is a personal favourite (my recipe for which you can find online), but it is hard to go past this classic flan.

SERVES: 6 PREP: 10 MINS (PLUS 10 MINS STANDING & OVERNIGHT CHILLING)
COOKING: 1½–2½ HOURS

400 g caster sugar
1 teaspoon lemon juice
900 ml full-cream milk
½ lemon, zest peeled into strips
1½ teaspoons vanilla bean paste
½ cinnamon stick
5 eggs
2 egg yolks
boiling water

Before we start, a word of advice. To achieve maximum silkiness, the flan is cooked at a low temperature. Given the vast temperature variances in home ovens, the flan can take anywhere between 1 and 2 hours to cook perfectly!

Preheat the oven to 160°C/140°C fan-forced.

Start by making a caramel. Sprinkle 200 g of the sugar evenly over the base of a large heavy-based saucepan and heat over medium–high heat. Add the lemon juice and 60 ml (¼ cup) water and stir until the sugar has dissolved. Bring to the boil and cook for 8–10 minutes or until golden.

Pour the caramel into the base of a 7.5 cm deep, 28 cm × 11 cm ceramic loaf dish or Pyrex mould (silicon is great too). Place in a large roasting tin. Pour enough cold water into the roasting tin to reach halfway up the side of the loaf dish or mould to help the caramel to cool (add some ice to the water in the base if you're in a hurry).

Combine the milk, lemon zest, vanilla and cinnamon in a small saucepan over medium heat and heat until steam is coming off but it's not boiling. Strain into a large heatproof jug and discard the lemon zest and cinnamon. Place the jug in a large bowl filled with iced water and set aside, stirring occasionally, for 10 minutes to let the heat escape.

Using an electric mixer fitted with the whisk attachment, whisk the eggs, egg yolks and remaining sugar until pale and fluffy. Gradually add the cooled milk and whisk until well combined. Pour through a sieve over the caramel in the dish or mould.

Drain the cold water from the roasting tin. Return the loaf dish or mould to the roasting tin, then pour enough boiling water into the roasting tin to reach halfway up the side of the loaf dish or mould. Bake for 1–2 hours until set. To test if the flan is set, give it a gentle shake – the surface shouldn't wobble or shimmer. If it does, return the flan to the oven and keep going until the middle is firm. Set aside to cool slightly, then place in the fridge to set overnight to allow the eggy taste to settle.

Run a knife around the sides and turn the flan out onto a long platter (make sure it has sides to catch all the caramel that runs out). Cut into slices and serve.

FOOD NERD FACT: Churros are not one of Spain's great desserts. They are a morning food, to be eaten in the sun with your coffee or hot chocolate, preferably in some grand square with a copy of something gripping by Javier Marias in your lap, or at a pinch, dunked into hot chocolate after a night of clubbing in Madrid.

GREECE

There are two great jokes about Greek food designed to annoy even the most placid Greek. First is Guy Grossi's classic line that 'Greek food is just Italian with extra lemon juice'; the other comes from Lebanese–Australian comedian Rob Shehadie who likes to ask, 'what's so Greek about a Greek salad that's made with Italian roma tomatoes, Lebanese cucumbers, Danish feta and Spanish olives?' The grain of truth here is that southern Italy and Sicily were once colonies of Greece and Venetian merchants traded extensively around the Greek islands, so there are similarities between Greek and southern Italian cooking that stretch past climatic influences alone.

Proud Greeks, however, will delight in telling you that everything from olives and fish soup (see page 179) to lasagne and pizza all originated in Greece. And while these claims might be best taken with a good pinch of salt (probably hand-harvested Nostimo Greek sea salt from Kythera), the Greek kitchen is so much more than the dips and burnt meats that dominate taverna menus in Australia.

Besides the grill, there are braises and bakes, fried and baked pastries, and all manner of things that have been stuffed – tomatoes, zucchini, eggplants, capsicums (see page 182) – or rolled up, such as dolmades or prawns in kataifi pastry.

Proteins include seafood – calamari, whole fish and that bacon of the sea, octopus – and lamb, goat, poultry, rabbit and pork (especially for souvlaki), which are all used across the islands and mainland. Popular vegetables include potatoes, eggplants, capsicums, artichokes, lady's finger (okra), green beans, celery, beetroot, silverbeet, tomatoes and cucumber. Cucumber has a special place on the Greek table whether as the centrepiece of the classic 'village salad' (that we call 'Greek') or mixed with slightly drained Greek yoghurt to make tzatziki. And if you haven't drunk shots of aniseedy ouzo with fresh batons of cucumber and tender barbecued octopus, I would question if you have ever lived.

The core flavourings of Greece reflect Venetian, Roman, Phoenician and Arab influences as well as that of the Byzantine Empire, which was at the centre of so many spice routes. This explains why flavourings range from spices, such as cinnamon, coriander, cumin, nutmeg and cloves, to garlic and key herbs, such as oregano, mint, dill, bay leaf and parsley. Acidity is certainly also important in the Greek savoury kitchen, whether it comes from yoghurt, wines or vinegars, or from something as simple as lemon squeezed over roast lamb (see page 187) or the famous egg and lemon soup 'avgolemono'.

Pair that lemon with mint and dill and a Greek cheese, such as a creamy feta, grilled kefalograviera or haloumi (just warmed to bring out its milkiness), and toss through a Greek pasta, such as hilopites egg pasta or short 'grains' of orzo; piled on chunks of tomato or cucumber, or mix with horta (wild, foraged greens) to fill trays of spanakopita or triangles wrapped in Greek filo. For our purposes, though, please stick to silverbeet or well-drained wilted spinach!

In the carb world pita breads and varied regional country breads join local pastas, beans (such as fava and the butter bean or lima bean-like 'gigantes'), grains, including cracked wheat (bulgur) and nuts, such as almonds, walnuts and pine nuts, in the Greek pantry.

There is a simplicity and directness about Greek food that makes it quite easy to fake, as it is driven by salty and sour flavours supported by a sweetness from honey (especially in desserts) and the fragrance of judiciously used herbs and spices as the following recipes show. If you want to add Greek-style flourishes to your meal try these ideas.

FAKING IT TIPS

1. Add feta, chopped dill and mint and a good squeeze of lemon juice to pretty much anything to give it a Greek flavour. For example, do this to prawns in a tomato sauce and it becomes prawn saganaki.
2. Be sparing with your marinades and rubs for meat. Salt, lemon and olive oil is enough for lamb, while pork can handle the addition of coriander seeds.
3. Put something grilled in flatbread. Add cucumber, tzatziki and fresh mint to lamb; a rough dip made from mashing roast beetroots with feta and fresh dill to pork; and a crumble of feta, some walnuts and a drizzle of honey to roasted chunks of eggplant.
4. Long, slow cooking will bring out delicious complex flavours in braises, whether its lamb and artichokes, or a stifado (see page 176). Here, the Greeks are more adventurous with their flavourings, but remember that you can always freshen up finished stews or braises with a squeeze of lemon and a blizzard of complementary herbs, such as oregano or parsley.
5. Avoid giving me 'tsipouro'. This highly alcoholic, often moonshined, version of ouzo brings out the absolute worst in me. Far better to brew me a mint or sage tea with herbs straight from your garden.

SHOPPING LIST

Although a lot of ingredients can be found at your local supermarket, there is no substitute for Greek cheese, Greek honey and Greek dried oregano. Especially look out for a big tub of brined feta – ideally one that's barrel-aged, as that's the best.

For the pantry, look out for traditional Greek pastas and 'gigantes', which are large, dried white beans that are great to have on hand. Soak overnight in cold water, then cook and serve in a tomato sauce or add to the Greek national tomato soup 'fasolada'. If you can find it, buy some 'tarhana', which is a grain-like mix of cracked wheat or flour and fermented milk.

Buy cod's roe from your local deli to make Taramasalata (see page 170). White tarama is the more superior option here, although the pink stuff will do at a pinch.

Buy a jar of vine leaves and practise stuffing and wrapping using different ingredients. Dolmades is the obvious choice, but vine leaves are also used to wrap fish, which are then grilled and kept wonderfully moist by the leaves.

Frozen filo pastry is readily available and can be applied to any number of Greek recipes that require a pastry element. This might take the form of the family favourite Spanakopita (see page 184), which makes a perfect midweek meal. Also pop your Greek pita breads in the freezer – they will last for ages but defrost quickly.

'Likkel Fishies' with Citrus Salt

(a bit like the chips of the sea)

Imagine if you could combine the crispiness of chips with the sea-salty maritime breeze of fish – like a one-bite fish 'n' chips but without the batter!?! That's what we've achieved here with a little bit of Greek ingenuity and a big bag of whitebait. Serve on or in a cone of newspaper for added authenticity.

Oh, and don't be scared of the cooking time. Two hours of that is drying the lemon rinds for the citrus salt, which you can do while you are getting on with your life. If you can't be bothered waiting around, just serve these crispy 'likkel fishies' sprinkled with grated lemon zest, along with lemon wedges and fine salt, or a lemon-hit mayo.

SERVES: 6 AS AN APPETISER **PREP:** 15 MINS (PLUS COOLING) **COOKING:** 2 HOURS 15 MINS

cottonseed, vegetable or extra virgin olive oil, for deep-frying
500 g whitebait, as small as possible (henceforth we shall refer to these as 'likkel fishies') (see TIPS)
100 g (⅔ cup) plain flour or gluten-free flour (see TIPS)
2 lemons, cut into wedges, to serve

CITRUS SALT
2 lemons
2 teaspoons coriander seeds
20 whole black peppercorns
2 tablespoons sea salt

To make the citrus salt, preheat the oven to 140°C/120°C fan-forced. Line a baking tray with baking paper.

Use a vegetable peeler to remove the rind from the lemons in strips, leaving the bitter white pith behind. Save the lemons to squeeze over later or keep them for another use. Scatter the rind on the prepared tray and bake for 2 hours or until the rind becomes brittle and easily snaps. Don't let the rind brown. Set aside to cool completely.

While the rind cools, toast the coriander seeds in a dry frying pan over medium heat for 1–2 minutes or until aromatic. Transfer to a bowl and set aside to cool.

Place the cooled rind in a small food processor or spice grinder, add the toasted coriander seeds, peppercorns and salt and blitz to a fine powder. This can also be done using a mortar and pestle, but the results won't be as fine.

Pour the oil into a deep heavy-based saucepan, wok or deep-fryer and heat over medium–high heat to 180°C on a cook's thermometer.

Use paper towel to pat the likkel fishies dry. Place the flour in a large bowl and, working in batches, toss the likkel fishies in the flour to coat. Dust off any excess.

When the oil has reached the right temperature, add the fish in batches and fry for about 2 minutes or until golden and crispy. Remove with a slotted spoon and drain on a large plate lined with paper towel. Don't add too many likkel fishies to the oil at once, as overcrowding the pan will make them stick together. Also they won't cook evenly, and that is bad. While hot, sprinkle the now-crispy likkel fishies with the citrus salt. Transfer to a serving plate or paper cone.

Take to the table and serve hot with lemon wedges and any remaining citrus salt.

TIPS

Gluten-free flours such as rice, potato or tapioca can be used instead of the plain flour.

You can use frozen whitebait. Just thaw and pat dry with paper towel.

The citrus salt will keep for up to 4 weeks in an airtight container, so it's a great one to make ahead of time. It goes really well with calamari or sprinkled over roast, grilled or barbecued chicken and fish.

You can buy dried yuzu zest from Japanese grocers if you don't have the time or the inclination to make your own citrus salt.

Taramasalata with Barbecued Potato Skewers

In the ubiquitous 'trio of dips' on every Greek taverna menu taramasalata reigns supreme. Yet if we called it by its English translation, 'fish egg salad', I'm not sure it would have sold so well. But then where would we be if most Greeks knew that 'baba ghanoush' is originally Arabic and translates as 'pampered daddy' (which is about the best name ever), or that tzatziki comes from an Armenian word meaning 'herbed yoghurt'?

Tarama is, of course, a minefield. A bright pink fishy minefield. There's the tarama dyed the colour of bubblegum that I buy from the supermarket to spread on cheap white toast with lots of butter, then there's the posh stuff that's 'real' and properly Greek, and doesn't make snooty foodies stick their noses in the air. This is the one you are about to make. It's not that hard and you can use a mortar and pestle if you feel like you need a more authentic experience and want to get all 'yia yia' on me. Just remember that sometimes what we're used to is better than what's authentic – and don't be embarrassed to slather these potatoes with hot pink, shop-bought tarama if that's what makes you happy.

SERVES: 4 **PREP:** 10 MINS **COOKING:** 25 MINS

8–12 baby coliban (chat) potatoes
120 g piece crustless ordinary white country loaf
1 small garlic clove
boiling water
100–120 g white or pink fish roe paste (see TIPS)
⅓ small white onion, super finely chopped
60 ml (¼ cup) lemon juice, plus extra to taste
125 ml (½ cup) grapeseed, vegetable or sunflower oil (or a combination)
extra virgin olive oil, for brushing
sea salt

Place the potatoes in a microwave-safe bowl and add 1 tablespoon water. Cover with plastic wrap and microwave on high for 12 minutes or until just tender. Set aside to cool slightly. Halve the potatoes.

While the potatoes cook, make the dip. Place the bread in a bowl and cover with water. Set aside for a few minutes to soak. (I just hope you followed my instructions and used a slice of country loaf and not sourdough because you thought it wouldn't make a difference, because it WILL! If you use sourdough your dip is likely to end up heavy and stodgy. Have you always been so reckless with instructions? Were you a disobedient child? Oh, your poor mother ... she must have despaired.)

While your bread soaks, blanch the garlic clove in a bowl of boiling water for 40 seconds. Drain and finely grate half the clove, discarding the remaining half.

Remove the bread (that is now definitely something white and soft and not too artisan) and squeeze out most of the water. Blitz the bread, grated garlic, roe, onion and lemon juice in a food processor until smooth. Keep the motor running, then add the oil in a thin steady stream until well combined and smooth. Taste and balance with more lemon juice if needed. Transfer to a serving bowl, then cover and place in the fridge.

Thread the potatoes onto metal skewers. Brush the potato with olive oil and sprinkle with salt. Preheat a barbecue grill or chargrill pan over medium–high heat. Add the skewers, flat-sides down, and cook for 6–8 minutes or until golden. Turn over and cook for a further 3 minutes. Transfer to a serving plate and serve with the taramasalata.

This tarama makes a great pre-dinner nibble, is wonderful served with scallops or prawn gnocchi (see my recipe online), or serve it as part of a Greek share feast.

TIPS

This dip gets better with age, as the flavours intensify. Cover and store in the fridge for up to 2 weeks.

Instead of using white or pink roe, you could use salmon or trout roe.

White roe is available from Mediterranean delicatessens.

Marnie's Keftedes in Tomato Sauce

BEWARE: These Greek meatballs are very addictive. The first time my food muse Marnie made them, she ate ten of them before bedtime. The next morning, she got up to find the other 30 gone, which is what happens when you have a teenage son in the house.

NOTE: The fresh tomatoes in the sauce are worth the effort, so please follow these instructions at least for the first time, rather than just opening a can of peeled cherry toms. Not that I would blame you if you did use the tinned toms the seventh time you were making this, because you needed to feed the herd quickly so you could continue bingeing on some Danish noir cop series or some violent slash 'n' shag historical drama (with or without dragons, long boats or bodices).

SERVES: 4–6 **PREP:** 20 MINS (PLUS 30 MINS STANDING) **COOKING:** 1 HOUR

800 g (about 8 medium) extra-ripe tomatoes
100 ml extra virgin olive oil
2 garlic cloves, finely chopped
125 ml (½ cup) white wine or water
½ teaspoon ground cinnamon
1 teaspoon caster sugar
1 teaspoon sea salt
freshly ground black pepper
chopped herbs (such as oregano, flat-leaf parsley or mint), to serve

KEFTEDES

150 ml full-cream milk
125 g fresh breadcrumbs
500 g pork mince
500 g beef mince
1 brown onion, coarsely grated
1 garlic clove, crushed
½ bunch flat-leaf parsley, leaves finely chopped
6 mint leaves, finely chopped
2 teaspoons ground cumin
1 teaspoon dried mint leaves
1 teaspoon ground cinnamon
2½ teaspoons sea salt
lots of freshly ground black pepper
2 eggs, lightly whisked
olive oil, for frying

Start by making your keftedes. Pour the milk over the breadcrumbs in a bowl and set aside for 2 minutes to soak. Use your hands to squeeze out the excess liquid and place the breadcrumbs in a large bowl. Discard the liquid. Add the remaining keftedes ingredients (except the oil) and use one hand to mix until well combined. You can use both hands, but that's not the way my favourite Greek 'yia yia' taught me.

Set the mix aside at room temperature for 30–60 minutes to allow all the spices to flavour the meat. Roll dessertspoons of the mince mixture into about 40 rugby ball-shaped balls, using the spoon to help shape them.

Pour enough oil into a frying pan to come 1 cm up the side and heat over medium heat. Working in about four batches, add the meatballs and cook, turning, for 10–12 minutes or until cooked through and golden. Transfer to a tray lined with paper towel and cover loosely with foil to keep warm. My tip is to keep the balls turning for the first minute or so to brown all sides, as this will help keep the rugby ball shape.

Now make your sauce. Cut a small cross in the base of the tomatoes. Bring a large saucepan of water to the boil, add the tomatoes and blanch for 1 minute. Remove with a slotted spoon. Peel the skin from each tomato and discard. Roughly chop the flesh, removing the core membrane as you chop.

Heat 60 ml (¼ cup) of the oil in a large frying pan over low heat. Add the garlic and cook, stirring, for 1–2 minutes or until the garlic is soft and translucent but not coloured. Add the tomato, wine or water, cinnamon, sugar, salt and pepper. Increase the heat to medium and bring to a simmer, then reduce the heat to low and cook, stirring occasionally and breaking up the tomatoes as they cook, for 10–15 minutes or until the liquid has reduced by half. Taste and adjust the seasoning if necessary. If you prefer a smooth tomato sauce you could blitz it with a stick blender or in a food processor, but I like to keep mine a little chunky.

Pile the keftedes on a serving platter or in a large bowl. Pour over the sauce and drizzle with the remaining oil. Sprinkle with fresh herbs and serve.

TIP

If you prefer to bake the keftedes, reduce the amount of oil in the pan, give the balls a quick sear on all sides, then transfer to a baking tray lined with baking paper. Bake in a preheated 200°C/180°C fan-forced oven for 8 minutes or until cooked through.

Moussaka Made Vegetarian

Not everyone loves lentils, and silverbeet could be classed as another divisive ingredient, but together under the mantle of one of the fluffiest bechamels you'll ever taste, they make a team that will convince even the most ardent carnivore teenager that they both have culinary merit!

When we were developing this dish the big dilemma was whether to egg or not to egg that bechamel, but food muse Marnie found that adding the egg at the very last minute resulted in a higher bechamel that maintained its fluff during cooking. It does take a bit of pfaffing around to make, but it is the gift that keeps on giving and will last all week!!! One day let me tell you about how this bechamel became part of moussaka lore.

SERVES: 6–8 **PREP:** 30 MINS (PLUS 30 MINS COOLING) **COOKING:** 1 HOUR 30 MINS

1 kg (about 4–5) desiree potatoes, peeled
1 kg (about 3–4) large eggplants
140 ml extra virgin olive oil
sea salt
1 red onion, cut into 1 cm pieces
6 garlic cloves, finely chopped
2 rosemary sprigs
1 teaspoon ground cinnamon
1 teaspoon ground allspice
lots of freshly ground black pepper
2 tablespoons red wine vinegar
12 × 15 cm white silverbeet stalks, cut into 1 cm pieces (use the leaves in another recipe, such as the Lamb stifado on page 176 or the Family spanakopita on page 184)
500 ml (2 cups) tomato passata
2 cups cooked brown lentils (you will need about 1 cup of dried lentils)
2 roasted red capsicums, store-bought or roast them yourself, coarsely chopped

BECHAMEL
600 ml full-cream milk
¼ whole nutmeg, finely grated or ½ teaspoon ground nutmeg
1 fresh or dried bay leaf
70 g butter
75 g (½ cup) plain flour
60 g kefalotyri, parmesan or pecorino, coarsely grated
sea salt and ground white pepper
2 eggs, lightly whisked

Preheat the oven to 210°C/190°C fan-forced.

Place the potatoes in a saucepan of cold water. Bring to the boil and cook for 15–20 minutes or until the potatoes are just cooked. Drain and cool slightly, then cut them into 5 mm thick slices. Set aside.

Meanwhile, cut the eggplants lengthways into 5 mm thick slices. Brush both sides with a generous amount of oil and place in a single layer on a few baking trays. Sprinkle with salt. Bake for 25–30 minutes or until the slices are soft and golden. Alternatively, you could cook the slices on a barbecue grill or in a chargrill pan.

While the eggplant is baking, heat 2 tablespoons of the remaining oil in a frying pan over medium heat. Add the onion and cook, stirring occasionally, for 4–5 minutes or until soft. Add the garlic and rosemary and cook for a further minute or so until aromatic. Stir through the cinnamon, allspice, 2 teaspoons of salt and plenty of pepper. Increase the heat to high and stir in the vinegar. Let it bubble away for a few minutes until it has reduced slightly, then add the silverbeet stalks and stir until well combined. Add the passata and bring to the boil, then reduce the heat to low and stir through the lentils and capsicum. Cook, stirring, for 3–4 minutes or until the lentils are heated through. Season to taste and set aside.

Lightly grease a 30 cm × 23 cm baking dish with the remaining oil. Spoon half the lentil mixture into the dish. Lay half the potato on top, slightly overlapping them, then top with half the eggplant. Repeat the layers with the remaining lentil mixture, potato and eggplant.

Have all the bechamel ingredients ready to go and don't wander off. Pour the milk into a saucepan, add the nutmeg and bay leaf and warm the milk over low heat without letting it boil. Strain through a fine sieve into a heatproof jug. Discard the bay leaf.

Either clean the same saucepan or use another to melt the butter over low heat. Add the flour bit by bit and stir for a couple of minutes until it comes together and tans and colours slightly. Gradually add the milk, whisking well after each addition, ensuring each splash of milk is incorporated before adding the next. Add the cheese and whisk for a further 5 minutes or until melted and the sauce has thickened. Season well with salt and pepper. Lastly, whisk in the egg until smooth and well combined.

Pour the bechamel over the last eggplant layer to form a thick blanket. Bake for 45 minutes or until the top has lots of colour. Remove from the oven and set aside for 30 minutes before slicing.

Lamb Stifado

This is a seriously rich dish, but then so many Greeks are. Their government, not so much ...

SERVES: 6 **PREP:** 20 MINS **COOKING:** 1 HOUR 50 MINS

100 ml extra virgin olive oil, plus extra to drizzle
18–24 small brown pickling onions, depending on their size
2 teaspoons sea salt
1.2 kg boneless lamb shoulder, cut into 4–5 cm pieces
5 garlic cloves, thinly sliced
2 tablespoons tomato paste
2 teaspoons ground cumin
lots of freshly ground black pepper
1 × 400 g can crushed tomatoes
250 ml (1 cup) red wine
250 ml (1 cup) beef or vegetable stock, plus extra if needed
2 tablespoons red wine vinegar
2 cinnamon sticks
8 whole cloves
2 fresh or dried bay leaves
400 g dried orzo or other small pasta, such as risoni

Heat 60 ml (¼ cup) of the oil in a heavy-based flameproof casserole dish over medium heat. Add the onions and a pinch of the salt. Cook, tossing occasionally, for 5–7 minutes or until lightly browned. Transfer to a bowl.

Add 1 tablespoon of the remaining oil to the dish and increase the heat to medium–high. Add half the lamb and cook, tossing and seasoning with half the remaining salt, for 2–3 minutes or until browned. Repeat with the remaining oil, lamb and salt.

Return all the meat to the dish and add the garlic. Cook, stirring, for 1 minute or until aromatic. Add the onions, tomato paste, cumin and pepper and stir to combine. Add the crushed tomatoes, wine, stock and vinegar. Add the cinnamon sticks, cloves and bay leaves and stir to combine.

Bring to the boil, then cover with a lid or foil lined with baking paper and reduce the heat to low. Cook, stirring occasionally, for 1½ hours or until the lamb is tender. (If it starts to look a little dry add a touch of water or more stock.)

When the lamb is almost ready, bring a large saucepan of salted water to the boil over high heat. Add the pasta and cook for 1 minute less than it says on the packet, or until al dente. Drain and toss in a little extra oil.

Take the stifado to the table and serve with a share bowl of pasta, or spoon the pasta onto a large platter and top with the stifado.

TIPS

This dish also works well with beef – try cuts, such as gravy beef and chuck.

If you can't find small brown pickling onions, you can use golden shallots instead.

For optional extra veg, thinly slice the leaves of half a bunch of silverbeet (maybe the leftover leaves from the moussaka on page 174), baby spinach or kale and stir through the lamb just before serving.

An alternative to a side of pasta would be boiled chat potatoes or a simple green leaf salad.

Kakavia – The First Fish Soup

To be truly Greek is to take credit for every great invention from democracy to pasta. I think I read somewhere (I'm pretty sure it was in *Coastline*, Lucio Galletto's marvellous book on Med cuisine) that as well as olive oil, the Greeks also invented the fish soup that inspired the bouillabaisse of France and the cazuelas or sopa de mariscos of southern Spain.

I have learnt from bitter experience, working with a man who has unabashed pride in his national heritage, that it's occasionally worth checking some of these more outlandish claims with Dr Google – firebrand self-belief does not always equate with truth – but in the case of this fish soup called 'kakavia' it seems undoubtedly true. But then that's what you'd expect when a Greek fact is told to you by a bloke from Liguria in Italy.

I am not sure that the Greeks invented toast, but I know a man who will tell you that they did. He's from Mulgrave. I love you, my brother!

SERVES: 4 **PREP:** 30 MINS (PLUS 10 MINS INFUSING) **COOKING:** 20 MINS

pinch of saffron threads
100 ml extra virgin olive oil, plus extra for brushing
1 brown onion, finely chopped
3 garlic cloves, 2 cloves thinly sliced, 1 clove left whole
2 medium carrots, finely chopped (you need about 1 cup)
2 celery stalks, finely chopped (you need about 1 cup)
2 thyme sprigs, leaves stripped
1 fresh or dried bay leaf
250 ml (1 cup) white wine
1 × 250 g punnet cherry tomatoes or 2–3 tomatoes, chopped
500 ml (2 cups) good-quality fish stock
400 g skinless firm white fish fillets (such as snapper), pin-boned, cut into large pieces
8 medium green prawns, unpeeled
20 small black mussels, scrubbed and debearded
250 g pipis, purged (see TIP) (optional)
sea salt and freshly ground black pepper
½ bunch flat-leaf parsley, finely chopped
sliced crusty bread or baguette

Place the saffron threads in a bowl and add 200 ml water. Set aside for at least 10 minutes to infuse.

Heat the oil in a large deep frying pan over medium–low heat. Add the onion and cook, stirring, for 4–5 minutes or until soft. Add the sliced garlic and cook, stirring, for 1 minute or until aromatic. Add the carrot, celery, thyme and bay leaf and cook, stirring, for a further 3 minutes. Increase the heat to medium. Add the wine and simmer for about 5 minutes or until the liquid has reduced slightly.

Add the saffron water, tomatoes and stock to the pan. Bring to a gentle boil over medium heat, then reduce the heat to low. Add the fish and prawns and simmer for 1 minute, then gently stir through the mussels and pipis (if using). Cover with a lid and cook for a further 3 minutes or until the fish is cooked through and the mussels and pipis have opened. Discard any unopened mussels and pipis. Season to taste and gently stir through the parsley.

Once you start cooking the seafood, it's time to start making your toasts. Preheat a barbecue grill or chargrill pan over high heat. Brush the bread slices with a touch of extra oil and cook for 1–2 minutes on each side or until toasted and charred. Rub one side with the whole garlic clove to give it a hint of flavour.

Ladle the soup into bowls and serve with the toasted bread.

TIP

If your pipis haven't been purged when you buy them, you will need to do it yourself… ideally the night before. Dissolve 70 g (¼ cup) cooking salt in 1 litre water in a large bowl. Add the pipis, place in the fridge and leave to purge for as long as you can – at least several hours. Rinse well before using.

Slow-Cooked Pork Souvlaki

I once lived in a goat herder's stone hut in an olive grove on the Greek island of Sifnos, and it was a pretty serene time of my life. The days were mainly spent lying around in the sun and thinking poetic thoughts. I'll draw a discreet veil over the nights.

I feel that this version of a souva recreates this mood. With no standing at the barbie and not even any skewering to be done, this also becomes the perfect lazy souva where prep is at a minimum but flavour is maxed out. Just like me back then, the pork just lies around, contemplating the heat for hours on end. I'm not sure if the pork shoulder thinks poetic thoughts, but if it does, it's probably something lovelorn and beautiful in its melancholy. Either that or it's contemplating how well its tan is going ... I suspect pork might be as shallow as me.

SERVES: 8 (with leftover meat for the next day)

PREP: 25 MINS (PLUS 4 HOURS MARINATING & COOLING) **COOKING:** 4 HOURS 10 MINS

2 teaspoons whole black peppercorns
⅓ cup coriander seeds
1 tablespoon cumin seeds
2 tablespoons sea salt
10 garlic cloves
150 ml extra virgin olive oil, plus extra for brushing
2 kg boneless pork shoulder, rind removed, leaving a layer of fat
60 ml (¼ cup) apple cider or white wine vinegar
2 fresh or dried bay leaves
2 teaspoons caster sugar
8 medium pita breads
2 baby gem lettuces, leaves separated

SPICED YOGHURT

250 g Greek-style yoghurt
1 small garlic clove, crushed
1 teaspoon ground cumin
1 tablespoon lemon juice
extra virgin olive oil, for drizzling

GREEK SALAD

6 medium tomatoes, halved, cored and cut into large pieces
1 × 250 g punnet qukes, thickly sliced
24 pitted Kalamata olives
¼ red onion, thinly sliced
60 ml (¼ cup) red wine vinegar
150 g feta, cut into 1 cm thick slices
½ teaspoon dried mint leaves
2½ tablespoons extra virgin olive oil

Place the peppercorns in a mortar and use a pestle to grind until roughly crushed. Add the coriander and cumin seeds and grind until roughly crushed (it doesn't need to be too fine). Add the salt and grind to combine, then add the whole garlic cloves and smash until well combined. Add the oil and stir to combine. (You can also do this with a coffee mug on a chopping board if you don't have a mortar and pestle, but beware of the peppercorns pinging out.)

Place the pork in a large ceramic or glass dish. Add the garlic mixture and give it a good massage all over to coat. Imagine you are applying Hawaiian Tropic to your favourite backpacking crush from back in the day and slather it on. Cover and place in the fridge for at least 4 hours or overnight to marinate.

While the pork is marinating, make the spiced yoghurt. Combine all the ingredients in a bowl, then place in the fridge for at least 2 hours or, for the best results, overnight to intensify the flavours.

Preheat the oven to 180°C/160°C fan-forced. Remove the pork from the fridge and bring to room temperature.

Add the vinegar, bay leaves and 125 ml (½ cup) water to the dish with the pork. Sprinkle the sugar over the top. Cover the dish with baking paper and then with foil, tucking the edges tightly around the dish to seal, then bake for 4 hours or until the meat is falling apart. Remove from the oven.

Preheat the grill on high. Remove the baking paper and foil from the dish, then place the pork under the grill for 1–2 minutes or until it starts to brown around the edges. Transfer the pork to a large plate. Cover loosely with foil and set aside to rest for 15 minutes. Reserve 125 ml (½ cup) of the roasting liquid and discard the rest. Leave your grill on to warm the bread.

While the pork is resting, make the salad and warm your pitas. Combine the tomato, qukes, olives and onion in a serving bowl. Drizzle with the red wine vinegar, then arrange the feta slices on top and sprinkle with mint. Drizzle over the oil. Brush the pita breads with a little oil and grill for a few minutes or until warmed through.

Use two forks to shred the pork and place in a large serving bowl. Add the lettuce leaves and take it to the table, along with the salad and warmed pita bread. Drizzle a little oil over the spiced yoghurt, then let your guests assemble their own souvlaki, topping the pita breads with lettuce, salad, pork and yoghurt. Wrap and tuck in!!

TIPS

To intensify the flavours, marinate the pork and make the spiced yoghurt a day ahead.

Leftover pork is great in a sandwich the next day, or gently reheat and serve with a fresh salad.

Stuffed Capsicums

Stuffing vegetables and rolling stuff in vine leaves. These two techniques take on an important cultural significance in this particular corner of the world. I didn't know this when my mum would serve up roasted capsicums that were slightly slumped by the twin assault of roasting and stuffing; I just thought it was a tasty dinner, and the balance of the salty, meaty filling was 'ace' with the crimson flesh, its sweetness intensified by the oven.

I fear that the joy of the stuffed capsicum – like that of the baked potato or leeks rolled in ham and baked in a cheese sauce – has been lost to this generation. So let's bring it back! If it's going to be a campaign, we need a better hashtag than #getstuffed. Your inspiration is required, so make the dish, photograph it and post it on Insta tagged @mattscravat with your idea of the perfect #hashtag for the campaign.

MAKES: 4 LARGE OR 6 MEDIUM **PREP:** 20 MINS **COOKING:** 2 HOURS

125 ml (½ cup) extra virgin olive oil, plus extra for brushing and drizzling
1 white onion, finely chopped
2 celery stalks, finely chopped
2 garlic cloves, finely chopped
400 g lean beef mince
2 medium zucchini, coarsely grated
4 thyme sprigs, leaves stripped
3 teaspoons dried Greek oregano leaves
1 teaspoon dried mint leaves
½ whole nutmeg, finely grated
1½ teaspoons ground cinnamon
2 teaspoons sea salt
lots of freshly ground black pepper
100 g (½ cup) long-grain white rice
1 × 400 g can crushed tomatoes
150 ml chicken or beef stock, plus extra if needed
1 cup coarsely chopped flat-leaf parsley
25 large mint leaves, thinly sliced
75 g pine nuts, lightly toasted
4 large or 6 medium red capsicums (look for straight sides with stalks if possible)

Preheat the oven to 220°C/200°C fan-forced.

Heat 60 ml (¼ cup) of the oil in a large frying pan over medium–low heat. Add the onion and cook, stirring, for 3 minutes, then add the celery and cook, stirring, for 2 minutes or until just soft. Add the garlic and cook, stirring, for a further 2 minutes or until aromatic. Spoon the mixture into a bowl and set aside.

Increase the heat to high. Heat half the remaining oil in the same pan. Add half the beef and cook, breaking up the meat with a wooden spoon, for 5 minutes or until nicely browned. Transfer to a bowl. Repeat with the remaining oil and beef.

Return all the beef to the pan and stir in the zucchini, thyme, dried oregano and mint, nutmeg, cinnamon, salt and pepper. Cook for 1 minute or until well combined. Stir in the onion mixture, then add the rice, tomatoes and stock and bring to the boil. Immediately reduce the heat to low and continue to cook, stirring occasionally, for 15 minutes or until the rice has absorbed the liquid and the mixture looks moist but not saucy. You can always add a little more stock if needed. The rice will still have a little resistance to the bite, but don't worry as it will continue to soften in the oven.

Stir the parsley, mint and pine nuts into the mince mixture. Season again if needed and remove from the heat.

While the filling is cooking, prepare the capsicums. Use a sharp knife to slice around the top of each capsicum to create a lid. Try to do this neatly as this top will go back on. Carefully hollow out the middle, removing the seeds and membrane with a spoon. Brush the capsicums all over with oil, including the lids.

Use a tablespoon to fill the capsicums with the hot mince mixture, but don't overload them as the filling will expand during baking. Top with the capsicum lids.

Dig out a high-sided ceramic or cast-iron baking dish that will snugly fit the capsicums in a standing position. Transfer the capsicums to the dish and drizzle with a little extra oil. Cover the dish with baking paper and then with foil (the baking paper stops the capsicums from sticking to the foil) and tightly seal. Bake for 1 hour, then uncover and bake for a further 30 minutes. The capsicums will be soft and nicely browned. Remove from the oven and leave to cool down a bit.

Serve just as they are or with the Greek salad on page 180.

Family Spanakopita

The recipe where I finally use some feta ... (you will have seen from the previous pages that Greek food is so much more than cucumber, lemon, feta and baked lamb!).

SERVES: 6–8 **PREP:** 30 MINS **COOKING:** 1 HOUR

100 g butter, melted
2 × 800 g bunches silverbeet, white stalks removed, leaves coarsely chopped
1 tablespoon olive oil
1 brown onion, finely chopped
2 garlic cloves, crushed
500 g fresh ricotta
200 g feta, crumbled
4 spring onions, white and dark green parts sliced into coins
¼ cup chopped dill
finely grated zest of 1 lemon
4 eggs
sea salt and freshly ground black pepper
9 sheets filo pastry

Preheat the oven to 180°C/160°C fan-forced. Grease a 22 cm × 18 cm baking dish with a little of the melted butter.

Rinse the silverbeet under cold running water. Working in batches and with water still clinging to the leaves, add the silverbeet to a microwave-safe bowl. Cook on high for 3–4 minutes or until wilted. Transfer to a colander to drain and leave until cool enough to handle, then squeeze out any excess water and give it another rough chop. You should have about 400 g cooked chopped silverbeet.

Heat the oil in a frying pan over medium heat. Add the onion and garlic and cook, stirring, for 5 minutes or until soft. Transfer to a large bowl. Add the silverbeet, ricotta, feta, spring onion, dill, lemon zest, eggs, salt and pepper and mix until well combined.

Brush one filo sheet with melted butter, then top with another sheet and brush with butter. Repeat until you have a stack of six sheets. Line the base and sides of the prepared dish with the filo stack, and trim off any overhanging pastry. Spoon the silverbeet filling into the dish and smooth the surface.

Butter and stack the remaining filo sheets as you did before, then trim to the same size as your dish and place on top of the filling.

Use a small sharp knife to score the top of the filo diagonally and brush with the remaining butter. Bake for 40 minutes or until golden. Remove from the oven and set aside for 5 minutes, then cut into slices to serve.

TIPS

To save time, buy a 500 g packet of frozen cooked spinach. Let it thaw, then squeeze out the excess water. If preferred, replace with the same quantity of frozen kale.

You can turn this bake into small triangles for entertaining. To make 52 triangles you will need to increase the filo to 39 sheets and the butter to 250 g. Brush one filo sheet with melted butter, then top with another sheet and brush with butter. Repeat until you have a stack of three sheets. Cut crossways into four even strips. Place 1 tablespoon of the silverbeet mixture at the short end of a filo strip. Fold over to form a triangle, then continue folding, keeping the triangle shape, to enclose the filling. Repeat with the remaining filo, butter and filling. Place the triangles on lined trays, brush with butter and bake for 25–30 minutes or until golden.

Slow-Cooked Greek Lamb & Potatoes with Lemon

This is a classically simple but delicious Greek dish. You could finish it with crumbled feta, chopped dill and mint, but only if you needed some prettiness for your Instagram post and it would be a little cliched, detracting from the minimalist simplicity of roast lamb, lemon and soft, creamy potatoes.

SERVES: 6 **PREP:** 15 MINS **COOKING:** 4 HOURS 15 MINS

2.5 kg lamb leg or shoulder
1.5 kg potatoes, peeled and halved (quartered if large)
2 brown onions, quartered
125 ml (½ cup) chicken stock
2 tablespoons extra virgin olive oil, plus extra to serve
juice of 1 lemon
1 teaspoon dried Greek oregano leaves
2 rosemary sprigs, leaves stripped
sea salt and freshly ground black pepper
steamed green beans, to serve

Preheat the oven to 120°C/100°C fan-forced. Score the fat on top of the lamb in a diagonal pattern.

Place the potato and onion in a large roasting tin and drizzle with the stock. Place the lamb on top and drizzle with the oil and half the lemon juice. Sprinkle the oregano over the lamb, and the rosemary over both the lamb and potatoes. Season with salt and pepper.

Cover the tin with foil and roast for 3½ hours. Remove the foil and turn the potatoes over in the pan juices.

Increase the oven temperature to 220°C/200°C fan-forced. Roast, uncovered, for a further 30 minutes or until the lamb is golden. Transfer the lamb to a serving platter, cover loosely with foil and leave to rest for 10 minutes.

Return the potato and onion to the oven and roast for a further 10–15 minutes or until golden. (There will be a little juice left in the tin, but this is mainly rendered lamb fat.)

Toss the steamed beans in the remaining lemon juice and a little extra oil.

Add the potato and onion to the serving platter with the lamb and serve with the dressed beans.

TIPS

For a lighter summer version, slow-roast the lamb as above, then serve on a wooden board with a salad of roast beetroot, pistachios, crumbled feta and finely chopped dates. Dress with finely grated orange zest, a good squeeze of orange juice, some dollops of Greek-style yoghurt and lots of chopped flat-leaf parsley. You will find this recipe on tenplay.com.au.

Reckon that some feta, mint and dill would look nice sprinkled over the top of this dish. It's obvious and unsophisticated.

Baklava Therapy

Like so many of the desserts in this book, the making of baklava is a calming process not to be rushed. Much of the time is taken up prepping the layers upon layers of filo that make it so very special. So take your time, enlist some help and see this more as a kitchen yoga or meditation session than a mad rush to get dinner on the table. While Greek heroes would discuss their problems with the Delphic oracle, I think they would have found it just as helpful to make baklava.

This baklava can be easily frozen to keep longer as the recipe does make quite a lot. Wrap it in plastic wrap and foil, then freeze for up to 3 months. When you're ready for that dessert choice, you can cut the prep time down to 2 minutes!

MAKES: ABOUT 40 PIECES **PREP:** 50 MINS (PLUS 6 HOURS COOLING) **COOKING:** 35 MINS

500 g walnuts
100 g caster sugar
2 tablespoons ground cinnamon
1 whole clove, ground (or a good pinch of pre-ground cloves)
finely grated zest of 1 lemon
60 ml (¼ cup) orange blossom water
250 g clarified butter, melted (see TIP)
2 × 375 g packets filo pastry
finely chopped pistachios, for decorating

HONEY SYRUP

300 g honey
100 g caster sugar
1 teaspoon lemon juice

Preheat the oven to 200°C/180°C fan-forced. Blitz the walnuts in a food processor until finely chopped. Transfer to a bowl and add the sugar, cinnamon, clove, lemon zest and orange blossom water. Mix until well combined, then set aside.

Use a large ovenproof dish that is the same size as the filo pastry; if it's a little smaller you can trim the excess filo when you have finished layering, so don't worry about it now. If you have a round baking dish you will need to hang the excess over the side.

Play some soothing music and empty your mind of all the petty nags of the day. Brush the bottom of the baking dish with a little of the melted butter, and let all your cares melt away like the lines your pastry brush makes in the butter. Line the base of the dish with a sheet of filo, brush with a little butter and top with another sheet of filo.

Continue to layer the filo, brushing with butter between each layer until you have a stack of 15 sheets. With each layer put to rest any one unhelpful thought that has been bothering you. I generally find that no one has the capacity for more than 15 unhelpful thoughts, but if you do, there are still 20 more sheets to come. Spread the walnut filling over the pastry and smooth it out with the back of a spoon. Cover the filling with a sheet of filo, brush it with a little butter and top with another sheet. Continue to layer until you have 20 sheets of filo on top. Trim any excess pastry, if you need to.

Use a small knife to score the pastry through the top pastry layers, but not all the way to the base (these score lines will help you cut it into portions later). You can do this in diamonds or rectangles. Sprinkle a little cold water over the top, as it helps to stop the filo curling up while baking. Bake for about 35 minutes or until golden brown.

Meanwhile, make your syrup. Combine the honey, sugar, lemon juice and 250 ml (1 cup) water in a small saucepan and stir over low heat until the sugar has dissolved.

Remove the baklava from the oven and evenly pour the syrup over the top. Set aside for 6 hours before cutting. Sprinkle with chopped pistachios to serve.

TIP

It's not strictly Greek, but you can buy clarified butter (or ghee) at the supermarket. It's a nifty shortcut, but if you want to make your own, melt 310 g unsalted butter over low heat and simmer until foam rises to the surface. Use a spoon to skim the top and remove the foam. Very slowly pour the remaining butter through a fine sieve lined with muslin, leaving any solids in the bottom of the pan. Discard these too or toss through pasta with grated parmesan.

Bougatsa

The ancient city of Siris in Macedonia wasn't just an important strategic stronghold; it's also famous for championing the Greek answer to the vanilla slice. In fact, history tells us that it was Greek bakers, who left Constantinople as part of the population exchange after the Greco–Turkish War (1919–1922), who actually brought the pastry with them. Dig deeper, and it seems that meat bougatsa were being made in Constantinople back when it was still called Byzantium and was part of the Greek empire, so this should reassure any proud Hellenes who are worried that their favourite bougatsa is actually Turkish.

What won't reassure them is the news that the name, also pronounced 'pogatsa', is descended from the same Latin root word for hearth (focus), which gave us the word 'focaccia'.

That is all I know about bougatsa. It's not a lot, but now you probably know more than most people on this planet!

SERVES: 8 **PREP:** 45 MINS (PLUS 30 MINS COOLING) **COOKING:** 50 MINS

1 litre full-cream milk
180 g caster sugar
½ teaspoon vanilla extract
finely grated zest of ¼ orange
185 g (1½ cups) fine semolina
2 eggs, lightly whisked
80 g clarified butter, melted (see TIP on page 188)
1 × 375 g packet filo pastry
icing sugar and ground cinnamon, for dusting

Combine the milk, sugar, vanilla and orange zest in a large saucepan and heat over medium–high heat until the sugar has dissolved and the milk has come to the boil. Immediately reduce the heat and add the semolina in a steady stream, stirring constantly. Cook, stirring, for a few minutes until it thickens and comes back to the boil, then remove from the heat and set aside for 5 minutes to cool slightly.

Add the eggs to the semolina mixture and quickly combine. Set aside.

Preheat the oven to 200°C/180°C fan-forced. Grease a 5 cm deep, 30 cm × 20 cm baking dish with a little of the melted butter. Line the base and sides with one sheet of filo, allowing the excess to hang over the sides. Brush the filo with a little butter. Continue to layer with gentle, rhythmic, repetitive movements, brushing with butter between each layer until you have a stack of eight sheets of filo.

Pour the cooled custard into the filo-lined dish. Watch how it gently rolls into every corner with a steady confidence that you should take as inspiration and metaphor for how we should all live our lives.

Fold the overhanging pastry sheets over the custard to enclose it like you were tucking in a favourite child – not the one who drew on the bathroom mirror with your favourite lipstick or decided it would be funny to pour milk into your golf bag so you had something to drink the next time you played a round.

OK, now breathe and let the frustration you felt after that act fade away.

Top the custard with another sheet of filo, allowing it to hang over the sides of the dish. Brush with butter. Breathe. Continue to layer, brushing each layer with butter using that same gentle, calming rhythm until you have layered eight sheets. Trim off the overhanging pastry so it fits neatly in the dish.

Use a small knife to score the top few sheets of filo into portions; this will help when cutting the bougatsa later.

Bake for 45 minutes or until golden brown. Set aside for about 30 minutes to cool slightly.

Dust the top with icing sugar and cinnamon before cutting into pieces to serve.

ITALY

Invasion, colonisation, trade, migration, climatic breadth and geographic and political barriers influence every country's cuisine, whether it's Spain, India or Mexico. And all countries' cuisines are an amalgam of many regional variations and specialties, but given that Italy has only existed as a country since 1871, these differences are perhaps more marked than many other cuisines. This is what helps make Italian food so freaking delicious, but it also means that Italians can have stand-up rows about why their region's version, or their mother's version, of a dish is the only way to make it.

So much of the Italian food we love today comes from the tradition of 'cucina povera' – the cash-strapped rural or urban working-class kitchen – whether it's osso bucco, originally made by poor tannery families with the shanky offcuts of the animal hide, or pasta sauces that revolve around nothing more than tomatoes, olive oil and something to flavour it, such as porky pancetta, garlic, anchovies and olives or chilli flakes. It helps that classic Italian ingredients, such as anchovies, tomatoes and parmesan are all very high in umami. (Witness the Matriciana recipe on page 218, which only uses the fat rendered from cooking the pancetta or bacon to flavour the sauce.)

This frugal necessity also sees the same ingenious methods used with stale bread, whether grilled for bruschetta or turned into a Tuscan soup or salad with ripe tomatoes. When it comes to leftovers, Italians really are the champs, and this can be seen in soups, such as the Ribollita on page 211 and minestrone, which are no more than canny ways of using up whatever veg you have lying around that's heading towards its use-by date.

This approach of the classic Italian kitchen also ensures that foraging and growing your own food, and cooking from scratch are both very much part of cultural and family identity, whether it's a day set aside for making tomato sauce or salami or heading out into the woods and hillsides to gather truffles, mushrooms (such as the wonderful porcini) and wild, often bitter, greens.

Another side of the rural heritage of the Italians is the many tasty ways they preserve excess for the less-bountiful months. Milk is transformed into huge rounds of parmesan; gooey cheeses, such as melty fontina or taleggio; soft, milky mozzarella or ricotta; or something more pungent, such as gorgonzola. Pigs are turned into prosciutto, pancetta, guanciale, salami, lardo, tubs of pristine, white homemade lard, souse and strings of salsicce. And this is just the tip of the charcuterie iceberg, which includes mortadella and bresaola, along with many others.

When it comes to other proteins, beef, chicken, veal, lamb and goat all feature alongside an impressive range of seafood – amazing red prawns, calamari, sea urchin roe, tuna and all manner of local fish – given the extraordinary amount of coastline of this long-skinny-boot-kicking-a-badly-deflated-football country.

In terms of aromatics, herbs and spices, such as thyme, oregano, rosemary, parsley, basil (which reaches its apotheosis as a Genovese pesto), sage, nutmeg, fennel seeds and black pepper (much prized by the Romans), all feature prominently at times. Vegetables include silverbeet, potatoes, fennel, artichokes, spinach, kale, celery, carrots, onion, broccolini, rape, bitter chicory, cauliflower and beans, such as borlotti and cannellini (Tuscans especially love their beans and are known as the 'bean eaters'). Fruit is widely consumed with cherries, peaches, pears, blood oranges, grapefruit, strawberries and grapes at the fore, the last of which might be turned into vincotto or balsamic vinegar – perfect for drizzling onto a Tuscan bean stew.

FAKING IT TIPS

1. Add olive oil, tomatoes, garlic, cheese and basil to a bake, braise or pasta dish. Add prosciutto to complete the picture, if you like, or use pecorino and chilli flakes for a more southern bent.
2. Pretty much every Italian meat braise, stew or sauce starts with a fried base of two-parts diced onion, one-part carrot and one-part celery (or fennel if the protein is seafood). Once translucent, add garlic, along with anchovies or anything porky to add flavour.
3. Keep your meats for roasting or grilling free from spice rubs, although a marinade of lemon, garlic, olive oil and a hardy herb, such as rosemary for lamb, oregano for chicken or parsley for beef is a nice addition. Always season your meat with lots of salt flakes after grilling.
4. Serve lamb with a black olive tapenade and grilled beef with a salsa verde made with fresh herbs pounded with vinegar or lemon juice and your choice of garlic, capers and/or anchovies.
5. Simplicity is the central tenet of Italian cookery, so keep the ingredients to a minimum. Unless it's a minestrone, in which case throw in any odds and sods you have.
6. Don't overload pastas with sauces. The sauce should be seen as a condiment.
7. Serve dishes with a simple side salad, such as fennel, radicchio and orange, witlof, parmesan and balsamic, or finely shredded cabbage, torn mint and parmesan dressed with no more than salt and oil. Or opt for a simple side veg, such as spinach with lemon juice and garlic or roast potatoes with garlic and rosemary.

SHOPPING LIST

It's easy to stock your shelves with Italian flavours, as most ingredients feature regularly in our cooking repertoires in one form or another and can be readily bought at the supermarket. Perhaps the most obvious here is pasta, and few households would be without a packet of spaghetti or penne lurking somewhere in the pantry. For a change, look out for more unusual and interesting pasta shapes to mix things up, and seek out fregola (a fancy couscous-like Sardinian pasta) and polenta (especially white polenta). For risottos, buy starchier rices, such as vialone nano and carnaroli will result in a creamier end result.

Canned tomatoes are another obvious choice, but, if you can, look out for canned cherry tomatoes or the prized San Marzano tomatoes the next time you visit your local Italian deli, as they will take any pasta sauce to the next level. While you're there, buy some pancetta, prosciutto and true salsicce (Italian sausage).

Finally, for an umami hit, stock up on salted capers, dried porcini and jarred anchovies, and save your parmesan rinds to add to soups and sauces for an extra depth of flavour.

Caponata Baked Eggs

So many of the good things of summer jolly along together in a caponata, which is a Sicilian sweet and sour dish. I think of it as summer sunshine in a bowl.

Some caponatas include a little chocolate for texture. I don't like that. So we didn't. I'd far rather add eggs to poach in the rich tomatoey goodness, which turns the caponata from a side dish into a perfect light lunch or supper. It's what my mum used to do way back when we were kids. Sigh, 'I love you, Mum'.

Anyway, there's enough silkiness with the eggplant here. And when it comes to big flavours, all those olives, capers, tomatoes and the classic Sicilian agro-dolce hit means there's more than enough going on to stop anyone wondering where the bacon is.

And save those squares of bitter chocolate to go with the short black after dinner ... but never with a latte! You can't fake your way out of that faux pas or 'passo falso', as the Italians might say.

SERVES: 4 **PREP:** 15 MINS **COOKING:** 30 MINS

100 ml extra virgin olive oil
1 large eggplant, cut into 1.5 cm pieces
sea salt and freshly ground black pepper
2 celery stalks, finely chopped
1 brown onion, finely chopped
1 red capsicum, deseeded and cut into 1.5 cm pieces
½ bunch flat-leaf parsley, leaves picked and stalks finely chopped
2 garlic cloves, crushed
2 teaspoons dried oregano
1 × 400 g can whole peeled tomatoes
250 g mixed cherry tomatoes, halved
55 g (⅓ cup) pitted Kalamata olives
2 tablespoons baby capers, rinsed and drained
2 tablespoons vincotto (or 2 tablespoons white wine vinegar mixed with 1 tablespoon brown sugar)
4 eggs
45 g (¼ cup) pine nuts, toasted
toasted crusty bread, to serve

Preheat the oven to 200°C/180°C fan-forced.

Heat half the oil in a shallow flameproof casserole dish or large ovenproof frying pan over medium–high heat. Add the eggplant and season well. Cook, tossing occasionally, for 5–6 minutes or until golden. Transfer to a bowl.

Heat the remaining oil in the pan, add the celery, onion, capsicum and parsley stalks and cook for 3–4 minutes or until soft. Add the garlic and oregano and cook for a further 1 minute or until aromatic. Add the canned tomatoes, cherry tomatoes, olives, capers and vincotto and stir to combine, then return the eggplant to the pan, along with 125 ml (½ cup) water, and season with pepper. Bring to a simmer, then reduce the heat to medium and cook, stirring occasionally, for 6–8 minutes or until the eggplant is tender and the liquid has reduced slightly.

Remove the pan from the heat. Use the back of a spoon to make four indentations in the caponata, then crack an egg into each indent.

Transfer to the oven and bake for 8 minutes or until the egg whites are just cooked. Scatter with the parsley leaves and pine nuts, and serve with toasted crusty bread.

TIPS

Get ahead and make the tomato base to have on hand. It keeps well in an airtight container in the freezer for up to 3 months. When you need it, thaw it in the fridge overnight and you are ready to go. It makes a delicious bruschetta topping, too.

Caponata makes a fine home for leftovers, such as roast chicken, and is great in a pasta bake with pecorino, mozzarella and penne cooked for 3 minutes less than it says on the packet. You can also chop frankfurters or leftover cooked sausages into it for a quick supper, served with garlic- and oil-rubbed grilled bread.

Chicken Saltimbocca Tray Bake

They aren't mentioned in the title of this dish, but this tray bake is actually all about the crispy-edged potatoes.

Are you drooling yet?

They're so special because the salty prosciutto fat and the chicken drippings meld with the sage butter, making these some of the best, most flavour-packed potatoes you'll ever let leap into your gob ...

Bet you are now!!!

SERVES: 4 **PREP:** 20 MINS **COOKING:** 50 MINS

50 g unsalted butter, melted
8 sage leaves, very finely chopped, plus extra small leaves to serve
2 garlic cloves, crushed
finely grated zest and juice of 1 lemon
2 tablespoons extra virgin olive oil
sea salt and freshly ground black pepper
800 g sebago or desiree potatoes, scrubbed
8 slices prosciutto
8 large chicken thigh fillets
garlic buttered zucchini, to serve (see TIP)

Preheat the oven to 200°C/180°C fan-forced. Line a large shallow roasting tin with baking paper.

Combine the butter, chopped sage, garlic, lemon zest and 1 tablespoon of the oil in a bowl. Season with salt and pepper.

Using a mandoline or sharp knife, very thinly slice the potatoes – ideally about 3 mm thick. Spread, slightly overlapping, over the prepared tin and brush with two-thirds of the butter mixture. Bake for 15 minutes while you prepare the chicken.

Lay one slice of prosciutto on a chopping board and top with a chicken thigh, boned side up. Brush the chicken with a little of the remaining butter mixture, then wrap in the prosciutto and secure with a toothpick. Repeat with the remaining prosciutto, chicken and butter mixture.

Remove the tray from the oven and use a spoon to make small gaps in the potato to pop in each chicken parcel – make sure the potatoes are not entirely covered. Brush the chicken parcels with the remaining oil.

Reduce the oven temperature to 180°C/160°C fan-forced. Roast for a further 35 minutes or until the potato is golden and the chicken is cooked through. Set aside for 5 minutes to rest.

Drain the buttery pan juices and combine with the lemon juice.

Remove all toothpicks from the chicken parcels! Then, and only then, slice the chicken. Serve the chicken and potato topped with the buttery lemon sauce and extra sage leaves.

TIP

Serve with zucchini. Cut into rounds and either grill, steam or cook slowly in a covered pan with lots of garlic and a little butter. They should sweat to a lovely sweet softness that's perfect with all the crispy saltiness!

Gooey Three-Cheese, Garlic & Silverbeet Piadina

'My arms ache, and I'm dusted with more flour than Banquo's ghost in a bad school production of Macbeth. I've just spent the day trying out a sheaf of recipes for doughs to make a decent piadina, and now I understand why the 'adzores' (housewives of the Emilia-Romagna region of Italy, which is home to this peasant flatbread), so often have arms the size of the local Parma hams. The reward for all that kneading, kneading, kneading and rolling, rolling, rolling is, eventually, after no little trial and fractious doughy errors, a pretty perfect crescent of hot, light and slightly plumped bread. It's filled with gooey melted Italian cheese and a handful of rocket, and pulled freshly cooked from a dry cast-iron pan, the crowns of the little bubbles in the dough tanned like the pate of a balding Noosa gentleman. One bite and it is easy to understand why in the 70s, piadina moved from Romagna's peasant hearths to being a perfect snack served at a thousand beachside shacks along the region's Adriatic coast.'

I wrote this after my first piadina-making foray almost 15 years ago and now, finally, a piadina makes it into one of my cookbooks. This one is the ultimate Italian cheese toastie, thanks to the three cheeses and loads of garlicky silverbeet. Once you've made it, you will make it again and again, but with a whole manner of different fillings or exotic Italian cheeses with names like taleggio, asiago or stracchino (a traditional piadina cheese and like a less pungent taleggio), all of which melt beautifully.

MAKES: 4 **PREP:** 15 MINS **COOKING:** 20 MINS

1 bunch silverbeet (you need about 250 g leaves)
150 g fontina, chopped (or brie, which is a lot easier to find and works almost as well, even if it is French ... or from King Island ...)
150 g mozzarella, coarsely grated
70 g (1 cup) finely grated parmesan
2 tablespoons extra virgin olive oil, plus extra for brushing
1 leek, white and light green parts, thinly sliced
2 garlic cloves, crushed
1 tablespoon very finely chopped rosemary leaves
1 tablespoon red wine vinegar
4 flatbreads, such as Greek pita bread

Preheat the oven to 100°C/80°C fan-forced.

Use a small knife to cut the white stalks from the silverbeet leaves. Finely chop the leaves and discard the stalks, or quick pickle them (see TIPS).

Combine the fontina, mozzarella and parmesan in a bowl.

Heat the oil in a large frying pan over medium heat. Add the leek and cook, stirring, for 2–3 minutes or until soft. Add the garlic and rosemary and cook for 30 seconds, then add the silverbeet leaves and toss to combine. Cook, stirring, for 1–2 minutes or until the silverbeet starts to wilt. Stir in the vinegar. Drain any excess liquid from the pan and transfer the silverbeet mixture to a bowl. Wipe the frying pan clean.

Place a flatbread on a chopping board. Brush one side with extra oil, then flip it over. Spoon one-quarter of the silverbeet mixture over half of the flatbread and top with one-quarter of the combined cheeses. Fold the naked side over to enclose the filling.

Heat the frying pan over medium–high heat. Using a spatula, lift the piadina into the pan and cook for 1–2 minutes or until golden underneath. Flip over and cook the other side for a further 1 minute or until the cheese has melted. Pop into the oven to keep warm and repeat with the remaining flatbreads, silverbeet mixture and cheese.

TIPS

Make your own cheat's piadina breads using my two-ingredient recipe on page 264. Or for more authentic piadina breads, look for my dead-easy recipe online (search Matt Preston piadina).

TO QUICK-PICKLE THE SILVERBEET STALKS: *trim the ends, cut into finger-width chunks and fry in a little olive oil until they soften. Sprinkle over a little caster sugar and a pinch of salt, then cook, stirring, for another 2 minutes. Add a good splash of wine vinegar and cook until it's either evaporated or soaked into the stalks. Serve on the side with the piadina. You can add toasted pine nuts and currants at the beginning or the end if you are feeling fancy.*

Calabrian Meatlovers Lasagna 2.0

The original lasagne was created by the Romans. According to an ancient recipe I uncovered their 'lasanis' was squares of pasta cut into strips as wide as three fingers. The sheets (or 'bed of towels' as the translation puts it!) were layered with 'caseum grattatum' (that's grated cheese, according to my trusty online translator of ancient Latin).

You've got to love a good online translator – well, until it throws up the English translation of 'lasanis'. This comes out as 'wash room' or 'chamber pot', which makes our lasagne sound a whole lot less appetising! Maybe it was something about all those sheets of pasta piled up in the earthenware cooking pot.

Anyway, I digress ... the lasagne we know best is the version from Emilia-Romagna, with bechamel and bolognese, but the canny Calabrians make their lasagna (note that in the south of Italy lasagna ends with an 'a' not an 'e') with layers of oozy mozzarella instead of bechamel, and include layers of chopped boiled egg and ham or mortadella as well as mince. In this version, I've added prosciutto for saltiness and extra meatiness.

SERVES: 6 **PREP:** 20 MINS **COOKING:** 1 HOUR 10 MINS

2 tablespoons extra virgin olive oil, plus extra for greasing
1 brown onion, coarsely grated
1 large carrot, coarsely grated
sea salt and freshly ground black pepper
3 garlic cloves, finely grated
1 tablespoon chopped thyme leaves
1 tablespoon chopped rosemary leaves
500 g pork and veal mince
1 × 700 ml bottle tomato passata
250 ml (1 cup) red wine
500 g (5 cups) coarsely grated mozzarella
70 g (1 cup) finely grated parmesan
12 dried lasagne sheets
80 g thinly sliced prosciutto, cut into 4 cm pieces
80 g sliced mortadella, cut into 4 cm pieces
4 hard-boiled eggs, sliced
small flat-leaf parsley leaves, to serve (yes, chopped larger leaves are also fine)

Heat the oil in a large saucepan or flameproof casserole dish over medium–high heat. Add the onion and carrot, season with salt and pepper and cook, stirring, for 3–4 minutes or until soft. Add the garlic, thyme and rosemary and cook for a further 1 minute or until aromatic.

Add the mince and cook, breaking up any lumps with the back of a wooden spoon, for 4–5 minutes or until well browned. Add the passata, wine and 500 ml (2 cups) water. Bring to a simmer, then reduce the heat to medium and cook, stirring occasionally, for 10 minutes or until the sauce has thickened slightly. Remove from the heat and set aside to cool slightly. (The mince mixture will have more moisture than a traditional lasagne; as there is no bechamel you need this extra liquid to cook the pasta.)

Preheat the oven to 180°C/160°C fan-forced. Grease a 6 cm deep, 30 cm × 22 cm baking dish with a little oil. Combine the mozzarella and parmesan in a bowl.

Spoon about ½ cup of the mince mixture over the base of the dish and cover with four of the lasagne sheets. Top with one-third of the remaining mince mixture, then one-third of the prosciutto and mortadella, one-third of the egg and one-third of the cheese mixture. Repeat the layering twice, but before the final layer of egg and cheese, drizzle over 60 ml (¼ cup) water.

Cover with a sheet of baking paper and then foil, and bake for 40 minutes.

Increase the oven temperature to 220°C/200°C fan-forced. Remove the paper and foil and bake for a further 8–10 minutes or until golden. Scatter with parsley to serve.

TIP

If you want to make this ahead and freeze it, you can take it up to the point where you remove the paper and foil for the final bake. Let it cool completely, then cover with a double layer of plastic wrap and freeze for up to 3 months. Thaw overnight in the fridge. Cover with a layer of baking paper and foil and reheat in a preheated 180°C/160°C fan-forced oven for 20 minutes, then remove the paper and foil and bake until golden.

Pork & Fennel Polpette with Spaghettini

In Italy, meatballs are served in tomato sauce, possibly with bread on the side. Serving them on spaghetti is an American mafia-movie sort of thing to do. You know, the evocative shot, just before someone gets whacked, of a meatball rolling in slow motion off the tangled pile of pasta to bounce, roll and splash its vivid vermilion way across the red and white checked tablecloth of a classic Little Italy trattoria in Chicago or New York.

In less artistic mob movies this would be intercut with equally slo-mo shots of the Cosa Nostra kingpin getting offed by his crosstown rivals all dressed in sharp suits and homburgs. At the end of the scene the meatball would come to rest against the victim's lifeless hand ... You're not sure if that splatter is tomato sauce or gore.

I include this recipe to prove that Italian food is more often 'food made by Italians' – wherever they may be – rather than 'food made in Italy'. This is important because Italy is only a comparatively recent thing, and Italian food has always been open to evolution, whether through invasion, importation or migration. Classic Italian dishes with chilli or tomato, for example, only exist thanks to the one-time rule of the country's south by the Spanish, who had discovered these now-essentials of the Italian kitchen in the New World, along with capsicums, beans and chocolate.

SERVES: 4 **PREP:** 20 MINS **COOKING:** 30 MINS

80 ml (⅓ cup) extra virgin olive oil
2 garlic cloves, thinly sliced
1–2 teaspoons dried chilli flakes, to taste (I like 1½ teaspoons)
1 teaspoon fennel seeds, crushed using a mortar and pestle
4 roma tomatoes, coarsely chopped
1 × 700 ml bottle tomato passata
1 parmesan rind, plus extra finely grated parmesan to serve
½ bunch basil
sea salt and freshly ground black pepper
400 g dried spaghettini
sliced red chilli, to serve (optional)

PORK MEATBALLS
1 zucchini
1 teaspoon fennel seeds, crushed
500 g pork mince
50 g (⅔ cup) finely grated parmesan
25 g panko breadcrumbs
1 garlic clove, crushed
1 egg

To make the meatballs, coarsely grate the zucchini. Place in a piece of paper towel, then squeeze out the excess moisture. Place the zucchini in a food processor, add the remaining ingredients and blitz until well combined. With wet hands, roll 1½ tablespoon portions of the mixture into balls (you should have about 20 meatballs). Arrange on a tray lined with baking paper and place in the freezer for 5 minutes to firm up.

Heat half the oil in a large deep frying pan over medium–high heat. Add the meatballs and cook, turning, for 4–5 minutes or until well browned. Transfer to a plate.

Heat the remaining oil in the pan, add the garlic, chilli flakes and fennel seeds and cook, stirring, for 20 seconds or until aromatic. Add the chopped tomato and cook, stirring occasionally, for 2–3 minutes or until they start to break down. Add the passata, parmesan rind, half the basil (stalks and all) and 125 ml (½ cup) water. Bring to a simmer, then reduce the heat to medium and cook, stirring occasionally, for 5 minutes or until reduced slightly. Return the meatballs to the pan and cook for 15 minutes or until the sauce has thickened. Season.

Meanwhile, bring a large saucepan of salted water to the boil over high heat. Add the pasta and stir in 250 ml (1 cup) cold water to separate the pasta and stop it sticking. Return to the boil, then reduce the heat and simmer for 1 minute less than it says on the packet, or until al dente. Drain, reserving 80 ml (⅓ cup) of the cooking water.

Remove the basil and parmesan rind from the sauce and discard. Add the pasta to the pan, along with the reserved cooking water, and toss to combine.

Serve topped with grated parmesan, the remaining basil leaves and sliced chilli (if using).

TIP

Ditch the pasta and serve these meatballs in a ciabatta roll, loaded with lots of basil with fresh tomato and melting Swiss cheese – the ultimate Italian sub.

Pear Salad with Gorgonzola Polenta Chips

Pear salad has become as big a cliche these days as blokes with beards, or those sportsmen whose public apologies skillfully admit nothing and apologise for even less, or those celebrities who claim they have mental health problems when their problem is actually their extensive (often nasal) self-medication.

Yet, adding the golden crunch of polenta chips to this old Italian favourite turns things around and, even better, they both go perfectly with the creaminess of a nice blue cheese. Also, changing the usual rocket for bitter leaves, such as radicchio, really helps the sweetness of the pear and the saltiness of the cheese to shine.

One word of warning: you'll need to start the polenta chips a few hours before you want to eat, as the polenta needs to cool and set. This is not a dish to make if you need dinner on the table in 15 minutes.

SERVES: 4 **PREP:** 20 MINS (PLUS 2 HOURS CHILLING) **COOKING:** 15 MINS

- 125 g instant polenta
- 65 g gorgonzola, crumbled
- 25 g unsalted butter
- sea salt and freshly ground black pepper
- sunflower or vegetable oil, for shallow-frying
- juice of ½ lemon
- 2 pears
- 1 small head radicchio, leaves separated
- 1 witlof, leaves separated
- 1 cup baby basil leaves
- 2 tablespoons chopped roasted walnuts

SOUR CREAM DRESSING

- 2 tablespoons sour cream
- 25 g gorgonzola, crumbled
- 2 tablespoons extra virgin olive oil
- juice of 1 lemon
- freshly ground black pepper

Grease and line a 20 cm square baking tin or dish with plastic wrap.

Pour 500 ml (2 cups) water into a large saucepan and bring to the boil over high heat. In a steady stream, add the polenta and whisk until smooth. Cook, stirring constantly, for 2 minutes, then remove from the heat. Add the gorgonzola and butter and stir until melted and well combined. Season well with salt and pepper.

Pour the polenta into the prepared tin or dish and smooth the surface with the back of a spoon or palette knife. Place in the fridge for at least 2 hours or until firm and well chilled. Lift out the polenta and place on a chopping board. Cut into 2 cm thick chips, then place on a baking tray lined with baking paper. Freeze for 5 minutes to firm up.

Pour oil into a deep frying pan to a depth of 2 cm and heat over medium–high heat until hot. Add the polenta chips in batches and cook, turning gently, for 3–4 minutes or until golden and crisp all over. The chips will burst a little, creating crunchy pockets, which is what you want. Drain on paper towel and leave to cool slightly.

For the dressing, place the sour cream and gorgonzola in a bowl and mash with a fork. Add the oil, lemon juice and 1 tablespoon water, and season very well with pepper.

Pour the lemon juice into a bowl of water. Using a very sharp knife or a mandoline, slice the pears very thinly, leaving the cores behind, and place in the acidulated water to prevent it from going brown.

Arrange the radicchio, witlof, basil and sliced pear on serving plates. Finish with the crispy polenta chips and walnuts, and drizzle the dressing over the top to serve.

TIP

If you prefer to bake your polenta rather than fry it, try polenta crisps instead. Place dollops of the cooked polenta on a baking tray lined with baking paper and spread evenly with the back of a spoon. Finely grate over 25 g parmesan, then bake in a preheated 200°C/180°C fan-forced oven for 20 minutes or until dark golden. Allow to cool, then tear into pieces.

Secret-Ingredient White Polenta with Mushroom Sauce

While it may look like mashed potato this is, in fact, polenta, and it's just as comforting. More common in northern Italy and the Abruzzo, it is made from ground white corn and is often used to make sweet porridge, although it also makes a great savoury winter bowl. The porridge is cooked in milk and is very rich and delicious, so I've added that richness to the savoury polenta, using milk powder in an out-of-whack ratio to water to make it extra creamy.

Skim milk powder is the most wonderful secret ingredient to have in your pantry – to find out why read my 11 Magical Ways with Skimmed Milk Powder online at delicious.com.au.

SERVES: 4 **PREP:** 15 MINS **COOKING:** 35 MINS

150 g (1 cup) white polenta
180 g (1½ cups) full-cream or skim milk powder
15 g dried porcini mushrooms, chopped
250 ml (1 cup) boiling water
80 ml (⅓ cup) extra virgin olive oil
200 g small portobello mushrooms
400 g Swiss brown mushrooms, halved if large
4 thyme sprigs, leaves stripped
2 garlic cloves, crushed
75 g unsalted butter
sea salt and freshly ground black pepper
125 g taleggio (or other soft cheese, such as brie), skin removed, chopped

TARRAGON GREMOLATA

2 tablespoons finely chopped tarragon
2 tablespoons finely chopped flat-leaf parsley
finely grated zest of 1 lemon
2 tablespoons chopped roasted hazelnuts

Combine the polenta and milk powder in a bowl. Pour 1.25 litres water into a large saucepan over medium–high heat and bring to a simmer. Add the polenta mixture in a steady stream, whisking constantly until it thickens. Reduce the heat to low and cook, stirring every few minutes, for 30 minutes or until smooth and cooked through.

While the polenta is cooking, place the dried porcini in a heatproof bowl. Pour over the boiling water and leave to soak for 10 minutes.

Heat 1½ tablespoons of the oil in a large frying pan over medium–high heat. Add the portobello mushrooms and cook for 2 minutes each side or until almost tender. Transfer to a plate. Heat the remaining oil in the pan, add the Swiss brown mushrooms in batches and cook for 2–3 minutes or until well browned, transferring each batch to a plate when cooked. Return all the Swiss brown mushrooms to the pan.

Add the thyme, garlic and 25 g of the butter and cook, tossing, for 2 minutes, then add the portobello mushrooms, porcini and sieved soaking water, and season. Simmer for 8–10 minutes or until the mushrooms are tender and the sauce has reduced by half.

For the gremolata, life is even simpler: just combine all the ingredients in a bowl.

By now your polenta should be cooked. Add the taleggio, remaining butter and 100 ml water and stir until the cheese has melted and everything is combined. Season to taste. Serve immediately topped with the mushroom mixture. Sprinkle with the gremolata, sigh a lot and be grateful it's winter.

TIPS

To speed up the process, you can buy instant polenta at the supermarket. It may not be white, but if you're short of time you can have this recipe on the table in around 20 minutes.

To beef up this dish, serve with beef sausages or barbecued steak.

Hazelnut Chicken Milanese with Quick Pickled Salad

'Cotoletta alla Milanese' is an Italian schnitty – meat that is breaded and fried. While the schnitty comes from Austria and has been bouncing around there since the 1700s, in 1 BC the ancient Romans also had a thing for beating out meat, then breading and frying it, so let's not get caught up in a silly 'who stole what from whom' turf war. It's just more proof that food wouldn't be what it is today without a little cultural appropriation.

This version gets extra crunch and kick by adding hazelnut meal to the crumb instead of just the traditional breadcrumbs, and the fresh pickled salad cuts through the greasiness of the fried chicken nicely. That's a proudly Australian idea!

SERVES: 4 **PREP:** 25 MINS (PLUS 15 MINUTES STANDING) **COOKING:** 15 MINS

4 small (about 160 g) chicken breast fillets
25 g sea salt
75 g (½ cup) wholemeal plain flour
2 eggs
55 g (½ cup) hazelnut meal
45 g (½ cup) dried breadcrumbs
freshly ground black pepper
sunflower oil, for shallow-frying
lemon wedges, to serve

QUICK PICKLED SALAD

3 celery stalks
¼ teaspoon dried chilli flakes
2 tablespoons white wine vinegar or white balsamic vinegar
sea salt
1 bunch flat-leaf parsley, leaves chopped
1 zucchini, shaved with a vegetable peeler into ribbons
2 tablespoons extra virgin olive oil

Place one chicken breast fillet between two sheets of baking paper and use a rolling pin to bash lightly until it is 2 cm thick. Repeat with the remaining fillets.

Combine the salt and 500 ml (2 cups) warm water in a bowl. Add the chicken to the brine and set aside for 15 minutes or longer. This will make the chicken juicier and tastier, as Gina proved to devastating effect on the last season of *MasterChef*.

Meanwhile, make a start on the pickled celery salad. Use a vegetable peeler to shave the celery into long ribbons. When you get down to the bottom and can't shave it any more, finely chop the rest. Place in a bowl with the chilli flakes, vinegar and a pinch of salt. Set aside to pickle.

While the celery is pickling, make your schnitzels. Place the flour in a bowl and lightly whisk the eggs in a second bowl. Combine the hazelnut meal and breadcrumbs in a third bowl. Season each bowl.

Pat the chicken dry. Working with one piece at a time, coat it in flour, then the egg, then the hazelnut mixture and place on a baking tray.

Pour the oil into a deep frying pan to a depth of 2 cm and heat over medium-high heat. Add the chicken in batches and cook for 2–3 minutes each side or until golden and crisp. Transfer to a plate lined with paper towel to drain.

To finish the salad, add the parsley, zucchini and oil to the pickled celery mixture and toss to combine.

Serve the chicken with the salad and lemon wedges.

TIPS

Use almond meal if you can't get your hands on hazelnut meal.

You could also serve this dish with burrata or torn buffalo mozzarella to add a delicious creaminess.

I know a Milanese isn't usually served with mayo, but it is in my house! A garlic and parmesan mayo works particularly well: combine 180 g (⅔ cup) mayonnaise with 2 tablespoons finely grated parmesan and 1 crushed garlic clove. Seriously!

If you want a change from the pickled salad, I recommend shredded radicchio dressed with no more than lemon juice and salt, just like they do at the venerable old Milano institution, Trattoria Milanese Dal 1933.

Roasted Garlic Ribollita

This hearty Tuscan soup is made using a range of leftover vegetables and stale bread. It really is 'cucina povera' (peasant cooking) at its very best. This version is a very substantial soup and very warming, thanks to the roasted garlic, which adds a wonderful creaminess as well as a sweet, subtle garlic flavour.

Feel free to substitute vegetables, depending on what needs to be eaten in the vegetable crisper drawer, BUT DON'T, WHATEVER YOU DO, leave out the anchovies. They add a great saltiness and savoury flavour that absolutely make the dish, and still won't leave it tasting like fish!

!!!!!Embrace the hairy fish!!!!!

SERVES: 4 **PREP:** 30 MINS **COOKING:** 30 MINS

1 small garlic head
60 ml (¼ cup) extra virgin olive oil
6 anchovies in olive oil, drained and oil reserved, anchovies finely chopped
1 carrot, finely chopped
1 brown onion, finely chopped
1 celery stalk, finely chopped
½ bunch flat-leaf parsley, stalks and leaves separated, finely chopped
1 tablespoon very finely chopped rosemary leaves
1 tablespoon very finely chopped thyme leaves
2 fresh or dried bay leaves
2 × 250 g punnets cherry or grape tomatoes
½ bunch kale, leaves chopped
1 × 400 g can cannellini beans, rinsed and drained
1 parmesan rind
500 ml (2 cups) vegetable or chicken stock
2 slices ciabatta, plus extra toasted slices to serve
25 g finely grated parmesan, plus extra to serve
sea salt and freshly ground black pepper

Preheat the oven to 200°C/180°C fan-forced.

Separate the garlic into cloves and place in the centre of a piece of foil. Drizzle with 1 tablespoon of the oil and wrap in the foil to enclose. Roast for 20 minutes or until very soft.

While the garlic roasts, heat the remaining olive oil and 1 tablespoon of the reserved oil from the anchovy jar in a saucepan over medium heat. Add the carrot, onion and celery and cook, stirring, for 3–4 minutes or until soft. Add the chopped anchovies, parsley stalks, rosemary, thyme and bay leaves and cook, stirring, for 1 minute or until aromatic. Add the tomatoes and kale and cook, stirring, for 2–3 minutes or until the kale has wilted. Add the beans, parmesan rind, stock and 500 ml (2 cups) water. Bring to the boil, then reduce the heat to low. Cover and simmer gently for 15 minutes or until the flavours have infused.

While the soup simmers away, remove the garlic from the foil, squeeze the flesh from each clove into a bowl and mash with a fork. Very finely chop the ciabatta (or whiz in a food processor) and add to the soup with the garlic, grated parmesan and 250 ml (1 cup) hot water. Stir until combined and season. Cook for a further 5 minutes or until the bread has broken down and thickened the soup. Discard the parmesan rind.

Ladle the soup into serving bowls and top with the chopped parsley leaves and extra grated parmesan. Serve with toasted ciabatta and a big hug.

TIP

To make this gluten free, leave out the bread and mash some extra cannellini beans to help thicken the soup.

Simple Pumpkin Pappardelle Pasta with Lamb Ragu

Making your own pasta is a luxury *[Ed: Is it really? Me: Yes it is; you need the luxury of time and expensive equipment]*, but it doesn't have to be hard. You don't even need a pasta machine! This recipe uses just pumpkin and flour to make a deliciously vibrant orange pasta.

If you don't have the time or patience to roll your own pasta, you can pair the lamb with store-bought pasta, but opt for fresh if you can to take full advantage of the rich ragu.

SERVES: 4 PREP: 30 MINS (PLUS 30 MINS RESTING) COOKING: 2 HOURS 45 MINS

- 125 ml (½ cup) extra virgin olive oil
- 700 g boneless lamb leg, cut into 2.5 cm pieces
- 60 g piece flat pancetta, coarsely chopped
- 1 brown onion, finely chopped
- 2 garlic cloves, finely chopped
- 1 tablespoon finely chopped oregano
- 1 × 400 g can whole peeled tomatoes
- 70 g (¼ cup) tomato paste
- 250 ml (1 cup) red wine
- sea salt and freshly ground black pepper
- 100 g pepitas
- finely grated parmesan, to serve

PUMPKIN PAPPARDELLE

- 300 g peeled and deseeded Kent pumpkin, cut into 3 cm pieces
- 350 g (2⅓ cups) plain flour, plus extra for dusting
- sea salt

Heat 1½ tablespoons of the oil in a heavy-based saucepan over medium–high heat. Add half the lamb and cook, turning, for 4–5 minutes or until browned, then remove and repeat with another 1½ tablespoons of oil and the remaining lamb. Reduce the heat to medium, add the pancetta and onion and cook for 3–4 minutes or until soft. Add the garlic and oregano and cook for 1 minute or until aromatic. Return the lamb to the pan and add the tomatoes, tomato paste, wine and 125 ml (½ cup) water. Reduce the heat to low, cover and cook for 2 hours or until very tender. Season with salt and pepper.

To make the pappardelle, place the pumpkin in a microwave-safe bowl and cover with plastic wrap. Microwave on high for 4 minutes or until the pumpkin is very tender. Mash well with a fork and set aside to cool slightly.

Place the pumpkin in a food processor with the flour and season with salt. Blitz until the mixture comes together and forms a dough. If you find the dough is a little dry, add 1 tablespoon water or enough to just bring the mixture together. Transfer the dough to a lightly floured surface and knead for 5 minutes or until smooth (work in a little more flour if it seems a bit wet). Cover with plastic wrap and place in the fridge to rest for at least 30 minutes.

Uncover the lamb and cook for 30 minutes or until the sauce has reduced slightly. Using a fork, break up the meat, then stir to combine. Set aside and keep warm.

Heat the remaining oil in a small frying pan over medium heat. Add the pepitas and cook for 1–2 minutes or until the oil starts to turn green and the pepitas are toasted.

Divide the dough into six portions and place one portion on a lightly floured surface. Roughly roll the dough out, then fold it into thirds. Repeat this process, rolling the dough a little thinner each time, rolling and folding, rolling and folding, rolling and folding and, finally, rolling out until it is as thin as possible (or just do the rolling and folding once; it won't be as silky, but it will take a quarter of the time). Hand-cut the pasta into wide ribbons, then transfer to a lightly floured tray. Repeat with the remaining dough.

Bring a large saucepan of salted water to the boil over high heat. Add the pasta and stir in 250 ml (1 cup) cold water. Return to the boil, then reduce the heat and simmer for 2 minutes or until al dente. Drain, reserving 80 ml (⅓ cup) of the cooking water.

Return the pasta to the pan, along with the reserved cooking water and ragu, and toss to combine. Divide among serving bowls and sprinkle over the grated parmesan and pepitas, and finish with a drizzle of the pepita oil.

Bologinese

It is highly debatable whether spag bol is actually Italian. Sure, the Italians had a dish called 'ragu bolognese', but it was all beef, chicken livers, mushrooms and even cream served on wide tagliatelle. Much more a ragu than a sauce. It's more likely that the tomatoey mince sauce we know and love to serve on spaghetti originated in the UK and the US (yes both), where southern Italian migrants (who loved 'red sauces') worked with locally available ingredients, such as tinned tomatoes and dried spaghetti, to create something vaguely approximating the flavours of home. The technique here is all solidly Italian, even if the dish might not be. If you haven't made this bolognese before, you are in for a treat.

SERVES: 6–8 **PREP:** 20 MINS **COOKING:** 4 HOURS 20 MINS (and worth every minute)

40 g butter
olive oil, for frying
2 carrots, finely chopped
3 brown onions, finely chopped
4 bacon rashers, finely chopped
2 celery stalks, finely chopped
1 tablespoon brown sugar
4 garlic cloves, crushed
70 g (¼ cup) tomato paste
1 kg beef mince
500 ml (2 cups) red wine
3 fresh or dried bay leaves
a few splashes of Worcestershire sauce
1 lemon, zest peeled into a 4 cm strip, lemon halved
800 g canned diced tomatoes
500 ml (2 cups) beef stock, plus extra if needed
sea salt
375 g dried egg tagliatelle
150 g (1½ cups) grated parmesan

To make the soffritto (or base), combine the butter and a little oil in a large frying pan over medium–high heat. When the butter has melted, throw in the carrot, onion and bacon and cook, stirring, for 2 minutes. Add the celery and cook for another 5 minutes or until the vegetables are soft and slightly translucent. Sprinkle over the brown sugar and stir to combine. Add the garlic and tomato paste and move this around the pan to cook out for 3 minutes. Scrape this tomatoey soffritto into a bowl.

Splash a little more oil into the pan. When it's hot, add the mince and cook, stirring, over high heat until browned, breaking up any lumps with the back of a wooden spoon. Scrape the meat into the soffritto bowl.

Add the wine to the pan and simmer to deglaze, scraping up any bits caught on the bottom. When the wine has reduced by half, return the meat and soffritto to the pan and add the bay leaves, Worcestershire sauce, lemon zest, tomatoes and stock. Season with salt and a good squeeze of lemon juice from one of the lemon halves.

Cover and bring to the boil, then remove the lid and turn the heat right down. Cook very gently for up to 4 hours, stirring occasionally to ensure the sauce doesn't catch and burn. If it gets too thick, stir in some more stock. The sauce is ready when it smells irresistible and is thick, glossy and a wonderful dark-red colour. Taste and season with a little more salt and lemon juice if needed. Now you can either serve it straight away, or cool and place in the fridge for the next day.

About 15 minutes before the bolognese is ready, bring a large saucepan of salted water to the boil over high heat. Add the pasta and stir in a cup of cold water to separate the pasta and stop it sticking. Return to the boil, then reduce the heat and simmer for 1 minute less than it says on the packet or until al dente. Drain, reserving 250 ml (1 cup) of the cooking water. Return the pasta to the pan.

Add a generous ladle (about 2 cups) of the bolognese sauce to the pasta and toss, moistening with a little of the reserved pasta water so it isn't clumpy. Feel free to use as much or as little sauce as you like. Sprinkle with parmesan, and serve with a green salad and bread for mopping up the leftover sauce, if you like.

TIP

Bolognese is THE perfect freezer dish. Place in an airtight container and freeze for up to 3 months. Thaw overnight in the fridge and reheat in a saucepan over low heat. Pop your spaghetti on and you'll have dinner on the table in under 12 minutes.

Borlotti Bean Gnocchi with Cavolo Nero Pesto

The best thing about writing cookbooks is working with friends, like the brilliant team that has pulled this one together. Warren, Emma, Marnie, Kate, Karlie and Michelle are all food experts, whose knowledge and skill in their chosen areas far eclipse mine. Thanks guys!

What's especially exciting is when they quietly send in an extra recipe of theirs that fits perfectly, and I would never have thought of in a million years. So it is with this genius borlotti bean gnocchi – the brainchild of Warren Mendes, whose fingerprints are all over the recipes in this book. Do try them!

And then try them again with your favourite sticky duck or lamb ragu; a fricassee of peas, beans, parmesan and pancetta dotted with the best balsamic vinegar; or grilled tomatoes and zucchini with loads of olive oil, salt and lemon. These clever gnocchi are extremely versatile!

SERVES: 4 **PREP:** 25 MINS (PLUS 15 MINS RESTING) **COOKING:** 15 MINS

2 × 400 g cans borlotti beans, rinsed and drained
1 egg white
1 teaspoon sea salt
60 g plain flour, plus extra for dusting
shaved pecorino, to serve
chopped toasted pistachio kernels, to serve

CAVOLO NERO PESTO

90 g (2 cups) finely chopped cavolo nero leaves (see TIPS)
1 garlic clove
boiling water
40 g (½ cup) finely grated pecorino
55 g (⅓ cup) pistachio kernels, toasted
2 tablespoons capers, rinsed and drained
185 ml (¾ cup) extra virgin olive oil
sea salt and freshly ground black pepper

Tip the beans onto a double layer of paper towel and top with another double layer. Press down to draw out the moisture from the beans. If the paper towel is soaked through, repeat this process.

Blitz the beans, egg white and salt in a food processor until combined. Transfer the mixture to a bowl and gently fold in the flour in batches.

Lay a large square of baking paper on your work surface and dust generously with flour. Place one-quarter of the dough on top, then add another square of baking paper and gently roll the dough between the paper into a long 2 cm thick sausage. Cut the dough into 2 cm pieces and set aside on a baking tray lined with baking paper. Repeat with the remaining dough.

To make the pesto, place the cavolo nero and garlic in a heatproof bowl and cover with boiling water. Set aside for 2 minutes, then rinse under cold water and drain. Use your hands to squeeze out any excess water. Transfer to a small food processor with the remaining ingredients and blitz until a smooth paste forms.

Bring a large saucepan of salted water to the boil. Add the gnocchi (in batches if you don't have a very large pan) and cook for 3 minutes or until they rise to the surface. Remove with a slotted spoon and transfer to a large bowl. Reserve 60 ml (¼ cup) of the cooking water.

Add the pesto and reserved cooking water to the gnocchi and toss to combine. Serve immediately, topped with shaved pecorino and chopped pistachios.

TIPS

You can also use spinach, kale or silverbeet leaves instead of the cavolo nero.

If you have a bit more time on your hands, these gnocchi are also delicious fried. After boiling, drain them well. Heat a little olive oil and butter in a frying pan, add the gnocchi in batches and cook, tossing, for 3–4 minutes or until golden. Return all the gnocchi to the pan, toss through the pesto, season and you're done.

Matriciana

The town of Amatrice is famous for two things. Many of the papal cooks over the centuries came from here and, just as significantly, so did the simplest and most delicious of all pasta sauces – sugo all'amatriciana. As they seldom pronounce the 'a' in this commune 65 kilometres north of Rome, you often find it written as 'sugo alla matriciana' on modern menus.

This 'food fact' is almost as boring as knowing the 'phonetics fact' that dropping, and not pronouncing, a silent vowel like this at the front of a word is called 'aphaeresis'.

I was first taught this as a 'cucina povera' (peasant cooking) dish by a disreputable Roman when we had no bacon left, just some rendered lard left over from frying the pig bits for carbonara the night before. This 'strutto' gave an equally meaty depth and lovely silkiness to a simple tomato and garlic sauce, and this is why I like to use the bacon just as a garnish for my matriciana.

SERVES: 4 **PREP:** 10 MINS **COOKING:** 20 MINS

sea salt
500 g dried rigatoni or penne
1 tablespoon extra virgin olive oil
300 g bacon or pancetta (or fancy guanciale if you can find it), cut into batons
1 red onion, finely chopped
6 garlic cloves, crushed
2 × 400 g cans whole peeled tomatoes, ideally cherry
1 lemon, zest peeled into a 4 cm strip, lemon juiced
100 g pecorino (or parmesan if you prefer), finely grated

Bring a large saucepan of water as salty as the sea to the boil over high heat. Add the pasta and stir in a cup of cold water to separate the pasta and stop it sticking. Return to the boil, then reduce the heat and simmer for 2 minutes less than it says on the packet or until al dente.

While your water is coming to the boil, heat the oil in a frying pan over medium–high heat. Add the bacon or pancetta and cook for 3–4 minutes or until crispy. Remove with a slotted spoon and drain on a plate lined with paper towel.

Add the onion to the pan and cook in the rendered fat for 5 minutes or until softened. Add the garlic and cook for 1 minute or until aromatic. Mash in one of the cans of tomatoes, then add the other (without mashing) and the strip of lemon zest. Cook for 10 minutes or until reduced and thickened.

While the sauce is reducing, check the pasta – it should be cooked but still with a little resistance. Scoop out and reserve 250 ml (1 cup) of the cooking water.

If you want to warm your bowls and keep your pasta good and hot to serve, here is a little trick I have picked up. Place your serving bowls in the sink and put the colander on top. Drain the pasta through the colander, allowing the cooking water to warm your bowls. Brilliant! (Just remember to dry the bowls before serving up!)

Add the pasta to the tomato sauce, splash in a little of the reserved pasta cooking water and toss to coat the pasta. Taste and season with salt and lemon juice.

Scoop into the serving bowls, top with the crispy bacon or pancetta and finish with a good sprinkling of pecorino.

TIP

Herbs – especially marjoram or oregano – make this meal prettier but will double the price of the dish if you have to buy a sleeve of herbs from the supermarket. Plant a herb garden and save $$$$$$!

Panna Cotta with Peppery Strawberries

The height of luxury in ancient Rome was dunking strawberries in pepper, so pull up a couch, comfortably recline and enjoy this most wibbly of generously proportioned panna cottas.

SERVES: 4 **PREP:** 30 MINS (PLUS 10 MINS STANDING & 4 HOURS CHILLING) **COOKING:** 35 MINS

3½ gold-strength gelatine leaves
200 ml full-cream milk
1 vanilla bean, split
395 ml pouring cream
230 g (1 cup) caster sugar
2 × 250 g punnets strawberries, hulled and halved
200 ml prosecco
juice of 1 lime
freshly ground black pepper

Soak the gelatine leaves in cold water and set aside for 5 minutes to soften.

Place the milk and vanilla bean in a small saucepan and bring just to boiling point, then immediately remove from the heat. Take out the vanilla bean and use a small knife to scrape the seeds into the milk. Stir well.

Squeeze the gelatine leaves to remove any excess water. Add the gelatine to the hot milk and stir until dissolved. Be patient and make sure it has completely dissolved, then set aside for about 5 minutes to cool slightly.

Use a balloon whisk to whisk the cream and 80 g of the sugar into the milk mixture. Strain through a sieve into a jug, then pour into a 500 ml (2 cup) jelly mould. Place in the fridge for 4 hours or until completely set.

Meanwhile, place half the strawberries in a small saucepan with the prosecco, lime juice, a pinch of pepper and the remaining sugar. Bring to the boil over medium heat, then reduce the heat to low and simmer for about 20 minutes. Strain through a sieve over a bowl, reserving the sauce and setting the solids aside (see TIP). Leave the sauce to cool completely.

Remove the panna cotta from the fridge and have your serving plate ready. Fill your sink with hot water, deep enough to dip the base of the mould into. Lower the base and side of the mould into the water, being VERY careful not to let it submerge completely and wet the panna cotta. Keep it there for 5 seconds. Place the serving plate over the mould and flip it over. Say a prayer to all you hold holy and the mould should lift off with a few gentle shakes.

Top with the strawberry sauce and fresh strawberries, and finish with an extra pinch of pepper.

TIP

The remaining pulp from the sauce can be used as jam for your morning toast or served over gelato for a quick dessert.

Patrizia's Tiramisu

One of my favourite cooks of all time is Patrizia Simone, whose restaurant in Bright was a place of food pilgrimage, and whose generosity saw her family take me in like a long-lost son when I was in Perugia. They cooked for me the old way, using nothing more than a small fireplace for six amazing courses, took me foraging for white truffles in the hills behind Gubbio and taught me volumes about the beauty of the Umbrian table.

When Patrizia's restaurant closed after many decades as an icon of Victoria's north east and the building was being gutted, a friend who knew how much it meant to me salvaged a rusty old cast-iron frying pan from the skip. The pan is one of two mementoes I have of my time there. The other is this impeccable recipe for tiramisu. I have tried others and I've developed others, but none have ever come close to Patrizia's classic.

SERVES: 8 **PREP:** 30 MINS (PLUS OVERNIGHT CHILLING)

4 eggs
80 g caster sugar
2 tablespoons marsala
1 teaspoon vanilla extract
500 g mascarpone
300 ml freshly brewed strong black coffee, cooled
220 g small lady finger biscuits (savoiardi)
400 ml pouring cream
Dutch-processed cocoa powder, for dusting
dark chocolate, for grating (optional)

Place the eggs and sugar in the bowl of your electric mixer and beat for 15 minutes or until thick and pale, adding the marsala and vanilla in the last minute of beating.

Place 350 g of the mascarpone in a separate bowl and add a little of the egg mixture. Stir to soften the mascarpone slightly – this will loosen it and make it much easier to fold into the remaining egg mixture, keeping it light and fluffy. Now gently fold the mascarpone mixture into the remaining egg mixture until combined.

Spread a small amount of the mascarpone mixture over the bottom of an 8 cm deep, 30 cm × 20 cm serving dish, or you could use a trifle bowl.

Pour the coffee into a bowl. Dip half the biscuits, one at a time, in the coffee for a few seconds and place them alongside each other in a single layer on top of the mascarpone mixture in your dish. Pour half the remaining mascarpone mixture over the top. Repeat with the remaining biscuits, coffee and mascarpone mixture to make another layer. If you are using a trifle bowl you will probably have at least three layers – just trim the biscuits to fit.

Use clean electric beaters to lightly whisk the cream to billowy soft peaks. Gently fold in the remaining mascarpone until just combined, then spoon it evenly over the tiramisu like a white blanket. Cover the dish with plastic wrap and put it in the fridge overnight to set.

Dust the top of the tiramisu with cocoa, then grate dark chocolate over the top to cover, if you like.

Keep the tiramisu in the fridge until about 30 minutes before serving, then remove it to bring the temperature up slightly. This will soften it and add to the glorious creaminess of the dish.

REST *of the* WORLD

This is a bit of a fudge of a section, but it also includes some of the very best food and flavours, which have echoed their way across the previous sections in this book. Mexico, India and the Middle East and North Africa have always been at the crossroads between culinary worlds – whether that's the ancient spice trade routes that ran through India for millennia or the collision between the Old and New Worlds, which saw an incredible selection of what are now everyday ingredients flood from Mexico to Spain, then Italy and on through Africa and beyond to the Middle East, as the ancient spice trade routes were reversed.

MEXICO

MIDDLE EAST
& NORTH
AFRICA
INDIA

MIDDLE EAST & NORTH AFRICA

On the surface of it, this is a foolish section as it covers lots of countries, which ribbon between the Mediterranean in the north, the deserts in the south and from the Atlantic Coast to the Persian Gulf. Of course, they all have their different delicacies, but with many of them on the same latitude, and with many shared religious, agricultural and cultural themes, the food of this swathe of countries has plenty in common. These themes are flavoured by the fact that the rich empires that historically controlled these lands straddled the valuable and ancient spice routes to Asia, and embraced the bounty that arrived from the south and east by dhow, camel or wagon.

Throughout this region, spices, such as coriander and cumin seeds, turmeric, dusky saffron, warm cinnamon and lemony sumac, dominate the cuisines, along with a dizzying selection of spice mixes, such as baharat and chermoula (see page 241), which you will find across the North African Maghrebi region. Most familiar is perhaps Egyptian dukkah (see page 242) which, at its most common, is cumin and coriander seeds crushed with salt, sesame seeds and a nut, such as hazelnuts or almonds. Then there's Moroccan ras el hanout (see page 234) where ginger, cinnamon, cumin and coriander are perfumed with a little nutmeg, cardamom, allspice and hot paprika. The spice mix za'atar differs from place to place, with Palestinians adding caraway and the Lebanese adding sumac to sesame seeds, salt and a dried herb, such as thyme, oregano or, originally, dried hyssop.

Another great feature of these cuisines is the need to dry and preserve ingredients given the brutal climate, hence the preponderance of dried fruit, such as dates, apricots, currants; sweet and sour molasses made from cooked-down pomegranate juice or grapes; brined and pickled goods, such as olives; dried or preserved lemons; simple salted or drained cheese, such as labne; or dried pulses, grains and legumes with chickpeas and fava beans featuring heavily, along with green wheat (freekeh) and cracked wheat (bulgur). Other key pantry staples include tahini (sesame seed paste), honey and nuts, such as almonds, pistachios and walnuts. Orange blossom water and rosewater often feature in desserts, while pastries, such as brik, filo and warqa (see page 244), are used throughout the region. Couscous, flatbreads, beans and rice boosting the carb count.

Lamb is the most popular meat, although goat and birds, such as chicken, quail and pigeon, also feature alongside seafood and those spicy mutton or even beef merguez sausages. These proteins will find their way onto the grill or roasted or baked in stews, such as Moroccan tagines.

Freshness comes from herbs, such as parsley, mint and coriander, the tart bite of lemon and orange, pomegranate gems, yoghurt and veg, such as zucchini, skinny Lebanese eggplants, carrots, onions and, of course, garlic. The zucchini and eggplant might find themselves stuffed or added to braises, or grilled, steamed or pounded into dips and sauces with the help of, perhaps, olive oil, tahini or yoghurt.

FAKING IT TIPS

1. Use the right spices. At its simplest this could be a simple mix of one part ground cumin and two parts ground coriander rubbed into that lamb shoulder for a slow-roast, sprinkled into that burger mince or used in the base of that pumpkin soup. Or up the ante by using any of the spice mixes discussed here.
2. Employ Tunisian chilli-spiced harissa paste to add warmth if required.
3. Pick the right carb as your accompaniment, whether that's couscous, flatbreads, freekeh or stewed chickpeas.
4. If you want to add sweetness, use dried fruit, caramelised onions or honey balanced against a sour squeeze of lemon, orange or a sweet and sour molasses, whether as a garnish or tossed through your carb of choice.
5. Garnish with a fresh herb, some nuts and/or something creamy, such as labne, yoghurt, a tahini-based dip, such as hummus, baba ghanoush, or even just a combo of yoghurt, tahini and lemon or garlic.

SHOPPING LIST

First up, you'll want some good-quality tahini – the fresher it is, the less chance it will be bitter. Ready-made spice mixes, such as baharat and ras al hanout, are easily available, so stock up on a few. They can differ dramatically in composition from region to region and source to source, so experiment until you find your favourites. Harder-to-find spices, such as black nigella seeds and dried rosebuds, make wonderful finishing touches and garnishes to loads of dishes. Look for high-quality saffron – ideally from Iran for the really good stuff.

In the citrus department, the finely chopped rind of preserved lemon adds freshness to salads, dressings and grains, while dried lemon adds a deep, earthy citrus flavour when added to slow braises. On the subject of dried fruit, also look out for tight, hard hunza apricots (which need to be soaked before throwing into your tagine).

Pantry staples should include grains, such as freekeh, faro and cracked wheat (bulgur), and dried pulses and legumes, such as fava beans and chickpeas along with canned varieties. Couscous is also great to have on hand, either the everyday small variety or the larger pearl, Israeli or Moghrabieh couscous. Also keep an eye out for pomegranate or date molasses, tubes or pots of different harissas, jars of vine leaves, interesting nuts (such as lemon-roasted pistachios or bright green slivered young pistachios) and the delicate flavours of rosewater and orange blossom water.

Finally, buy some frozen brik or filo pastry, or use fresh if it's available. Use some that day and freeze the rest.

Felafel

Felafel are so hot right now. It's their flexibility, you see. They can welcome all manner of ingredients, such as roast pumpkin or sweet beetroot, fresh herbs and any number of nuts, seeds, pulses and beans. Taking this vego favourite to new heights by customisation isn't a new thing; all across North Africa and over the generations there have been many variations. The Egyptians alone might use broad beans, dried fava beans, chickpeas or a mixture of these. The Egyptians also claim the creation of the first felafel and call it 'taameyya'. While based on this original, the recipe below sings with plenty of fresh herbs and fresh (well, probably frozen) broad beans for a greener, more vibrant ball of fried goodness that also has significant grunt in the flavour department.

SERVES: 4 **PREP:** 20 MINS (PLUS 1 HOUR CHILLING) **COOKING:** 30 MINS

300 g fresh or frozen broad beans, thawed and peeled
1 white onion, coarsely chopped
1 bunch flat-leaf parsley, leaves picked
1 bunch coriander, leaves picked
3 garlic cloves, peeled
2 teaspoons bicarbonate of soda
2 teaspoons sea salt
2 teaspoons ground coriander
1 teaspoon ground cumin
2 × 400 g cans chickpeas, rinsed and drained
50 g (⅓ cup) plain flour
2 tablespoons sesame seeds
vegetable or canola oil, for deep-frying

TO SERVE
fresh pita breads or flatbreads (to make your own, check out the TIP on page 264)
shredded iceberg lettuce
dill pickles or pickled turnips
garlic sauce (see TIPS; optional)

Place the broad beans, onion, fresh herbs, garlic, bicarbonate of soda, salt, ground coriander and cumin in a food processor, and blitz using the pulse button until finely chopped. Add the chickpeas and keep pulsing, scraping down the side every now and again, until a good uniform mixture forms. Transfer to a large bowl, stir through the flour and place in the fridge for 30 minutes to chill and firm up. This helps make rolling the felafel easier.

Line a baking tray with baking paper. Place the sesame seeds in a bowl.

Use wet hands to roll heaped tablespoons of the chickpea mixture into balls (or shape with a felafel mould if you have one). Roll the felafel in the sesame seeds and arrange on the prepared tray. Place in the fridge for 30 minutes to firm up again.

If you want to serve a garlic sauce with the felafel (see TIPS), now would be an excellent time to make it.

Pour enough oil into a large heavy-based saucepan to come two-thirds of the way up the side and heat over medium–high heat to 180°C on a cook's thermometer. Working in batches of four or five at a time, add the felafels and cook, turning occasionally, for 6–8 minutes or until golden brown. Transfer to a large plate lined with paper towel to drain.

Serve the felafels in warmed pita breads or flatbreads with shredded iceberg and your choice of pickles. Finish with a drizzle of garlic sauce (if using).

TIPS

To make a garlic sauce, peel the cloves of 1 whole garlic head and cut them in half. Place in a bowl, cover with boiling water and set aside to blanch for 1 minute. Drain and refresh in iced water. Place in a stick blender jug with the juice of ½ lemon and ½ teaspoon salt and blitz until smooth. Gradually add 100 ml sunflower oil and blitz until well combined. Add another 100 ml oil and the juice of ½ lemon. Season.

Feel free to vary your choice of accompanying sauce or dip. Homemade yoghurt with tahini or cucumber, store-bought tzatziki or smoky baba ghanoush all work well, as does pretty much any vegetable hummus (try beetroot or roast pumpkin).

In addition to everything else these felafels have to offer, they also freeze well. Place the uncooked balls in an airtight container and freeze for up to 3 months. Thaw for only 30 minutes before deep-frying.

Ful Medames

Is it a salad or a dip? Should it be garlicky or lemony? Should it be mashed or not? The answers depend on where you come from. The Syrians like it unmashed and sharp with lots of lemon, fresh tomato and parsley. Many Egyptians like theirs mashed with a tomatoey sauce and extra onion and garlic. While the ful of the Torah and Bible was just beans with oil and garlic. With the lemon hit of the Syrian ful and a reassuring mixture of creaminess and whole beans, I am hoping that this is the ful everyone will enjoy.

SERVES: 4–6 **PREP:** 15 MINS **COOKING:** 10 MINS

4 garlic cloves, 3 cloves lightly smashed, 1 clove crushed
2 × 400 g cans fava beans (see TIPS), rinsed and drained
1 bunch flat-leaf parsley, stalks thinly sliced, leaves finely chopped
2 teaspoons tahini
60 ml (¼ cup) lemon juice
½ teaspoon ground cumin
1 teaspoon sea salt
60 ml (¼ cup) extra virgin olive oil
1 × 400 g can chickpeas, rinsed and drained
½ white onion, finely chopped
½ teaspoon smoked paprika
2 tablespoons natural yoghurt

TO SERVE
4 pita breads, cut into triangles
lemon wedges
quartered cherry tomatoes

Place the smashed garlic cloves, fava beans, chopped parsley stalks and 310 ml (1¼ cups) water in a medium saucepan over high heat. Bring to the boil, then reduce the heat to medium–low and simmer for 6–8 minutes. Remove from the heat. Take out half the beans and use a stick blender or potato masher to roughly mash the remaining ingredients in the pan. Gently return the whole beans to the mashed mixture.

Combine the crushed garlic, tahini and lemon juice in a large bowl. Stir in the bean mixture until well combined, then add the cumin, salt and half the oil. Cover and keep warm.

In a separate bowl, combine the chickpeas, onion, paprika, remaining oil and 2 heaped tablespoons of the chopped parsley leaves. Save the remaining parsley leaves for another use.

Spoon the warm bean mixture into a shallow serving bowl and top with the chickpea mixture and yoghurt. Serve with pita breads, lemon wedges and a bowl of quartered cherry tomatoes.

TIPS

Top with a fried egg for a flavourful breakfast or brunch dish.

Look for canned fava beans (ful) in Middle Eastern grocery stores. If you can't find them, use butter beans or kidney beans.

Lamb Tagine *with* Preserved Lemon & Olives

In Morocco and Tunisia, chicken and lamb tend to marry with dried fruits and nuts. But here, with the intensely scented preserved lemon and juicy green olives, we get the flavours of North Africa at a lighter pace. Go easy on the preserved lemon as it can transform into an overpowering soapiness. It's taken me ten years to come round to the joys of preserved lemon and, to be honest, I'm still a little suspicious of it. And let's not mention that it smells to me of 'toilet lollies'.

SERVES: 4–6 **PREP:** 15 MINS **COOKING:** 3 HOURS 10 MINS

1.5 kg boneless lamb shoulder or leg, cut into 5 cm chunks
sea salt and freshly ground black pepper
2 tablespoons extra virgin olive oil
1 brown onion, coarsely chopped
4 garlic cloves, crushed
1 carrot, finely chopped
1 teaspoon ground coriander
1 teaspoon ground ginger
½ teaspoon ground cumin
½ teaspoon ground turmeric
150 g green olives (manzanilla or mammoth)
1 preserved lemon, rind finely shredded, flesh discarded
½ bunch coriander, stalks and leaves finely chopped
½ bunch flat-leaf parsley, stalks and leaves finely chopped
1 cinnamon stick
1 litre chicken stock, plus extra if needed
1 lemon, halved
buttered potatoes and steamed carrots, or your favourite grain, to serve

Sprinkle the lamb with 1 teaspoon of salt. Heat the oil in a large heavy-based saucepan or tagine over medium–high heat. Add the lamb and cook, turning, for 8 minutes or until beginning to brown. Add the onion, garlic, carrot, ground coriander, ginger, cumin, turmeric and ½ teaspoon of pepper and cook, stirring occasionally to prevent the spices from burning, for 1 minute or until the lamb has released all of its fat and juices.

Add the olives, preserved lemon, fresh coriander, parsley, cinnamon and stock and stir to combine. Reduce the heat to low and simmer, covered, for 1½ hours. Remove the lid and give it a stir, then taste and adjust the seasoning if necessary. Uncover and cook for a further 1½ hours or until the liquid has reduced and the flavours have intensified. Add more stock or water if it seems a little dry. Remove from the heat and squeeze in the juice of half the lemon. Thinly slice the remaining lemon half.

Garnish the tagine with the lemon slices and serve with buttered potatoes and steamed carrots, or your favourite grain.

TIP

Tagines also work well in a slow cooker. Just pop all the ingredients in (except the lemon slices) and cook on low for 6 hours.

FOOD NERD FACT: A prominent cooking technique from North Africa and Maghreb cuisine is the use of meats and fish with fruit extracts from citrus, grapes, dates, pomegranates and figs. It keeps the protein and vegetables well hydrated and sweetens the dish as it cooks.

Couscous Royale

Promoting concerts was part of my first job back in London, and during this period I spent time with one of my heroes, rockabilly legend Sleepy LaBeef. Sleepy is a mountain of a man with a voice as dark, rich and smooth as a good caramel. Born in the tiny and oddly named Arkansas town of Smackover (we share a birthday!), he is nicknamed 'the human jukebox', as he has a prodigious knowledge of early rock 'n' roll tunes. Sleepy has stories about times spent with all the great names and quirky lesser lights who wrote the songs, making him one of the ultimate dinner companions. I bring this up not to name drop, but because before his show we ate couscous royale together and discussed its similarity to the rice dishes from his side of the pond, such as jambalaya and Hoppin' John, both likely descended from either the Moorish world or the wistful food of homesick West African-born slaves. Local rices had been harvested in West Africa for over a thousand years before the more common Asian strains arrived in sub-Saharan Africa. That's all.

SERVES: 4 **PREP:** 15 MINS **COOKING:** 1 HOUR 45 MINS

100 ml extra virgin olive oil
4 chicken drumsticks
4 Moroccan-flavoured lamb sausages (merguez would be fine)
2 × 200 g lamb rump steaks, cut into thick strips
1 brown onion, thinly sliced
3 garlic cloves, chopped
1 tablespoon tomato paste
2 teaspoons ras el hanout (see TIPS)
1 × 400 g can crushed tomatoes
pinch of saffron threads
1 litre chicken or beef stock
1 × 400 g can chickpeas, rinsed and drained
2 carrots, cut into large chunks
2 zucchini, halved lengthways
2 celery stalks, cut into large chunks
sea salt and freshly ground black pepper
2 tablespoons harissa paste
380 g (2 cups) couscous

Heat 1 tablespoon of the oil in a large heavy-based saucepan or tagine over medium–high heat. Add the chicken and cook for 3–4 minutes each side or until browned. Transfer to a plate. Heat 2 tablespoons of the remaining oil and add the sausages and steak. Cook the sausages, turning regularly, for 4–5 minutes or until nicely browned, and the steak for 1–2 minutes each side. Add to the plate with the chicken. Don't panic about cooking the meat through at this point – it will get a chance later.

Reduce the heat to medium, add the onion and garlic and cook, stirring occasionally, for 8 minutes or until softened and lightly browned. Return the steak to the pan, add the tomato paste and ras el hanout and cook, tossing, for 2–3 minutes or until aromatic and well coated. Add the tomatoes, saffron and stock and bring to a gentle simmer. Simmer, stirring occasionally, for 30 minutes or until the liquid has reduced and thickened slightly. Return the chicken and sausages to the pan, add the chickpeas, carrot, zucchini and celery and stir to combine. Season. Cover and simmer for 30–40 minutes or until the the chicken is falling off the bone.

While your tagine simmers away, combine the harissa and remaining oil in a small bowl. Cook the couscous following the packet directions.

Spoon the couscous onto a large serving platter and top with the tagine and all the glorious sauce, or serve in separate bowls. Drizzle with the harissa oil and serve.

TIPS

The couscous is served quite wet in this dish, but if you prefer a drier result, serve the couscous on the side. Just know that the whole joy of the couscous royale is eating the meat and veg and then ladling on any extra sauce so the couscous is swimming in it.

What makes this dish is the funky blend of spices, and it's quite easy to make your own ras el hanout. Use a spice grinder or mortar and pestle to grind 1 teaspoon each of ground ginger, ground cinnamon, cumin seeds and coriander seeds with ¼ teaspoon each of grated nutmeg, cardamom seeds, hot paprika, ground turmeric, ground allspice and sea salt. Grind in 4 whole cloves and ½ teaspoon black peppercorns.

Cheat's Chicken B'stilla

(Pastilla)

It's a chicken pie, North-African style!

'Paloma' pigeon is traditionally used for b'stilla. It wasn't available for this recipe, so chicken got the job.

SERVES: 6–8 **PREP:** 30 MINS **COOKING:** 1 HOUR

about 150 g butter (or ghee), melted (see TIPS)
6 sheets brik, filo or homemade warqa pastry (see page 244)
1 tablespoon pure icing sugar
2 teaspoons ground cinnamon
simple side salad (see TIPS), to serve
harissa paste, to serve

FILLING

1 × 1.6 kg store-bought roasted or barbecued chicken
625 ml (2½ cups) chicken stock
40 g butter
2 teaspoons extra virgin olive oil
1½ brown onions, finely chopped
3 garlic cloves, coarsely chopped
sea salt and freshly ground black pepper
1 teaspoon ground ginger
½ cinnamon stick
4 eggs, lightly whisked
100 g medjool dates, pitted and coarsely chopped
100 g blanched almonds, toasted, finely chopped
1 teaspoon orange blossom water or finely grated orange zest

To make the filling, remove the skin from the chicken and discard. Shred the chicken meat and tear into small pieces. Transfer any bones to a saucepan, add the stock and bring to the boil.

Meanwhile, heat the butter and oil in a large frying pan over medium heat. Add the onion, garlic and a pinch of salt and cook, stirring occasionally, for 4–6 minutes or until the onion has softened. Add the ginger and cinnamon and cook for 2 minutes.

Your stock should be hot now. Carefully strain it through a sieve into the frying pan, discarding the bones. Simmer for 15 minutes or until the liquid has reduced by two-thirds. Remove from the heat and, whisking constantly and enthusiastically, add the egg. Stir in the chicken, dates, almonds and orange blossom water or zest. Return to low heat and cook, stirring constantly, until the mixture has thickened. Set aside.

Preheat the oven to 180°C/160°C fan-forced. Grease a 24 cm pie dish with a little of the melted butter. Place a layer of pastry over the base of the dish, allowing the sides to overhang. Brush the top with butter and repeat with four of the remaining sheets of pastry, brushing with butter as you go and fanning each sheet at right angles and slightly overlapping them to cover the dish. Spoon the chicken filling into the lined dish and use the back of the spoon to smooth and flatten the surface. Place the final sheet of pastry on top of the filling and brush with butter. Individually fold the overhanging pastry sheets back over the filling, brushing each sheet with butter as you go, until the filling is completely enclosed. Brush any remaining butter over the pastry lid.

Bake for 40 minutes or until golden and crisp. Set aside to cool slightly, then transfer to a serving plate.

Sift the icing sugar and cinnamon over the top. For a traditional finish, heat a metal skewer until jolly hot (holding it with an oven mitt, obvs). Lay the skewer on the sugared top to make a diamond pattern.

Serve with a simple side salad and spicy harissa paste on the side.

TIPS

The perfect salad for this b'stilla is loads of herbs, such as flat-leaf parsley, mint and coriander, tossed with chopped tomato, sliced celery and a squeeze of lemon juice.

To dramatically speed up the assembly process, put your melted butter in a clean, warm spray bottle and spray instead of brushing each layer of pastry. Don't tell the Greeks this, but this tip is also good for Bougatsa (see page 190), Baklava (see page 188) and Spanakopita (see page 184).

Freekeh Salad

I freakin' love freekeh. Over the last decade, this immature, roasted green wheat has become far more readily available here. These days, we even harvest our own freekeh in South Australia. Freekeh is notorious for taking longer to cook than it says on the packet, so if time is of the essence choose cracked freekeh, which cooks more quickly and actually absorbs more flavours. Personally, I prefer the wholegrain, but it takes more than twice as long to cook and requires a lot more water or stock. But then, it gives you time to properly hang the yoghurt to drain and become labne, rather than using the cheat's method in the TIPS below! Always a bright side.

SERVES: 4 **PREP:** 25 MINS (PLUS OVERNIGHT CHILLING) **COOKING:** 15 MINS

200 g natural pot-set yoghurt
2 eggplants, chopped into 2 cm pieces
60 ml (¼ cup) extra virgin olive oil
1 teaspoon ground cumin
200 g cracked freekeh
1 fresh or dried bay leaf
½ cinnamon stick
1 teaspoon sea salt
4 spring onions, white and dark green parts finely chopped
seeds of 1 pomegranate
1 bunch flat-leaf parsley, half the leaves finely chopped, the rest left whole
½ bunch mint, larger leaves finely chopped, smaller leaves left whole
2 tablespoons raw pistachio kernels, chopped
freshly ground black pepper
2 teaspoons tahini
juice of ½ lemon, plus extra wedges to serve
40 g (¼ cup) sunflower seeds
1 teaspoon sumac (or use lemon zest if you can't find this ground lemony berry)

DRESSING

4 cm knob of ginger, peeled and very finely chopped
1 tablespoon pomegranate molasses
juice of 1 lemon
juice and finely grated zest of ½ orange
1½ tablespoons extra virgin olive oil

Start making the labne the day before you want to eat the salad. Line a fine sieve with a double layer of muslin or a Chux and place over a bowl. Spoon the yoghurt into the muslin or Chux and tie the corners to enclose. Place in the fridge to drain overnight.

Preheat the oven to 210°C/190°C fan-forced. Line a large baking tray with baking paper.

Spread the eggplant over the prepared tray, drizzle with the oil and sprinkle with the cumin. Toss to combine. Bake for 15 minutes or until golden.

Meanwhile, place the freekeh in a sieve and rinse well under cold running water. Transfer to a medium saucepan and add the bay leaf, cinnamon stick, salt and 580 ml (2⅓ cups) water. Bring to the boil over high heat, then reduce the heat to medium and simmer, covered, for 12–15 minutes or until all the water has been absorbed and the freekeh is tender. Spread out over a large baking tray and let it cool slightly. Amazingly, this will give you just enough time to make the dressing!

To make the dressing, whisk the ingredients in a small bowl, seasoning with the salt and pepper.

Place the warm freekeh in a large bowl, pour over the dressing and toss to combine. Set aside to cool completely.

Add the eggplant, spring onion, pomegranate seeds, chopped parsley and mint and pistachios to the cooled freekeh and toss lightly to combine. Season.

Whisk the tahini, lemon juice and 1 tablespoon warm water in a bowl. Stir in the labne.

Place the freekeh salad on a serving platter and sprinkle over the sunflower seeds. Top with dollops of the labne mixture, then sprinkle sumac over the labne. Garnish with the remaining mint and parsley leaves and serve with lemon wedges.

TIPS

If you want to add some meat, my pick would be roast chicken or just-pink chunks of lamb backstrap brushed with pomegranate molasses and grilled on skewers.

To make speedy cheat's labne, you simply need to squeeze out the whey from the yoghurt. The easiest way to do this quickly is to place the yoghurt in a clean piece of doubled-up muslin or a Chux, twist up the edges and squeeze against paper towel to wring out the whey. When it comes to mixing in the tahini, be sparing when adding the water as this version leaves a wetter labne.

Chermoula Tray Bake

Ras el hanout, chermoula, dukkah, za'atar, baharat ... North Africa has no shortage of unique spice or herb mixes to act like a super-charged flavour boost, lifting simple dishes into something really special. Take this easy tray bake of fish and potatoes as 'exhibit A'.

SERVES: 4 **PREP:** 20 MINS (PLUS 1 HOUR MARINATING) **COOKING:** 40 MINS

2 × 800 g snapper or barramundi, scaled and gutted (see TIPS)
4 desiree potatoes, thickly sliced
2 tablespoons extra virgin olive oil
1 lemon, plus extra wedges to serve
1 green capsicum, deseeded and thickly sliced
2 fresh or dried bay leaves
pinch of saffron threads
sea salt and freshly ground black pepper
simple green salad, to serve

CHERMOULA
2 teaspoons cumin seeds
2 teaspoons coriander seeds
½ red onion, coarsely chopped
2 garlic cloves
2 cm knob of ginger, peeled and coarsely chopped
2 teaspoons harissa paste (see TIPS)
1 teaspoon sweet paprika
1 teaspoon black peppercorns
1 teaspoon sea salt
2 flat-leaf parsley sprigs
2 coriander sprigs
2 teaspoons honey
finely grated zest and juice of 1 lemon
1 long red chilli, thinly sliced (deseeded for a milder version)
2½ tablespoons extra virgin olive oil

To make your chermoula, place the cumin and coriander seeds in a small non-stick frying pan over medium heat and toast for a few minutes or until aromatic. Transfer to a blender. Add the remaining ingredients (except the chilli and oil) and blend to a smooth paste. Transfer to a bowl and stir in the chilli and oil.

Using a sharp knife, diagonally score the fish across the thickest part three or four times on each side. Place the fish in a glass or ceramic dish and rub the chermoula paste all over the inside and outside to coat. Cover with plastic wrap and marinate in the fridge for 1–2 hours.

Preheat the oven to 220°C/200°C fan-forced. Line a large roasting tin with baking paper.

Cook the potato in a saucepan of salted boiling water for 5 minutes or until starting to soften. Set aside in the hot water for a further 5 minutes to continue the cooking process (this should stop the slices breaking up). Drain and return to the pan. Drizzle with 2 teaspoons of the oil and stir to coat.

Arrange the potato in the base of the prepared tin (it doesn't matter if the slices overlap) and drizzle with the remaining oil. Thinly slice half the lemon and place on top, then add the capsicum and bay leaves, and sprinkle over the saffron. Squeeze over the juice from the remaining lemon half and season. Place the marinated fish on top and bake for 25–30 minutes or until the skin begins to shrink and fall away from the flesh and the flesh flakes easily when tested with a fork.

Take the roasting tin to the table and serve the fish and potatoes with a simple green salad and extra lemon wedges. Bags the cheeks!!!!

TIPS

If you can't get two big fish, try one big one (around 1.6 kg). The cooking time should be about the same, but keep an eye on it.

Harissa is a North African chilli paste that packs quite a punch. This fiery combination of chilli, paprika and oil can be found in the spice section of most supermarkets. Use it on chicken, in dressings and marinades, as a condiment for toasties, or add cream cheese and turn it into a dip. It also adds depth and heat to bean stews or tomato braises. It's a constant in my kitchen.

Cardamom Roasted Carrots *with* Haloumi, Parsley & Pistachio–Nigella Dukkah

Credit where credit's due ... when we were shooting the last book, Seddon's rather tasty Advieh was our local favourite for coffee, conversation and breakfast. This is where I first saw the combination of crispy haloumi with a nigella dukkah. I reckoned dukkah would go really well on these carrots, which have been looking for the perfect partner for a couple of years now. And I was right. This could be a sexy side for a roast or a barbecue, a light lunch or supper all on its own with the addition of a couple of eggs.

SERVES: 4 **PREP:** 15 MINS **COOKING:** 30 MINS

2–3 bunches rainbow carrots or baby carrots, scrubbed and trimmed, fat ones halved lengthways
1½ teaspoons ground cardamom
½ teaspoon ground white pepper
finely grated zest of ½ orange, resulting orange halved
⅓ cup finely chopped coriander
60 ml (¼ cup) verjuice or apple juice
2 tablespoons extra virgin olive oil
sea salt and freshly ground black pepper
2 garlic cloves, chopped
150 g haloumi, broken into small pieces to resemble chunky breadcrumbs
juice of ½ lemon

PISTACHIO–NIGELLA DUKKAH
40 g (¼ cup) sesame seeds
1 teaspoon coriander seeds
55 g (⅓ cup) raw pistachio kernels, chopped
35 g (¼ cup) nigella seeds
1 teaspoon sea salt

Preheat the oven to 210°C/190°C fan-forced.

Arrange the carrots in a large roasting tin and sprinkle with the cardamom, pepper, orange zest and half the coriander. Squeeze one of the orange halves over the top, then drizzle with the verjuice or apple juice and 1 tablespoon of olive oil. Toss until well coated, then season. Roast for 20–25 minutes or until the pan juices start to caramelise and the carrots brown and shrivel up slightly. Remove the tin from the oven and squeeze over the juice from the remaining orange half. Sprinkle with the garlic and roast for a further 5 minutes.

While your carrots are roasting, make the dukkah. Place the sesame seeds and coriander seeds in a non-stick frying pan over medium heat and toast, swirling the pan, for a few minutes or until aromatic. Keep them moving and don't leave them or they will burn! Transfer to a mortar and use a pestle to lightly grind the seeds. Stir in the pistachio, nigella seeds and salt until combined.

Pour the remaining oil into the same pan and heat over medium–high heat. Add the haloumi and cook, tossing, for 4 minutes or until crispy and golden. Transfer to a small heatproof bowl. Drizzle over the lemon juice, sprinkle with the remaining coriander and season with pepper.

Place the carrots on a large platter and drizzle with any pan juices. Sprinkle generously with the haloumi crumbs and dukkah, and serve.

TIP

If preferred, you can replace the carrots with parsnips or thin sweet potato wedges.

The nigella dukkah is also great sprinkled over chicken, other roast vegetables or your favourite breakfast eggs, so make double, if you like.

Mo Rock 'n' Rolls

(aka Middle Eastern Brik Cigars)

Here's a new skill to learn that you can use in lots of different ways. It's fun to make enough pastry for a small dinner, but I still feel guilty about a time an age ago when Sam Clark from Moro (that's London's pioneering Moorish Mediterranean restaurant with the great cookbooks, BTW) spent all night making warqa pastry for a dinner in Melbourne because the stuff we'd sourced for him just wasn't fine enough. Sorry Sam! Honestly, next time we'll all be able to help as this recipe will give you warqa that's so delicate it's almost translucent. Given this delicateness it is important to use a strong, high-gluten flour – sorry.

SERVES: 4–6 (MAKES 12 ROLLS) **PREP:** 30 MINS (PLUS COOLING) **COOKING:** 30 MINS

50 g (¼ cup) raisins, finely chopped
finely grated zest and juice of 1 lemon
1 tablespoon extra virgin olive oil
100 g butter
1 brown onion, finely chopped
500 g lamb mince
1½ teaspoons dried mint
1½ teaspoons ground allspice
1½ teaspoons ground cinnamon
30 g (¼ cup) finely chopped walnuts
sea salt and freshly ground black pepper
1 egg white, lightly whisked

WARQA PASTRY
300 g (2 cups) bread flour (or another high-gluten flour)
50 g (¼ cup) fine semolina flour
½ teaspoon sea salt
2 tablespoons extra virgin olive oil, plus extra for greasing

WHIPPED FETA AND MINT DIP
130 g feta, crumbled
80 g (½ cup) fresh ricotta
2 teaspoons finely chopped mint
2 tablespoons extra virgin olive oil
1 tablespoon honey

To make the warqa pastry, place the ingredients and 685 ml (2¾ cups) cold water in a blender and blend until smooth. Transfer to a jug, then set aside at room temperature to rest for 30 minutes.

Line a baking tray with plastic wrap. Heat a large flat grill or barbecue plate over a very low heat and lightly grease the surface with a little oil. Use a wide pastry brush to brush a thin layer of the batter onto the grill or plate, dotting extra batter over any holes that form. In my experience, the first couple are always too fat or too thin until you get used to your brush and the amount of batter per stroke to reach that nice thin evenness. Cook for about 2 minutes or until the edges are crisp and starting to curl. Use a spatula to gently transfer your paper-thin pastry sheet to the prepared tray. Repeat with the remaining batter to make 12 pastry sheets. Stack the sheets on top of each other, brushing each sheet with a little oil as you go to stop them sticking together. Set the stack aside to cool completely, then cover with plastic wrap and place in the fridge until required.

Combine the raisins, lemon zest and juice in a small bowl. Set aside for 10 minutes.

Heat the oil and 20 g of the butter in a frying pan over medium–low heat, add the onion and cook for 8–10 minutes or until soft. Add the lamb mince, dried mint, allspice and 1 teaspoon of the cinnamon. Increase the heat to high and cook, breaking up any lumps with the back of a wooden spoon, for 3–4 minutes or until the lamb is just cooked. Add the raisin mixture and walnuts and stir until well combined. Remove from the heat and season. Transfer to a bowl and place in the fridge to cool completely.

To make the whipped feta and mint dip, place the feta, ricotta, mint and oil in a food processor with 60 ml (¼ cup) water and blitz until smooth. Transfer to a small bowl, cover and place in the fridge.

Preheat the oven to 220°C/200°C fan-forced and line a baking tray with baking paper. Melt the remaining butter.

Place one pastry sheet on a clean surface. Brush with a little melted butter and fold in half vertically. Place 2 tablespoons of the cooled lamb mixture along one short edge, leaving a thin gap on both long sides of the pastry. Fold in each side, then roll up to enclose the filling, forming a cigar shape. Brush the end of the pastry with egg white to seal and place on the prepared tray, seam-side down. Repeat with the remaining pastry and lamb mixture, brushing with butter and egg white as you go. Lightly brush the pastry cigars with the remaining butter, then bake for 12–15 minutes or until golden and cooked through. Sprinkle with the remaining cinnamon.

Drizzle the honey over the whipped feta and mint dip, and serve with the hot cigars.

Orange Blossom Pavlovas

I love the word 'plump', and it's perfect for describing these little round pavs paired with all the bold flavours you'd expect from the souks and markets of North Africa, offering the sort of sweet, airy lightness that only the best dreams are made of ...

SERVES: 6 **PREP:** 25 MINS (PLUS 1 HOUR COOLING) **COOKING:** 1 HOUR

4 egg whites
¼ teaspoon cream of tartar
50 g brown sugar
150 g caster sugar
4 oranges, segmented
2 teaspoons orange blossom water
400 ml pouring cream
2½ tablespoons honey
1 teaspoon ground cinnamon

Preheat the oven to 130°C/110°C fan-forced.

Place the egg whites in a clean bowl. Using electric beaters, beat on low speed for 30 seconds or until bubbles begin to build and the mixture looks a bit foamy. Add the cream of tartar and increase the speed to medium. Gradually add the brown sugar, 1 tablespoon at a time, until well incorporated. Increase the speed to high and gradually add the caster sugar until well combined. Continue to beat on high speed for a few more minutes to ensure the sugar has completely dissolved.

Line a large baking tray with baking paper. Put a little blob of meringue under each corner to help the paper stick to the tray. Place six dollops of meringue mixture on the prepared tray, leaving plenty of room for spreading as they cook. Use the back of a spoon to pat them down slightly, making a shallow indent in the top of each one. Bake for 1 hour, then turn off the oven and leave the meringues in the oven with the door closed for at least another hour to cool. Don't be tempted to open the oven door.

While your pavs are cooling, prepare your toppings.

Combine the orange segments and 1 teaspoon of the orange blossom water in a bowl.

Pour the cream into a bowl, add 1 tablespoon of the honey and the remaining orange blossom water and lightly whip with a balloon whisk. Do not over-whip the cream or it will start to separate. Using a balloon whisk rather than electric beaters will give you more control.

When you are ready to serve, put a large dollop of cream onto each pavlova and decorate with the orange segments. Use a tea strainer to dust the tops with ground cinnamon and drizzle each pav with the remaining honey.

TIPS

If you are making one large pavlova, dollop the meringue in the centre of the baking paper and build it up into a pile. Once you have all the meringue on the tray, use the back of a spoon to pat it down into a circle about 3 cm smaller than you need it to be when cooked. It will spread out a bit as it cooks. Increase both the baking and cooling time to 2 hours.

Piping on some lemon or orange curd is also a nice twist.

Pistachio Yoghurt Cake

Perfect for tea, lunchboxes or dressed up for a dinner, this simple cake owes its sophisticated vibe to the elusive fragrance of orange blossom water. As Leonardo da Vinci always said, simplicity is the ultimate sophistication. Or, to be more accurate, 'la semplicita e la suprema sofisticazione', cos Leo didn't speak much English.

SERVES: 10 **PREP:** 15 MINS (PLUS 10 MINS COOLING) **COOKING:** 1 HOUR

butter, at room temperature, for greasing
225 g raw pistachio kernels
80 g blanched almonds
150 g (1 cup) plain flour, plus extra for dusting
1 teaspoon baking powder
½ teaspoon bicarbonate of soda
200 g natural yoghurt, plus extra to serve
finely grated zest and juice of 2 oranges
120 ml extra virgin olive oil
1 teaspoon orange blossom water
4 eggs
320 g caster sugar
pure icing sugar, for dusting

Preheat the oven to 190°C /170°C fan-forced. Grease a 23 cm springform tin with butter and lightly dust with flour, shaking off any excess.

Spread the pistachios on a baking tray and bake for 10 minutes or until just fragrant and lightly toasted. Set aside to cool.

Blitz the almonds and 200 g of the pistachios in a food processor until a fine meal forms (by this I mean very finely crushed).

Combine the flour, baking powder and bicarbonate of soda in a bowl.

Mix the yoghurt, orange zest, oil and orange blossom water in a second bowl.

Crack the eggs into a large bowl. Using electric beaters, beat on high speed for 1 minute or until thick and pale. Add 220 g of the sugar and beat on medium speed for a further 5 minutes or until the sugar has dissolved. Reduce the speed to low, add the flour mixture and beat until just combined. Add the yoghurt mixture and beat until just combined, then stir in the nut meal.

Pour the batter into the prepared tin and bake for 50 minutes or until a skewer inserted into the centre comes out clean.

While the cake is in the oven, make a glaze. Combine the orange juice and remaining sugar in a small saucepan and bring to the boil over medium heat, stirring until the sugar has dissolved. Set aside.

Remove the cake from the oven and set aside for 10 minutes to cool slightly. Pour the syrup over the warm cake while still in the tin and watch it all soak in. Remove the cake from the tin by tipping it upside-down onto a plate, then release the side and remove the base. Place your serving plate on the cake and flip it over again so it's right-side up.

Coarsely chop the remaining pistachios and sprinkle over the cake. Dust with icing sugar and serve warm with a good dollop of yoghurt.

INDIA

With its vast geographic, religious and climatic variations, it's no surprise that Indian cuisine is incredibly broad, with influences ranging from Portugal and the UK to Persia and the Middle East. For our purposes, however, it does boast certain flavours and ingredients that make an Indian-inspired dish immediately recognisable. And as long as you remember a few basics, such as that richer northern dishes use lots of lamb, ghee, chicken and earthy vegetables, and food from the south tends to be spicier, more often vegetarian or pescatarian and uses ingredients, such as tamarind, mustard seeds, coconut and curry leaves, you are halfway there to faking it.

The next thing to note is that Indian food is largely spicy but not crazily hot (barring a few famous dishes such as a Goan vindaloo, which is actually Portuguese in influence). Instead, flavourings are more used to bring a harmonious warmth and balance to dishes. Curries are thickened through slow cooking, the addition of nut flours and even the judicious blending of a portion of the curry to add richness and texture. Yoghurt is also a must for richness, whether used in curries or more often served on the side as 'curds' or a raita alongside tamarind, lime and coriander chutneys.

Popular proteins in Indian cuisine include lamb, chicken, fish, prawns, lentils and split peas. A little harder to find, but still widely available, are paneer cheese and goat meat. Cooking over the grill or in a tandoor oven, frying and braising are the most popular techniques for cooking proteins.

When it comes to vegetables, potatoes, eggplants, carrots, capsicums, onions, peas, cauliflower, tomatoes, lady's finger (okra) and spinach are all widely used.

Typical flavourings in Indian cuisine include fresh ginger and garlic (especially when crushed together and cooked down in a pan as a flavour base), mint, curry leaves, fresh coriander, fresh green chillies and dried red chillies. Spices, such as cardamom, coriander seeds, cumin seeds, cloves, turmeric, mustard seeds and the spice mix garam masala, are at the fore, while sweetness may come from sugar (white, brown or authentic Indian jaggery) or fruit (more often dried), and sourness is sourced from tamarind, citrus, green mango and amchoor (sour green mango powder), yoghurt, wine or local vinegars, such as coorg vinegar.

If you want to add crunch to a dish, pistachios, cashews and almonds all work, while the ideal carb partners for an Indian meal revolve around basmati rice and a dizzying selection of Indian flatbreads.

FAKING IT TIPS

1. Many curries share ingredients with European braises, but they are different thanks to their base and flavourings. So, start by frying mustard seeds as you heat the oil in the pan. Add onions and a minced paste of garlic and ginger – probably more of this than you think you need. Cook until this starts smelling fragrant, then add and cook your spices in the same way. You can take this same approach to customise your cauliflower or pumpkin soup.
2. Mix yoghurt with spices, blitzed herbs or pastes, such as Indian tandoori paste, to make simple rubs and marinades for grilling and roasting lamb or chicken. Serve with something sweet, something green and bread or rice on the side.
3. To thicken curries, slowly reduce over low heat or, if you can't wait, scoop out a cup of the hot curry (meat, gravy and veg), blitz to a thick paste and return to the pan to thicken.
4. To turn your burger into something from the subcontinent, add curry paste or toasted fancy curry powder to the chicken or lamb mince for your pattie. Nigella seeds are also a nice addition to chicken and cumin for lamb. Add a smear of coriander and mint chutney, some fresh cucumber and butter lettuce to the rolls or naan breads. A dollop of thick natural or Greek yoghurt is great too.
5. Always garnish with sliced green chillies.

SHOPPING LIST

In the spice arena, try to find dried red Kashmiri chillies, garam masala (which is the acceptable face of curry powder; or even better make your own – see page 253), fenugreek and amchoor, which is a great tenderiser for poultry and adds tang to chutneys and desserts. You'll also need mustard seeds to pop and sizzle in hot oil with curry leaves when tempering South Indian dishes. You could buy 'kala nemak' but, while authentic, this Indian black salt is a little sulphurous and thus smells of bad eggs. Spices, such as coriander seeds, cumin seeds, cardamom, turmeric and saffron are available at most supermarkets, but it's worth restocking at your local Indian grocer, especially if their spices look fresher and more fragrant. While you're there, look out for methi (fenugreek leaves) or mustard leaves for a change to spinach and other greens.

For the pantry, look for flours, such as atta, besan (chickpea flour) and ground cashew flour, to add richness to Mughal-style chicken curries. Also look for lentils, dried peas and pulses, edible silver and gold leaf, and Indian jaggery – a long-lasting, coarse Indian sugar with smoky molasses notes, which are welcome in any Indian-inspired recipe that calls for sweetness. Tamarind pulp and rosewater are widely available, but you'll find more unusual brands at Indian grocers. Also check out the exotic spice pastes and chutneys and pickles, such as green mango, lime, eggplant, date or prawn balichow, which will take even the dullest cheese sandwich or leftover roast to new heights. Ghee, or clarified butter, is also very authentic for frying, but its use in India is on the decline as the country becomes more health conscious.

You can also happily freeze many Indian ingredients. Leftover fresh curry leaves can be frozen so they are always on hand, and interesting, but harder-to-find, ingredients, such as frozen green chickpeas, can be deployed in many of the savoury recipes that follow. And remember that any number of Indian breads, such as paratha, roti and naan, freeze well and help to complete an Indian feast.

Butter Chicken

This is Australia's favourite curry. Let me tell you more about it.

Tandoori chicken was originally a Peshwari dish that spread after the 1947 Partition of India, when chefs, such as Kundan Lal Jaggi, left restaurants like Peshwar's Moti Mahal, a simple dhaba in Gora Bazar, to flee to uncertain futures in other cities. Jaggi landed in Delhi and, with the blessing of the original owner of Peshwar's Moti Mahal, he and two other refugee workmates, Kundan Lal Gujral and Thakur Das Mago, opened their own Moti Mahal.

By the 1950s, this restaurant had become a pioneering champion of such dishes as tandoori chicken, the seekh kebab, Punjabi black dhal, barrah kebab and butter chicken. Originally, the latter was basically a solution for what to do with yesterday's (now rather dry) tandoori chicken. Jaggi used a sauce of tomatoes, cream and butter to help hide/rehydrate the chicken. The original recipe used minimal spices – just cumin and chilli powder. Oh, and no honey or methi (fenugreek leaves). That's why there are none in my butter chicken.

SERVES: 4 **PREP:** 15 MINS **COOKING:** 50 MINS

90 g (⅓ cup) natural yoghurt
2 tablespoons tomato paste
¼ teaspoon chilli powder
3 large garlic cloves, minced
1 kg chicken thigh fillets, excess fat trimmed, cut into 2–3 cm chunks
1 kg very ripe tomatoes, coarsely chopped
1 large red onion, coarsely chopped
2 tablespoons coconut, vegetable or olive oil
3 green cardamom pods, bruised
2 tablespoons finely chopped ginger
1 tablespoon ground cumin
1 teaspoon ground coriander
80 g butter
1 tablespoon caster sugar
1 teaspoon garam masala (see TIPS)
sea salt
100 ml pouring cream
saffron rice (see TIPS) or steamed basmati rice, to serve

Combine the yoghurt, tomato paste, chilli and half the garlic in a large glass or ceramic bowl. Add the chicken and stir to coat well, then set aside.

Place the chopped tomatoes and onion in a large frying pan over medium heat. Bring to a simmer and cook, stirring occasionally, for 10 minutes or until the tomatoes have broken down.

Meanwhile, heat the oil in a small frying pan over medium–high heat. Add the cardamom pods, ginger, cumin, coriander and remaining garlic and cook for 1–2 minutes or until aromatic.

Add the spice mixture to the tomato mixture and stir to combine. Remove from the heat and set aside to cool for a few minutes. Transfer the mixture to a blender and blitz until pureed. Strain through a colander into a bowl, pressing with the back of a spoon to push as much of the mixture through as you can. Discard what is left in the colander.

Wipe out the tomato pan with paper towel, then add the butter and melt over medium heat until frothy. Add the chicken and cook for 5 minutes or until it turns white. Add the tomato mixture and stir in the sugar. Reduce the heat to low and simmer gently for 10 minutes or until the chicken is cooked through.

Stir in the garam masala and season to taste with salt. Simmer for another 10–20 minutes or until the sauce has thickened. Taste and add more salt if necessary. Stir in the cream just before serving. Serve with saffron rice or steamed basmati rice.

TIPS

This is a mild curry, but you can always add chilli powder with the other spices, or serve garnished with sliced fresh green chilli.

Traditionally, butter chicken has a smokiness to it. Cheat and add a few drops of liquid smoke or, alternatively, smoke the dish by putting a piece of red-hot charcoal in a small metal bowl and placing it in the dish with the raw chicken. Drip over coconut oil. It will smoke immediately, so cover it and leave for 10 minutes. This will not affect the cooking time. You can use the same technique to smoke the curry itself by floating the (scrupulously clean) metal bowl with the charcoal in the finished curry.

To make your own garam masala, place 2 tablespoons coriander seeds, 1 tablespoon cumin seeds, ½ teaspoon cloves, 1 teaspoon cardamom seeds, ½ teaspoon chilli powder, 1 teaspoon fennel seeds, 1 dried bay leaf and a thumb-sized stick of cinnamon in a mortar and use a pestle to grind to a coarse powder. Alternatively you can use a good-quality store-bought garam masala.

To make saffron rice, melt 50 g butter in a saucepan over medium–high heat. Stir in 400 g (2 cups) basmati rice, 4 bruised green cardamom pods and a large pinch of saffron threads. Add 750 ml (3 cups) water and a good pinch of salt. Bring to the boil and stir with a fork. Reduce the heat to low and cook, covered, for 17 minutes or until the water is completely absorbed and the rice is tender. Use a fork to separate the grains.

Cheat's Lamb Biryani

I once flew to Hyderabad to interview the woman widely regarded as the world's leading expert in biryani, that wonderful slow-cooked dish of mutton and spiced rice. This is not that recipe but a far quicker family-dinner version, inspired by the classic but colliding with another Mughlai dish of spiced lamb mince (keema). The dish is still baked 'dum phukt' style, but slightly more accessibly in the oven, rather than being buried in a fire pit. This technique involves attaching a pastry seal around the pan to ensure no steam escapes during cooking, kind of like making a basic pressure cooker. It looks great, but I'll let you in on a little secret; when we tested the recipe without the pastry seal it still tasted pretty darned good, so you *could* omit it. But then you'll miss the theatre of cracking open the pot.

SERVES: 4–6 **PREP:** 30 MINS **COOKING:** 1 HOUR 15 MINS

250 ml (1 cup) full-cream milk, warmed
1½ teaspoons ground turmeric
pinch of saffron threads
100 ml sunflower or vegetable oil
4 brown onions, thinly sliced
12 curry leaves
4 garlic cloves, thinly sliced
1 tablespoon finely chopped ginger
750 g lamb mince
sea salt and freshly ground black pepper
2 tablespoons garam masala (see TIP on page 253)
2 tablespoons tomato paste
300 g (1½ cups) basmati rice
4 green cardamom pods, bruised
1 cinnamon stick
80 g (½ cup) sliced dried apricots
65 g (½ cup) slivered almonds, toasted
natural yoghurt, to serve

PASTRY SEAL
225 g (1½ cups) plain flour
125 ml (½ cup) vegetable oil

Preheat the oven to 180°C/160°C fan-forced. Combine the milk, turmeric and saffron in a bowl and set aside.

To make the pastry seal, combine the flour, oil and 80 ml (⅓ cup) water in a bowl, then turn out onto a lightly floured surface and knead until smooth. Wrap in plastic wrap and place in the fridge until ready to use.

Heat three-quarters of the oil in a shallow flameproof casserole dish over medium–high heat. Add the onion and eight curry leaves and cook, stirring often, for 8 minutes or until the onion is dark brown. Use a slotted spoon to separately transfer the onion and curry leaves to a plate lined with paper towel to drain.

Reduce the heat to medium and add the remaining oil, then add the garlic, ginger and remaining curry leaves to the pan and cook for 30 seconds or until aromatic. Add the mince, season and cook, stirring, for 8 minutes or until well browned. Add the garam masala and tomato paste and cook for 2 minutes, then splash in 100 ml water. Reduce the heat to medium–low and simmer, stirring occasionally, for 15 minutes or until the mixture has thickened.

While your meat cooks, combine the rice, cardamom, cinnamon, 2 teaspoons of salt and 750 ml (3 cups) water in a medium saucepan. Bring to a simmer over medium–low heat and cook, covered, for 10–12 minutes or until all the water has been absorbed and the rice is tender. Set aside.

Scatter half the apricot, almonds and fried onion over the lamb mixture, then top with the rice. Scatter over the remaining apricot, almonds and fried onion. Drizzle over the milk mixture, tinting some of the rice yellow as you pour. Cover with a lid.

Roll the pastry to make a sausage shape long enough to fit around the lid, then press the pastry securely around the lid so that no steam can escape. Bake for 40 minutes. Crack the seal at the table so the steam escapes. Obviously do this with as much drama as you possibly can, but be careful not to burn yourself. Top with the reserved fried curry leaves and serve with a bowl of yoghurt on the side.

TIPS

Just in case you're wondering, you can eat the pastry, but it's not really there for consumption!

For a vegetarian version, just replace the lamb with 600 g par-boiled chunks of peeled waxy potato. Also add 50 g of roasted cashews to the rice when you cook it.

Warren's Tray-Baked Tandoori Chicken

Instead of marinating chicken in yoghurt and spices, this is a speedy solution for a midweek meal dreamt up by food guru Warren. What makes it so clever is that as the chicken cooks and renders, the tandoori butter drips down onto the onions, filling them with all the tandoori goodness, but with none of the time and hassle.

SERVES: 4 **PREP:** 15 MINS (PLUS 10 MINS RESTING) **COOKING:** 55 MINS

25 g unsalted butter, at room temperature
2 tablespoons tandoori paste
1 teaspoon sea salt
1 × 1.8 kg whole chicken
3 red onions, sliced into 8 mm thick rounds
½ teaspoon cumin seeds, crushed using a mortar and pestle
250 g baby truss tomatoes
½ bunch mint, leaves picked
store-bought or homemade Indian flatbreads (see page 264) or steamed basmati rice, to serve

RAITA
130 g (½ cup) thick Greek-style yoghurt
½ Lebanese cucumber, deseeded and finely chopped
1 tablespoon chopped mint
2 teaspoons lemon juice
sea salt and freshly ground black pepper

Preheat the oven to 200°C/180°C fan-forced. Line a baking dish with baking paper.

To make your raita, combine all the ingredients in a bowl and store in the fridge until you are ready to serve.

Combine the butter, tandoori paste and salt in a bowl.

Use kitchen scissors to cut either side of the chicken's backbone and remove it, then cut through the breastbone to create two halves. (You can always ask your butcher to do this for you if you are squeamish.)

Lay the onion slices overlapping slightly on the prepared tray and sprinkle with the crushed cumin seeds. Top with the chicken halves, skin-side up, then rub the tandoori mixture all over the chicken skin to coat. You do this in the dish so you don't make a mess if any of the butter falls off!

Roast the chicken for 25 minutes. Remove from the oven, then scoop up the juices in the base of the dish and spoon it over the chicken and onion to baste. Return to the oven and roast for a further 25 minutes.

Add the tomatoes and cook for a further 5 minutes or until slightly blistered. Remove from the oven and set aside to rest for 10 minutes.

Scatter the mint leaves over the chicken and tomatoes. Serve with flatbreads or basmati rice, a bowl of raita and don't forget to drizzle some of the pan juices over the chicken.

Pea & Pumpkin Samosa Pie

A samosa is such a popular Indian snack, I can't think of a single reason why we shouldn't turn it into a pie and serve it as the main event. Individual samosas are fried and have crispy pastry, so I have made a very easy butter-crisp cheat's pastry to echo that all-important crunch. I've kept the traditional peas and potato, but have added pumpkin and curry paste for a more generous, fragrant

SERVES: 4–6 PREP: 30 MINS (PLUS COOLING) COOKING: 40 MINS

1½ tablespoons ghee or vegetable oil
3 teaspoons panch phoron (see TIPS)
1 brown onion, thinly sliced
650 g jap, kent or butternut pumpkin, peeled, deseeded and cut into 2 cm chunks
1 desiree potato, peeled and cut into 2 cm chunks
120 g (⅓ cup) curry paste (I used tikka masala curry paste)
1 garlic clove, crushed
1 tablespoon plain flour
230 g (1½ cups) frozen peas
125 ml (½ cup) vegetable stock
1 egg, lightly whisked
coriander chutney, to serve (see TIPS)

CHEAT'S PASTRY

375 g (2½ cups) plain flour, plus extra for dusting
200 g unsalted butter, frozen
185 ml (¾ cup) iced water
2 teaspoons sea salt

To make the cheat's pastry, place the flour in a large bowl and coarsely grate over the frozen butter. Use your fingers to stir in the butter. Add the iced water and salt and stir with a wooden spoon until combined, then tip out onto a lightly floured surface and gently press together until a dough forms but there are still visible lumps of butter. Wrap in plastic wrap and place in the fridge until required.

Preheat the oven to 200°C/180°C fan-forced. Line a baking tray with baking paper.

Place the ghee or oil and 2 teaspoons of the panch phoron in a deep frying pan and heat over medium heat. Add the onion and cook, stirring, for 1 minute or until aromatic. Add the pumpkin and potato and cook for 4–5 minutes or until starting to brown. Add the curry paste and garlic and cook, stirring, for 2–3 minutes, then stir in the flour and add the peas and stock. Cook for 2 minutes or until the liquid has thickened. Remove from the heat and set aside to cool completely (you can speed this up by putting the mixture in the fridge).

Divide the pastry into two portions, with one slightly larger than the other. Roll out the smaller portion on a lightly floured surface to a 30 cm round. Place on the prepared tray. Roll out the larger portion to a 34 cm round.

Spoon the cooled pumpkin mixture onto the smaller pastry round, leaving a 2 cm border around the edge. Brush the border with a little egg. Top with the larger pastry round and press the edges to seal (you can crimp if you like). Trim any excess pastry, then brush with the remaining egg and scatter over the remaining panch phoron. Bake for 25 minutes or until golden brown. Cut the pie into wedges and serve with coriander chutney.

TIPS

Panch phoron is a five-spice blend of cumin seeds, brown mustard seeds, fenugreek, nigella seeds and fennel seeds. You can buy it from Indian specialty or spice stores. To make your own, pound 2 teaspoons each of fenugreek and fennel seeds using a mortar and pestle, then combine with equal quantities of cumin seeds, mustard seeds and nigella seeds. Store in an airtight container.

To make a simple coriander chutney, place a bunch of coriander leaves, a few mint leaves, a deseeded long green chilli and a little water in a food processor and blitz until finely chopped. Add fresh grated ginger to taste and season with salt, lemon juice and the tiniest bit of ground cumin to finish. Or combine 260 g (1 cup) natural yoghurt with 2 tablespoons of mango chutney and swirl through 2 tablespoons finely chopped mint.

Lamb Palak Paneer Chapati Wraps

(not just Indian Souvas)

I am sure that part of the reason spinach lost its popularity crown to kale, silverbeet and (for a while there) rocket was the tedium of removing those stalks. Use baby spinach, however, and there's no need. This makes knocking up a version of this North Indian classic to go with the lamb a cheat's breeze.

Three other kitchen 'wrinkles' bring more flavour to what could otherwise be a muted affair:

1) The paneer is seared to give it some colour (think golden haloumi) instead of adding it raw.

2) The lamb is coated in a very quick tomato paste marinade so that it scorches when cooked, adding a great smokiness to the dish.

3) Bombay snack mix adds great crunch and flavour to everything in its orbit, including this wrap.

SERVES: 4 **PREP:** 15 MINS **COOKING:** 15 MINS

250 g baby spinach leaves
2 long green chillies, deseeded
2 tablespoons vegetable oil
200 g paneer, cut into 1.5 cm cubes (use haloumi if you can't find paneer)
1½ tablespoons tomato paste
1 teaspoon ground coriander
1 teaspoon sea salt
4 × 125 g lamb leg or rump steaks
25 g unsalted butter
2 garlic cloves, crushed
1 tablespoon very finely grated ginger
1 teaspoon ground cumin
1 small red onion, coarsely grated
½ teaspoon ground turmeric
½ teaspoon chilli powder
4 store-bought or homemade chapatis, warmed
50 g Bombay snack mix (see TIPS)
½ bunch coriander, leaves picked

Bring a large saucepan of water to the boil over medium–high heat. Add the spinach and blanch for 30 seconds, then drain and refresh under cold water. Drain again, but don't wring out all the water. Place in a blender with the chilli and blitz until smooth.

Heat half the oil in a large non-stick frying pan over medium–high heat. Add the paneer and cook, turning, for 2–3 minutes or until golden. Transfer to a bowl and set aside.

Combine the tomato paste, ground coriander, salt and remaining oil in a bowl, then brush over the lamb. Heat the same frying pan over medium–high heat. Add the lamb and cook for 2 minutes each side or until slightly scorched. Transfer to a plate, cover with foil and leave to rest.

Wipe the pan clean with paper towel. Melt the butter over medium heat, then add the garlic, ginger and cumin and cook, stirring, for 2 minutes or until aromatic. Add the onion and cook, stirring, for 2–3 minutes, then stir in the turmeric and chilli powder. Add the spinach mixture and stir to combine. Bring to a simmer, add the paneer and cook until warmed through.

To serve, thinly slice the lamb. Spoon some of the spinach mixture onto each chapati, top with the lamb and sprinkle with the Bombay mix and coriander leaves. Wrap up the chapatis and serve.

TIPS

Bombay snack mix is available from supermarkets. It is usually a combination of spiced and fried lentils, roasted peanuts and fried chickpeas, and is dangerously moreish.

To make this a North Indian-style vego dish, add an extra block of paneer (or chunks of boiled waxy potato) to the spinach mixture. And leave out the lamb of course!

You could use mustard leaves or fenugreek leaves instead of spinach if you can find them. Or even microwaved broccoli!

If preferred, replace the chapatis with a packet of frozen flaky paratha.

The KFC Burger

(You won't believe it's vego)

In this recipe, KFC stands for KERALA FRIED CAULIFLOWER. It looks like a fried chicken burger, but take a bite and instead you'll discover a crispy cauliflower steak fragrant with curry spices. The presence of red wine vinegar and garlic is a nod to the Portuguese who settled in the state of Kerala and, in doing so, unexpectedly gave the world one of the great curries: vindaloo. The Portuguese also brought the chilli to India and Japan (where they would eventually also introduce tempura, such was their love of frying stuff), so I think they'd like this fried faux-burger. Even if it is a little off-piste, it's certainly on point (to use the two most-mouthed phrases on *MasterChef*).

SERVES: 4 **PREP:** 20 MINS **COOKING:** 15 MINS

1 cauliflower
1 small red onion, thinly sliced into rings
2 garlic cloves, thinly sliced lengthways
2 tablespoons red wine vinegar
sea salt and freshly ground black pepper
190 g plain flour
3 teaspoons curry powder
2 teaspoons onion powder
2 teaspoons garlic powder
½ teaspoon chilli powder
2 eggs
sunflower oil, for shallow-frying
4 brioche burger buns, cut in half and toasted
1 tablespoon wholegrain mustard
180 g (⅔ cup) natural yoghurt
1 small bunch coriander, leaves picked

Cut two 1.5–2 cm thick slices from the centre of the cauliflower to give you two large steaks – they need to be connected at the stalk. Reserve the outer sides of the cauliflower for another use.

Cut each cauliflower steak in half lengthways through the core so the florets hold together. Place on a microwave-safe plate and cover with plastic wrap. Microwave on high for 3 minutes or until almost tender. (Alternatively, you can steam them for 3 minutes.) Set aside to cool completely.

Meanwhile, place the onion and garlic in a bowl and toss with the vinegar and a pinch of salt. Set aside to pickle.

Combine the flour, curry powder, onion powder, garlic powder, chilli powder and 2 teaspoons salt in a bowl. Crack the eggs into a second bowl and lightly whisk. Working with one cauliflower steak at a time, dip them into the egg and then into the flour mixture to coat, shaking off any excess. Repeat to add a second coating.

Pour enough oil into a frying pan to come 1 cm up the side and heat over medium–high heat. Add two cauliflower steaks and cook for 2 minutes each side or until golden. Transfer to a plate or tray lined with paper towel to drain. Repeat with the remaining steaks.

Spread the burger bun bases with mustard, then a little yoghurt and top with the pickled onion and garlic. Add a fried cauliflower steak to each bun and sprinkle with coriander. Spread a little more yoghurt over the top half of the bun and sandwich together. Serve.

Roasted Eggplant Curry *with* Garlicky Cashews

Roasting the eggplant brings out a little smokiness and helps it to keep its shape when cooking; it also gives this vego dish a real 'meatiness' – without any meat. The mustard seeds, curry leaves and coconut should be all the clues you need to identify this as South Indian in inspiration.

SERVES: 4 **PREP:** 20 MINS **COOKING:** 30 MINS

3 large (about 1.1 kg) eggplants, cut into 4 cm pieces
sea salt
1 tablespoon garam masala (see TIP on page 253)
2 teaspoons ground turmeric
80 ml (⅓ cup) sunflower or vegetable oil
1 teaspoon cumin seeds
2 teaspoons mustard seeds
2 sprigs curry leaves, leaves picked
1 brown onion, thinly sliced
2 garlic cloves, crushed
3 truss tomatoes, coarsely chopped
1 × 270 ml can coconut cream
coriander leaves, to serve
flatbreads (see TIP), to serve

GARLICKY CASHEWS

60 ml (¼ cup) sunflower oil
110 g (⅔ cup) raw cashews, coarsely chopped
1 garlic clove, crushed
1 teaspoon garam masala

To make the garlic cashews, heat the oil in a small frying pan over medium–high heat. Add the cashews and cook, tossing, for 2–3 minutes or until golden. Stir in the garlic and garam masala and cook for 30 seconds, then remove from the heat and drain on a plate lined with paper towel. Set aside.

Preheat the oven to 200°C/180°C fan-forced. Line a large baking tray with baking paper.

Place the eggplant in a bowl, add 1 teaspoon of salt, 2 teaspoons of the garam masala, half the turmeric and half the oil. Toss to coat. Scatter the eggplant over the prepared tray. Roast for 20 minutes or until slightly charred and tender, but still holding its shape.

While the eggplant roasts away, heat the remaining oil in a saucepan over medium–high heat. Add the cumin and mustard seeds and cook, stirring, for 30 seconds or until aromatic and the mustard seeds start to pop. Throw in the curry leaves and stir for 1 minute.

Add the onion and cook, stirring, for 3–4 minutes or until softened. Add the garlic and remaining garam masala and turmeric and cook for a further 1 minute or until aromatic. Add the tomatoes and cook, stirring, for 5 minutes or until they collapse and start to break down.

Your eggplant should be done now, so add it to the tomato mixture and stir to combine. Season with salt. Add the coconut cream and bring to a simmer, then reduce the heat to medium and cook for 5 minutes or until the liquid has reduced slightly.

Scatter the garlic cashews and coriander over the eggplant curry and serve with flatbreads.

TIP

If you want to make your own two-ingredient flatbreads here's how. Preheat a barbecue grill plate or large chargrill pan over medium–high heat. Place 300 g (2 cups) self-raising flour in a bowl. Add 260 g (1 cup) Greek-style yoghurt and stir until just combined. Turn out onto a well-floured surface and knead until smooth and well combined. Divide the dough into six portions. Use a well-floured rolling pin to roll out each portion to an 18 cm round. Chargrill for 2 minutes each side or until cooked, slightly puffed and nicely charred in places.

Golden Egg Curry

I discovered this super-intense curry on a trip to Andhra Pradesh. It's quick and easy to make but packs a massive punch of flavour. Serve with your favourite Indian flatbread, such as roti or paratha (or try my recipe for a super-simple flatbread on page 264). It's fine with rice, too.

SERVES: 4 **PREP:** 15 MINS **COOKING:** 35 MINS

100 ml vegetable oil
2 tablespoons brown or yellow mustard seeds
4 sprigs fresh curry leaves, leaves picked
500 g coarsely grated red onion, drained to remove excess moisture (you will need about 4 onions) (see TIPS)
4 large garlic cloves, finely grated
5 cm knob of ginger, peeled and finely grated
2 teaspoons dried chilli flakes or two dried red chillies
2 teaspoons ground coriander
1 teaspoon cumin seeds
1 tablespoon ground turmeric (or 2 tablespoons grated fresh turmeric if you can find it)
12 eggs
3 teaspoons hot paprika or chilli powder
8 flatbreads, store-bought or homemade (see TIP on page 264)
2 tablespoons tamarind pulp, concentrate or puree
2 tablespoons tomato paste
2 teaspoons caster sugar
sea salt
12 green long chillies, halved lengthways (but leave 7 of them connected at the stalk), deseeded
coriander leaves, to serve

Heat 1 tablespoon of the oil in a large frying pan over medium–high heat. Throw in the mustard seeds – they will start popping after a few seconds. Add half the curry leaves and cook for 1–2 minutes or until they turn bright green. Add the grated onion and fry, stirring occasionally, for 15 minutes or until softened and starting to brown. Add the garlic, ginger, chilli, ground coriander, cumin and 1 teaspoon of the ground turmeric (or 2 teaspoons fresh). Cook, stirring, for another 5 minutes.

Use this 20-minute window to cook your eggs in a large saucepan of boiling water for about 7 minutes or until hard-boiled. Dunk them in cold water to cool, then peel.

Heat 2 tablespoons of the remaining oil in a large frying pan over medium–high heat. Add the paprika or chilli powder and remaining turmeric and stir to combine. Add the peeled eggs and roll them around in the hot spiced oil for 3–4 minutes or until they are beautifully golden all over. Jiggle the pan regularly to keep them moving. It's OK if a couple of the sides become rather bronzed and give the eggs a sort of crust, but keep a close eye on them as they can stick and this will undo all that good work. Remove from the heat and cover to keep warm.

Warm or cook your flatbreads.

Back to your onions. Stir in the tamarind and tomato paste and cook, stirring, for 1–2 minutes or until heated through. Add the sugar and 1 teaspoon of salt to help take a little of the sharp, sour edge off the tamarind. Add 250 ml (1 cup) water and deglaze the pan, stirring any tasty brown stuck-on bits back into the sauce. After about 3 minutes of this pfaffing about, you will be left with a thick, intense curry sauce in which to paddle your eggs. Place the eggs around and about in the curry with their prettiest sides facing upwards. Cover loosely with foil to keep warm.

Quickly wipe out the pan you boiled the eggs in – be careful as it will probably still be hot. Pour in the remaining oil and heat over high heat. Add the green chillies and cook in the sizzling oil for 2–3 minutes or until bright green and blistered. Add the remaining curry leaves and cook for a few seconds or until they turn bright green. Use a slotted spoon to remove the leaves and chillies and scatter over the egg curry with wild abandon. Finish with a handful of coriander leaves and serve with the flatbreads.

TIPS

Dump the eggs and instead stir 250 ml (1 cup) hot fish stock into this rich, tangy sauce. Top with four well-oiled skinless, pin-boned blue-eye fish fillets (about 180 g each). Cover with foil and bake in a preheated 200°C/180°C fan-forced oven for 10 minutes or until just cooked through. Garnish with the fried curry leaves and green chillies.

Save the onion juice to add to marinades and dressings.

'Trishna' Prawns

For me, Mumbai is all about the street food, but one of the best meals I've had in a restaurant there was at the long-running Trishna. This recipe is my homage to them, although I use prawns as the local pomfret that they've made famous is unavailable here. They still work very well, especially with the punchy tomato chutney.

SERVES: 4 **PREP:** 15 MINS **COOKING:** 15 MINS

2 baby gem or cos lettuces, leaves separated
lime wedges, to serve
75 g (½ cup) chickpea flour (besan) or semolina
2 teaspoons ground turmeric
1 teaspoon chilli powder
sea salt
2 eggs
16 large green prawns, peeled and deveined
sunflower or vegetable oil, for shallow-frying

QUICK FRESH TOMATO CHUTNEY

1 tablespoon vegetable, peanut or rice bran oil
4 fresh curry leaves, very finely chopped
2 teaspoons brown or yellow mustard seeds
1 tablespoon tamarind puree
3 truss tomatoes, deseeded and chopped
1 small red onion, very finely chopped
½ teaspoon caster sugar, plus extra if needed

To make the chutney, heat the oil in a small saucepan over medium heat. Add the curry leaves and mustard seeds and cook for 1–2 minutes or until the seeds start to pop. Add the tamarind puree and stir for 1 minute, then throw in the tomato and onion and stir for 2 minutes to soften slightly. Gradually add the sugar to balance the sourness of the tamarind without obscuring it, tasting as you go; depending on your palate you might need more than ½ teaspoon. When you are happy, transfer the chutney to a heatproof bowl and set aside for the flavours to meld.

Arrange your lettuce leaves as cups on a large platter so they are ardently awaiting the oncoming crunchy prawns. Add a pile of lime wedges.

Combine the flour, turmeric and chilli powder in a bowl and season with salt. Crack the eggs into another bowl and lightly whisk. Season with salt.

Working with one prawn at a time, dip the prawns into the egg and then into the flour mixture to coat. Place on a plate.

Pour enough oil into a frying pan to come 1 cm up the side and heat over medium–high heat. Add the prawns in batches and cook for 2 minutes each side or until golden and very crunchy. Use a slotted spoon to transfer to a plate lined with paper towel to drain.

Serve immediately with the lettuce cups, chutney and lime wedges for squeezing over the top.

Shahi White Korma Karma

One of the richer and more decadent curries, korma is descended from the Persian-influenced cuisine of the Mughal Empire – an empire responsible for such beautiful buildings as the Taj Mahal in Agra, Jama Masjid in Delhi and Lahore Fort. In fact, a royal (that's what 'shahi' means) white korma with 'vark' (edible silver leaf) was served by Shah Jahan at the inauguration of the Taj Mahal.

If korma is the pinnacle of Mughlai cuisine – a cuisine that includes biryanis, keema matar (spiced mince), jalebi and lamb pasanda – then the Pearl Mosque in Agra was the pinnacle of their architectural achievement. Its soaring space is incredibly calm and so beautiful it brought me to tears the first time I saw it. A bit like the first time I tasted a true white korma.

SERVES: 4 GENEROUSLY PREP: 30 MINS (PLUS 10 MINS MARINATING) COOKING: 30 MINS

400 ml chicken stock, plus extra if needed
80 g (½ cup) raw cashews
1 brown onion, coarsely chopped
3 long green chillies (deseeded for a milder curry), chopped
4 large garlic cloves, chopped
4 cm knob of ginger, peeled and grated
1 kg chicken thigh fillets, excess fat trimmed, cut into 4 cm chunks
60 ml (¼ cup) grapeseed, rice bran or vegetable oil
50 g butter
10 saffron threads
6 green cardamom pods, crushed (you need about ¼ teaspoon seeds)
1½ tablespoons poppy seeds
1 tablespoon ground coriander
1 teaspoon ground cumin
100 g almond meal
1 strip lemon zest
4 whole cloves
200 g creme fraiche
sea salt, to taste
caster sugar, to taste
edible silver leaf (see TIP), to decorate
saffron rice (see TIP on page 253), to serve

Heat 100 ml of the chicken stock in a saucepan over low heat until it just comes to the boil. Place the cashews in a heatproof bowl, pour over the chicken stock and set aside.

Place the onion, chilli, garlic and ginger in the small bowl of a food processor or blender and blitz until finely minced.

Place the chicken in a glass or ceramic dish. Spoon the blitzed onion gunk into a piece of muslin or a Chux and twist hard over the dish to squeeze the juices over the chicken. Toss to coat, then set aside to marinate for 10 minutes. Keep the solids in the muslin or Chux as this will be the base for our korma. No waste here, friends.

Heat 2 tablespoons of the oil in a large flameproof casserole dish or heavy-based saucepan over medium heat. Add the squeezed onion mixture and cook, stirring constantly, for 3 minutes or until it starts to colour and smell fragrant. Scrape this to one side of the pan and add the butter to the other side. Once melted, add the saffron, cardamom seeds, poppy seeds, coriander and cumin and cook, stirring, for 1 minute or until aromatic. Again, keep it moving. Stir everything together, then scrape the mixture into a bowl and set aside.

Wipe out the food processor bowl or blender and add the almond meal, cashews and soaking liquid and blitz until finely chopped. With the motor running, gradually add another 100 ml of the chicken stock to create a fine slurry.

Heat the remaining oil in the casserole dish or saucepan over medium–high heat. Add the chicken and juices and cook, stirring occasionally, for 5 minutes or until the chicken starts to colour. Add the spice mixture and stir for 1 minute. Add the nut slurry and stir to combine, then pour in the remaining stock so the chicken is nicely saucy. Bring to the boil.

Stud the strip of lemon zest with the cloves and drop it in. Reduce the heat to low and simmer very gently for 15 minutes or until the chicken is cooked through. Add more stock if at any point the chicken stops looking saucy.

Fish out the lemon zest and discard. Stir through the creme fraiche a couple of minutes before serving to just heat through. Taste and season the korma with salt and sugar as needed. Decorate with torn pieces of silver leaf and serve with saffron rice.

TIP

Edible silver leaf is available from cake-decorating suppliers, Indian stores or online.

Rice Kheer

(Indian Rice Pudding with Saffron & Nuts)

Who knew rice pudding could be so regal?? I'd use even more exclamation marks for emphasis here, but it seems that I have exhausted my allocation for this cookbook. ***[Ed: Seeing as this is a rhetorical question I have changed them to question marks. You still have plenty of those left, so use as many as you like.]***

SERVES: 6 **PREP:** 10 MINS (PLUS 30 MINS SOAKING) **COOKING:** 50 MINS

100 g (½ cup) basmati rice, rinsed
1 litre full-cream milk
100 g caster sugar
40 g (¼ cup) slivered almonds
40 g (¼ cup) sultanas
¼ teaspoon ground cardamom
good pinch of saffron threads (about 40 threads), plus extra to decorate
chopped almonds and raw pistachio kernels, to decorate
edible silver leaf (see TIPS), to decorate (optional)

Place the rice in a large bowl, cover with water and set aside to soak for 30 minutes. Drain.

Pour the milk into a large saucepan and bring to the boil over medium heat. Add the drained rice and reduce the heat to low. Simmer, stirring every couple of minutes to prevent the rice from sticking to the pan, for about 45 minutes or until the milk has reduced by about one-third. Add the sugar, slivered almonds, sultanas, cardamom and saffron and cook for a further 5 minutes. Check that the rice is cooked to your liking, then set aside to rest for a few minutes.

Divide the rice among serving bowls and top with the almonds, pistachios, a few extra saffron threads and some torn edible silver leaf (if using). Serve warm or chilled.

TIPS

This rice is just as good cold as it is hot, so it's the perfect dessert to make ahead. Cover and store in the fridge until you're ready to go!

A few strands of saffron on top of the pudding will bleed yellow prettily across the dish.

To really fancy things up, serve the rice pudding with a kir royale, spritzed with a little rosewater.

Decorate with edible silver leaf if you have some left over from the korma on page 270.

Cardamom Brownies *with* Sweetened Condensed Milk Ice-Cream

I felt I could never eclipse the classic fudgy and malty chocolate brownie in my very first cookbook. So I never tried ... until now. Cardamom was born to cohabit with chocolate, but throw in a condensed milk ice-cream that references the classic Indian dessert kulfi and, my friends, we might have ourselves a new contender for the title.

SERVES: 8 **PREP:** 30 MINS (PLUS 6 HOURS FREEZING) **COOKING:** 2 HOURS 10 MINS

250 g butter, melted
2 tablespoons vegetable or olive oil
250 g brown sugar
200 g caster sugar
4 eggs
2 teaspoons vanilla extract
150 g (1 cup) plain flour
100 g Dutch-processed cocoa powder
½ teaspoon sea salt
10 green cardamom pods, crushed to remove the seeds, seeds ground into powder using a mortar and pestle
100 g dark chocolate, coarsely chopped

SWEETENED CONDENSED MILK ICE-CREAM

1 × 375 g can sweetened condensed milk
200 ml pouring cream
200 g creamy natural or Greek-style yoghurt
2 teaspoons vanilla extract
pinch of sea salt

Start by making your ice-cream. Place the unopened can of condensed milk in a large saucepan and fill with enough water to cover it generously. Bring to the boil over high heat, then reduce the heat to medium and simmer for 1½ hours. It is VERY IMPORTANT that the can stays fully submerged, so keep a close eye on it and top up the water if necessary. Set aside until the can has cooled completely, then open it to reveal a light-coloured caramel.

BEWARE! Don't EVER let the water boil away. My editor was emotionally scarred as a small child when her distracted mother let the saucepan boil dry when caramelising condensed milk like this. The can exploded, plastering the cupboards, ceiling and newly wallpapered kitchen walls with hot caramel. You have been warned. You could, of course, just buy some of that already caramelised-in-the-tin-by-the-manufacturer caramelised condensed milk, but I suspect this might be cheating. Even if it is sensible. Oh, and never ever use the microwave to caramelise a tin of condensed milk either ...

Use electric beaters to beat the cream and yoghurt, then add the cold caramel in a slow steady stream, beating until the mixture is well combined. Add the vanilla and salt and continue to beat for about 5 minutes or until the mixture is thick and pale. Pour into a freezer-proof container, then cover and freeze for at least 6 hours or until completely set.

Preheat the oven to 190°C/170°C fan-forced. Line a 30 cm × 20 cm lamington or slice tin with baking paper.

Combine the butter, oil and both sugars in a bowl. Use a balloon whisk to whisk in the eggs and vanilla until well combined. Sift the flour, cocoa powder, salt and ground cardamom seeds over the butter mixture and stir until just combined. Stir in the chocolate. Pour into the prepared tin and bake for 35 minutes. Set aside to cool slightly.

Cut the brownie into pieces (as big or as small as you like) and serve topped with scoops of condensed milk ice-cream.

TIP

If the ice-cream is very frozen and hard, place it in the microwave for about 30 seconds to soften slightly for perfect scooping. This ice-cream should keep for a couple of weeks in the freezer, but I suspect you'll eat it way before then.

MEXICO

Mexico's greatest gift has to be the amazing indigenous ingredients that have taken the world by storm over the centuries. Ingredients, such as avocados, chillies, tomatoes, tomatillos, capsicums, beans, sweet corn, sweet potato, vanilla and chocolate. Add iceberg lettuce, onions, radishes, squash, crunchy jicama, fleshy cactus paddles, chayote and even silverbeet, as well as fruits, such as pineapple, mango, soursop, custard apple, lime, orange, prickly pear, guava and banana, and nature's given you a lot to play with in the kitchen.

This trade wasn't all one way, however, and the presence and popularity of beef, chicken and pork is thanks to the Spanish involvement in Mexico. Modern Mexico takes the eat-everything, nose-to-tail approach to animals, but you'll also find eggs, fish, scallops and turkey, along with fresh cheeses and a Mexican version of sour cream, which all regularly feature on menus alongside the soft and squidgy animal bits.

Another distinctive element of Mexican cuisine is their obsession with dried and sometimes smoked chillies. You'll see stalls groaning with the weight of chillies in every market, with a dizzying selection on offer ranging in flavour from the fruity to the hot, smoky, or almost chocolate-like in flavour ... or maybe even all four! The Mexican spice cupboard is further bolstered with various exquisite chilli powders, along with other spices, such as cinnamon, coriander and cumin seeds, and dried herbs, such as Mexican oregano.

For crunch, you'll find pepitas, almonds and fried tortilla chips, while beans (especially black beans), ground corn tamales, tortillas, tacos and other flatbreads made with wheat or corn flour sort out the carb factor.

Varied ancient roots, very distinct regions and historical borders, which effectively reached up into what is now the USA, have blurred the very notion of what Mexican cuisine is and isn't. For me, it can be defined by four things:

1. The use of corn – fresh, dried and, above all, as a flour.
2. The use of chillies – both fresh and dried.
3. The brightness and freshness that comes from pairing ingredients, such as tomato and onion, lime and coriander, or using creamy avocado.
4. The fact that it is hard to recreate Mexican flavours outside of the country, as many of the key ingredients that are lauded in Mexico – such as particular herbs, flowers, chillies, cacti and escamoles – can't be easily sourced outside the region. Furthermore, the complexity and time-consuming nature of many dishes (such as mole sauces) means that the Mexican food we know here is a wee bit removed from the old country.

This means that faking it has its challenges, but because many people don't know about these complexities you should see this as a wide-open opportunity rather than a hindrance.

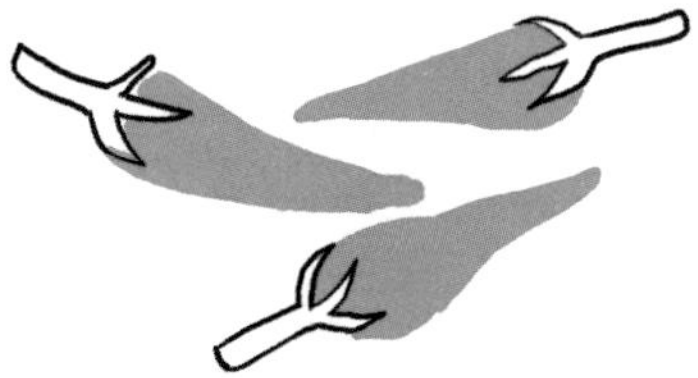

FAKING IT TIPS

1. Flavour a dish or sauce with good-quality dried and smoked or smoked and ground chillies and you are halfway there.
2. Add a punchy, crunchy salsa to the pulled pork (carnitas) in your tortilla and you are three-quarters of the way there.
3. Toss around some lime-crushed avocado and fresh coriander and some smart-arse will start shouting ¡arriba, arriba!
4. Cook things fast or very slowly.
5. Remember that at its most simplistic, Mexican food is often not defined by what it is but, rather, if it's served on a corn chip or a tostada, in a taco or a burrito, or even whether it's served with tortillas!

SHOPPING LIST

For a sexy selection of dried or smoked chillies, such as ancho, chipotle, pasilla, cascabel, mulato and guajillo, head to the internet and order online (dried chillies are dead cheap to post!). Dried Mexican oregano and other specialist herbs, such as epazote for your chilli con carne, are becoming more available now, as is chipotle powder and tins of chipotle in adobo sauce, along with other Mexican chilli pastes, and achiote paste or powder for reddening up the colour of dishes. Keep those corn husks or use banana leaves if you want to make tamales.

At an esoteric level, try 'huitlacoche' (often called the Mexican truffle), which is basically a plant disease known as corn smuts but tastes better than it sounds and looks!

When it comes to canned goods, look for large cans of green tomatillos. Canned black beans can also be used as a time-saver if your supermarket doesn't stock dried beans. Also look out for cactus paddles – known as nopales or nopalitos – which are often sold pickled in cans or jars.

If you want to get even more authentic, invest in a $30 tortilla press and make your own tortillas using masa harina – a white cornmeal flour that's more widely available these days. To save time, make a large batch and freeze them with a sheet of baking paper between each tortilla.

Buy a bottle or two of Mexican hot sauce.

For something sweet, if you can find them, tamarind and hibiscus syrups make refreshing coolers, while desserts are often flavoured with dark, hard cones of molasses-heavy Mexican sugar. Also look out for fruit pastes, such as guava and quince.

Los Tres Amigos – Soft Shell Tacos

There's a hole-in-the-wall in the historic centre of Mexico City where your hotel will advise you not to go after dark. This is the street-food place you dream of finding when you travel. The teeny cupboard kitchen that is Taqueria Los Cocuyos is also the place where you are most thankful for Google Translate, so you don't order an eyeball taco when you really wanted a chorizo one.

No such problem here, where a great chorizo taco is joined by a couple of classics for the ideal spread for Taco Tuesday ... yes, it IS a thing. Although a couple of greedy food chains around the world have tried to corporatise the concept by trademarking 'Taco Tuesday', so at home you might just have to call your midweek feast 'Tako Chewsday' instead.

Of course, you could always buy your favourite ready-made tortillas. We won't judge you. BUT ... if you make your own you'll find they are a wee bit superior, so the recipe is over the page. If you accept this challenge, give yourself an extra hour of prep time to make sure everything is ready at the same time.

SERVES: 4 **PREP:** 20 MINS **COOKING:** 20 MINS

12 corn tortillas (see page 281) or use store-bought tortillas
2 cups shredded iceberg lettuce
4 radishes, thinly sliced
125 g (½ cup) sour cream
3 limes, cut into wedges
your favourite hot sauce, to serve

QUICK CHICKEN FILLING

1 avocado
juice of 1 lime
1 long green or jalapeno chilli, deseeded and very finely chopped
1 bunch coriander, stalks and leaves separated
sea salt and freshly ground black pepper
2 chicken breast fillets
½ teaspoon ground cumin
½ teaspoon ground coriander
2 teaspoons extra virgin olive oil

SPICY CHORIZO FILLING

2 fresh chorizo sausages, meat squeezed out of its casing
1 tablespoon apple cider vinegar
½ white or red onion, finely chopped

BEEF AND CAPSICUM FILLING

2 teaspoons extra virgin olive oil
150 g beef minute steak
½ teaspoon sweet paprika
¼ teaspoon sea salt
½ yellow or red capsicum, deseeded and cut into strips

To make the chicken filling, coarsely mash the avocado with the lime juice and chilli in a bowl. Thinly slice the coriander stalks as if they were chives, and mix into the guacamole with a little salt to taste.

Slice each chicken breast in half horizontally to make thin fillets. Place each fillet between two sheets of baking paper and beat out to a size a little larger than your tortillas. You want it really thin!!!

Combine the ground cumin and coriander and dust over the chicken. Reserve in the fridge until needed, separated by baking paper. You'll cook these just as everything else is ready and your family or friends are sitting down to eat.

For the chorizo filling, preheat the oven to 100°C/80°C fan-forced. Cook the chorizo meat in a small frying pan over medium–high heat for 2 minutes or until the fat starts to render. Add the vinegar and cook, stirring, for 2 minutes or until the meat is cooked through. Use a slotted spoon to transfer the meat to an ovenproof bowl, reserving any pan juices. Add the onion to the bowl and stir to combine. Cover with foil and place in the oven to keep warm.

To make the beef and capsicum filling, lightly drizzle the oil over the steak and sprinkle on both sides with the paprika and salt. Heat the pan you used for the chorizo over high heat. Add the steak, then arrange the capsicum around it and cook the steak for 2 minutes each side for medium, stirring the capsicum occasionally. Transfer the steak to a chopping board and set aside for a few minutes to rest. Place the seared capsicum in a serving bowl. Cut the steak into thin slices and add to the capsicum.

When you are ready to eat, warm your tortillas in the oven, microwave or even the toaster, but DON'T let them get crispy! If you have made your own, cook them in a dry frying pan over medium–high heat for 2–3 minutes each side.

Reheat that pan – or use the flat grill of a barbecue if you are a purist. When it's really hot, add the oil and flash-fry the chicken to just cook through. This will take no time at all, so watch it like a hawk. Season and serve with the guacamole.

Place all your tortillas, fillings, lettuce, radish, sour cream, coriander leaves, lime wedges and hot sauce on the table and watch the hands go flying. Choose your own adventures.

Tortilla Time!

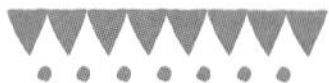

Making your own tortillas has its charm, but it's perhaps best if you grab a friend or two to enjoy it with. The corn flour is unique to work with; its silky-smooth texture doesn't have a mind of its own like gluten-based flours – it does what it's told and the smell is so aromatic, taking you back to the noisy taqueria bakery in the Oaxaca village of your imagination.

MAKES: 16 **PREP:** 15 MINS (PLUS 30 MINS RESTING) **COOKING:** 25 MINS

350 g masa harina (Mexican flour made from corn), plus extra for dusting
½ teaspoon sea salt

Combine the masa harina and salt in a large bowl. Gradually add up to 500 ml (2 cups) hot water and stir with a wooden spoon until a dough starts to form. Turn out onto a clean floured surface, then use your hands to roll it into a nice big smooth ball. Cover the dough with a damp tea towel and set aside to rest for 30 minutes.

Tear off a heaped tablespoon of the masa dough and roll it into a small ball. Place on a tray or plate and cover with a damp tea towel while you roll the rest. You should have enough dough to make 16 balls.

Press each ball through a tortilla press between two sheets of baking paper to form 14 cm rounds (use a zip-lock bag split in half if you don't have baking paper – this stops the dough sticking to the press). Stack them up on top of each other, lightly dusting masa flour between each tortilla. Limit each stack to five or six tortillas, otherwise they get compacted and stuck together from the weight.

Heat a large non-stick frying pan over medium–high heat. Add a few tortillas at a time and cook for 2–3 minutes each side or until toasted – they will start to puff up and develop some brown marks. Wrap in a clean, dry tea towel to keep them warm while you cook the remaining tortillas.

TIPS

If you don't have a tortilla press, you can hand roll your tacos, but this will take mucho time. These days tortilla presses are easy to find, either online or from kitchen shops, and are usually around the $30 mark. They make pressing out the dough a breeze and give the tortillas the perfect thickness.

The dough freezes well. Just wrap the dough balls in plastic wrap and thaw before pressing and cooking. Alternatively, flatten the dough into tortillas and stack with baking paper between each tortilla. These can be cooked from frozen.

If you have come home on a weeknight and don't have time to make the tortillas, a cheat's tip is to have a packet of bought ones in the cupboard. You'll cut your prep time in half. Pick just one of the fillings on the previous page for a fuss-free meal.

Adults-Only Tiger's Milk Ceviche

This Mexican ceviche is the hangover cure of the nation. Eaten in the mornings after a big session at the pulqueria, or after that lunch at the old-school workers' saloon bar turned into a night of singing sad songs and watching Los Camoteros play Las Pumas, all washed down with micheledas. (For the uninitiated, these are wonderful tankards of beer spiked spicy and savoury with everything from lime juice and hot sauce to a dash of soy.)

In Mexico, ceviche should always be loaded onto something crunchy before eating – whether that's tostadas (see page 301), totopos (baked tortillas) or even a humble Salada dry biscuit in some dirt-floor, dirt-poor local cantina. You'll also note that the fish is cut smaller for ceviche in Mexico, allowing for a quicker maceration and making it easier to load onto your corn chip.

Mexican ceviche is rather hot and not as sweet as the Peruvian version, which often comes with sweet potatoes (which takes us back to the nickname of the Puebla soccer team – 'Los Camoteros', or the sweet potato growers, but I digress), but then Mexico has a fiery, spicy and altogether more acidic culture. And I love it!

BTW, the sharp liquid leftover from curing the fish from the fish is known as 'leche de tigre', or tiger's milk, and is considered to have potent restorative qualities!

Note: Los Tigres is the nickname of San Nicolas de los Garza's football club in Monterey, and even though I can find no link between ceviche and Los Tigres (de la Universidad Autonoma de Nuevo Leon – to give them their full nickname), I do rather like the way a Mexican soccer theme is developing here. Especially given that Mexico City is the only city to have hosted two soccer World Cup finals. The reasons for this are too scurrilous to discuss here.

SERVES: 4 **PREP:** 25 MINS (PLUS 30 MINS STANDING)

125 ml (½ cup) lime juice
60 ml (¼ cup) orange juice
4 coriander sprigs, leaves picked, stalks finely chopped
sea salt
500 g skinless kingfish fillets, pin-boned, cut into 5 mm cubes (snapper, sea bream or sea bass will also do)
3–4 ice cubes
2 long green chillies, deseeded and finely chopped
1 Lebanese cucumber, peeled, deseeded and finely chopped
½ red onion, finely chopped
1½ tablespoons extra virgin olive oil
1 teaspoon dried Mexican or Greek oregano
1 avocado, finely chopped
1–2 red bird's eye chillies, thinly sliced (or ¼ habanero chilli)
12 corn tortillas (see page 281) or use store-bought tortillas, lightly pan-fried
hot sauce, to serve (just in case your state calls for more heat ...)

Start by making the leche de tigre. Combine the lime juice, orange juice, coriander stalks and 1 teaspoon of salt in a glass or ceramic bowl. Don't use a metal one!

Add the fish to the leche de tigre (gosh, I do love saying that; I think it might have to become my Mexican wrestling name), along with the ice cubes.

Stir well for about 1 minute or until the fish starts to go pale. Set aside for 20–30 minutes. During this time, the acid in the juice will 'cook' the fish slightly.

Strain the fish well, reserving the liquid. This liquid, loaded with fish juices, has become the much-prized leche de tigre hangover nectar.

Place the cured fish in a bowl and add the green chilli, cucumber, onion, oil and oregano.

Now add 1 tablespoon of the reserved leche de tigre at a time. The amount you need will depend on how wet you want your ceviche to be ... or how big the hangover is.

Divide the ceviche among serving bowls. Top with the avocado, a pinch of salt, the coriander leaves and as much of the red chilli as you think your guests can take, or need. Serve the tortillas and hot sauce in the middle of the table for everyone to fight over.

TIP

Leftover leche de tigre goes well in cocktails with mezcal and tequila, can be skulled neat as the best wake-up call, or just use it in your next salad vinaigrette.

The Best BBQ Corn Ever

Whether boiling away in a huge pot outside a rickety shack on a winding road up to the highlands of Sri Lanka, being cooked over coals as street-style 'bhutta' on a Mumbai corner, or being sold for $10 a pop by a bloke called Rainbow with a rat's tail and a nose ring at an alternative music festival somewhere in the Aussie bush, corn has to rate as one of the greatest all-time forms of vegetarian street food. And it probably all started with 'elotes'.

Mexican roadside corn is the perfect enterprise for even the poorest people in rural Mexico as all it requires is corn, a small gas burner and a large pot of boiling water. Oh, and 'queso cotija' to crumble over it.

As this is Australia, I like to cook the corn in their husks on the barbecue, as it keeps them plumper and juicier. And if you let the husk burn a little, you'll get a slightly smoky flavour, too.

Finding queso cotija in Australia is harder than finding a straight boomerang, but we've discovered that several other cheeses work well: dried ricotta salata, finely grated parmesan, a crumbled slab of really old barrel-aged feta that you might have forgotten about in the fridge, unwrapped to air-dry a bit, or even grated frozen feta. Over to you. Let me know which you prefer!

SERVES: 4 **PREP:** 10 MINS **COOKING:** 35 MINS

4 corn cobs, husks on
2 teaspoons smoked paprika
150 g finely grated parmesan
1 handful coriander leaves, finely chopped
2 limes, halved

CHIPOTLE MAYO

125 g (½ cup) good-quality whole-egg mayonnaise
1 tablespoon sauce from your jar or can of chipotle in adobo sauce
finely grated zest and juice of ½ lime

Preheat a barbecue with a lid to high to get it really cranking.

To make your chipotle mayo, combine the mayonnaise, chipotle sauce, lime zest and juice in a small bowl.

Gently pull back the corn husks and remove and discard the stringy silks. Pull the husks back over the corn and dampen the cobs and husks with a splash of water.

Place on the hot grill, put the lid down so you get a steam and burn action going and cook, turning occasionally, for 4 minutes on each side or until evenly cooked through.

Using a tea towel, very carefully pull back the husks until the corn is exposed (for fancy presentation, tear off thin strips of husk and use these to tie back the husks). Remove any silks still attached. Barbecue the corn cobs for a further 4 minutes each side or until charred.

Take the corn off the grill and smother with the chipotle mayo. Sprinkle with the paprika, parmesan and coriander, then squeeze over the lime halves and serve.

TIPS

Charcoal and wood-fired barbies are even better for flavour.

If there is no barbecue available where you are, throw the whole corn on the top rack of a preheated 220°C/200°C fan-forced oven, right at the back, and roast for 30 minutes. Or you can even just boil them whole with the husks on, like most of the street stalls in Mexico do now.

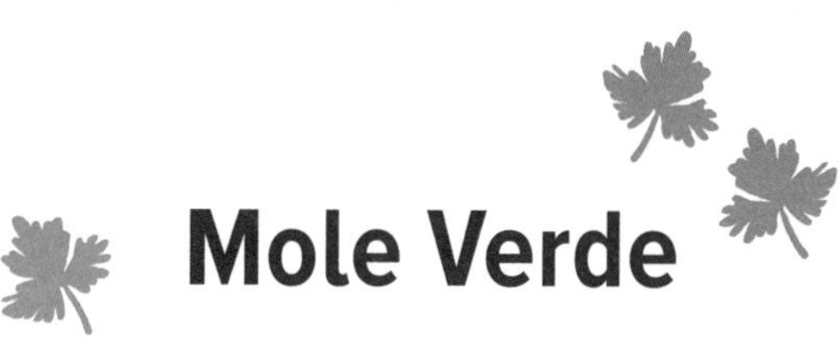

Mole Verde

Oaxaca (wah-hah-ka) is the home of the mole (molay), but making an authentic version of this green mole, which is the lightest of the six principal Oaxacan moles or sauces, is almost impossible in Australia. You see, there it is made with chayote (aka melon gourd or choko), lettuce leaves or even cactus paddles (which you can find in specialist delis if you'd like to experiment), and two distinctive Mexican herbs, hoja santa (oh-ha santa) and epazote (epa-zot-eh), which are not readily available here. (Drive-by food nerd fact: epazote is famously used in chillies and Mexican bean dishes for its carminative – or fart-reducing – properties.)

However, this whole book is all about faking it, and this recipe is no exception, delivering you a creditable mole verde with nuts, seeds and greenery from coriander, spinach and slightly more exotic canned tomatillos – or even dodgy unripe tomatoes.

SERVES: 4 **PREP:** 25 MINS **COOKING:** 50 MINS

1.2 kg chicken thigh fillets
1 brown onion, halved
10 whole peppercorns
6 whole allspice berries
2 fresh or dried bay leaves
sea salt
40 g (¼ cup) slivered almonds, toasted
45 g (¼ cup) pepitas, toasted
40 g (¼ cup) sesame seeds, toasted
1 × 800 g can tomatillos, drained (or chopped green tomatoes, or the least ripe tomatoes you can find)
2 jalapeno chillies (or 3 long green chillies), deseeded and coarsely chopped
½ green capsicum or 1 poblano chilli, deseeded and coarsely chopped
2 garlic cloves
1 cup coriander sprigs
50 g baby spinach leaves
¼ cup oregano leaves
1½ teaspoons ground cumin
steamed rice and corn tortillas (see page 281), to serve

Place the chicken, onion, peppercorns, allspice, bay leaves and 1 teaspoon of salt in a large saucepan and cover with 1.5 litres water. Bring to a simmer over medium–high heat and cook for 10–12 minutes or until the chicken is cooked through. Use tongs to transfer the chicken to a bowl and reserve the cooking liquid. Discard the bay leaves.

Place the almonds, pepitas, 2 tablespoons of the sesame seeds and 250 ml (1 cup) of the reserved cooking liquid in a blender and blitz until a smooth paste forms. Add the tomatillos, chilli, capsicum, garlic, coriander, spinach, oregano, cumin, 1 teaspoon of salt and another 250 ml (1 cup) of the reserved cooking liquid. Blitz until smooth.

Transfer the paste to a large non-stick saucepan and cook over medium–low heat, stirring constantly to prevent it from catching, for 8–10 minutes or until thickened. Add the chicken and another 250 ml (1 cup) of the reserved cooking liquid and simmer gently for a further 15–20 minutes. Have a taste and add a little more salt if needed.

Spoon the mole onto a serving plate and sprinkle with the remaining sesame seeds. Serve with rice and corn tortillas to mop up all that good greenness.

TIP

The sauce is just as good served with roasted or grilled chicken thighs. Or grilled prawns. Or with a bowl of warm tortilla chips and sour cream.

Pork Adobo

Every nation seems to venerate their grandmothers' cooking and this is a typical family recipe from the abuela of the Mexican family. Adobo means 'marinade', and it is another contender for the title of Mexico's national dish. It's the combination of dried chillies that gives each household's adobo its originality – some are fruity, others bitter or spicy. If I were an adobo, I'd be mostly the former and the latter, and only the middle when I look back at the time I was overlooked for a Gold Logie – again, and again, and again, and again, and again, and again, and again, and again, and again, and again, and again.

To make an authentic version at home, order the dried chillies from one of the many online Australian suppliers out there. Dried chillies are cheap to ship and are surprisingly reasonable for such an exotic, hard-to-find ingredient in our local shops.

SERVES: 4 **PREP:** 20 MINS (PLUS 20 MINS SOAKING & 3 HOURS MARINATING)
COOKING: 2 HOURS 15 MINS

1 kg boneless pork neck, shoulder or leg, cut into 3–4 cm pieces
2 teaspoons sea salt
2 tablespoons extra virgin olive oil
1 brown onion, coarsely chopped
3 garlic cloves, crushed
2 fresh or dried bay leaves
2 tablespoons tomato paste
1 litre chicken stock
3 large desiree potatoes, cut into quarters
1 red capsicum, deseeded and cut into 8 chunks
2 oregano sprigs
garden salad and corn tortillas (see page 281), to serve

ADOBO
4 dried ancho or pasilla chillies, deseeded (see TIP)
2 dried guajillo or mulato chillies, deseeded (see TIP)
2 teaspoons brown sugar
1 teaspoon dried oregano
1 teaspoon ground cumin
1 teaspoon sea salt
½ teaspoon freshly ground black pepper
250 ml (1 cup) chicken stock
60 ml (¼ cup) apple cider vinegar
finely grated zest of ¼ orange
juice of 1 orange

To make the adobo, soak the dried chillies in a bowl of hot water for 20 minutes. Drain, reserving the soaking liquid.

Remove the stalks if still attached and place the soaked chillies in a blender with the remaining adobo ingredients. Add 60 ml (¼ cup) of the reserved soaking liquid and blend until smooth.

Place the pork in a large bowl and toss with the salt. Add the adobe paste and stir until well coated. Cover with plastic wrap and place in the fridge for at least 3 hours or preferably overnight – the longer the better.

Heat the oil in a large heavy-based saucepan over medium heat. Add the onion, garlic and bay leaves and cook, stirring, for 8–10 minutes or until the onion is soft and beginning to turn golden. Add the tomato paste and cook, stirring, for 3–4 minutes or until the mixture is a rich dark colour. Add 750 ml (3 cups) of the stock and bring to a simmer. Gradually add the pork, along with any adobo paste left in the bowl. Increase the heat to medium–high and bring to a gentle simmer, then reduce the heat to low and simmer, partially covered, for 1½ hours or until the pork is tender.

Add the potato, capsicum and oregano and cook, partially covered and stirring occasionally, for 25–30 minutes or until the potato is cooked through. Add some or all of the remaining stock if it looks a bit dry or needs more sauce. (If you like, at this stage you can transfer the veggies to a serving bowl, cover and keep warm, then continue to cook the adobo for another hour until the sauce thickens further and the meat starts to fall apart, transforming it into the perfect enchilada, burrito or taco mix.)

Take the adobo to the table and let everyone help themselves. Serve with a garden salad and corn tortillas on the side for the mop-up.

TIP

Use two chipotle chillies from a can and 200 g diced tomato if you can't get the dried chillies.

PREPARE IN 20 MINUTES

Mexican Roast Pork for Sundays, Holy Days & Holidays

(aka Roast Chilli Pork Loin)

This is a special-occasion dish, ideal for showing people how much you love them. It can just be served with roast corn, tortillas and a tomato salad, or partner it with the pickle and salsas handily grouped together opposite.

SERVES: 4–6
PREP: 20 MINS (PLUS 2 HOURS SALTING, 30 MINS MARINATING & 15 MINS RESTING)
COOKING: 1 HOUR 35 MINS

- **1 × 2 kg boneless pork loin roll, skin finely scored**
- **1 tablespoon sea salt**
- **2 teaspoons ground chipotle powder or hot paprika**
- **1½ teaspoons ground coriander**
- **1 teaspoon dried chilli flakes**
- **1 teaspoon freshly ground black pepper**
- **3 garlic cloves**
- **2 tablespoons extra virgin olive oil**
- **2 large brown onions, each cut into 3 thick rings**
- **60 ml (¼ cup) apple cider vinegar**
- **Poblano chilli pickle, Salsa de maiz and Salsa de tomate (see opposite), to serve**

Lay the pork out flat on a plate or tray and rub the salt into the skin. Place in the fridge, uncovered, for 2 hours to dry out the rind. Skip this step if you are time-poor, but it does get you a foolproof crackling every time.

Combine the chipotle powder or paprika, ground coriander, chilli flakes, pepper, garlic and oil in a mortar and use a pestle to pound until a paste forms. You could also use a small blender if you have one.

Line a baking dish with baking paper. Brush the salt off the pork and place, skin-side down, in the dish, then rub the meat with the spice paste, without getting any on the rind. Turn the pork over so it is skin-side up, and place in the fridge to marinate for 30 minutes.

Preheat the oven to 220°C/200°C fan-forced.

Remove the pork to a plate, then place the onion slices in the dish and pop the pork back on top. Pour the vinegar and 125 ml (½ cup) water into the base of the dish.

Roast on the middle rack of the oven for 20 minutes, then reduce the temperature to 190°C /170°C fan-forced and roast for a further 1 hour 15 minutes or until the loin has shrunk and the crackling is starting to turn golden. Keep an eye on it, adding another 250 ml (1 cup) water if it looks like it's going to burn and leave you with some heavy scrubbing later.

Transfer to a chopping board, cover loosely with foil and rest for 10–15 minutes. Reserve half the onion slices for making your salsa de tomate (see opposite).

Cut the pork into thin slices and serve with the remaining onion slices and the pickle and salsas.

Chillies & Salsas

These three sauces will work with pretty much any roast meat, sizzled snag, grilled fish, tasty taco or barbecued piece of chook, but they go particularly well with the roast pork on the opposite page.

SERVES: 4–6 **PREP:** 20 MINS (PLUS COOLING) **COOKING:** 40 MINS

SALSA DE TOMATE

5 roma tomatoes
1 roasted onion (ideally from the Mexican roast pork recipe opposite), coarsely chopped
1½ teaspoons brown sugar
1 teaspoon dried Mexican or Greek oregano
½ teaspoon dried chilli flakes
2 teaspoons extra virgin olive oil
finely grated zest and juice of 1 lime
sea salt and freshly ground black pepper

Preheat the oven to 190°C /170°C fan-forced. Line a baking tray with baking paper.

Place the tomatoes on the prepared tray and roast for 15 minutes or until they soften and the skins start to shrivel. Set aside to cool slightly. Peel the skins from the tomatoes and discard, then remove the seeds and membranes.

Coarsely chop the tomato flesh and place in a serving bowl. Add the remaining ingredients and toss to combine.

SALSA DE MAIZ

2 corn cobs, husks on
4 coriander sprigs, finely chopped
3 spring onions, thinly sliced
1 long red chilli, sliced
40 g (¼ cup) pomegranate seeds
½ teaspoon sea salt
juice of 1 lime
1 tablespoon extra virgin olive oil

Cook the corn in a saucepan of salted boiling water for 10 minutes or until tender. Drain and set aside until cool enough to handle, then pull off the husks and silks. Use a sharp knife to remove the corn kernels and transfer to a serving bowl. Add the remaining ingredients and give it a good mix up.

POBLANO CHILLI PICKLE

4 poblano chillies (or 8 jalapenos – these are hotter, so be aware or go even hotter with 10 jalapenos!)
½ white onion, thinly sliced
6 whole peppercorns
1 garlic clove, thinly sliced
2 teaspoons caster sugar
⅓ teaspoon sea salt
80 ml (⅓ cup) apple cider vinegar

Blacken and blister the skins of the poblano chillies over a gas burner (see TIP). Set aside to cool slightly, then peel off the skins and discard. Cut the chillies in half and remove the seeds, then finely chop the flesh. Place the chilli, remaining ingredients and 1 tablespoon water in a saucepan over high heat and cook for 4 minutes or until the liquid has reduced slightly and thickened. Set aside to cool before serving or store in an airtight container in the fridge for up to 2 weeks.

TIP

If you don't have a gas burner, just pop the chillies under the grill, turning frequently until they crackle up a bit. Be careful to keep the skin away from the elements and watch it closely!

Chilli Con Carne Moderna

Chilli con carne can trace its first appearance back to the main square of San Antonio in the 18th century, when it was still under Spanish colonial rule and therefore part of Mexico. This doesn't stop the US and Mexico arguing over the ownership of the dish – in fact, it's one of the few Mexican things the Donald doesn't want to send back.

Over the last couple of years, CCC has been getting a bit of a modernist makeover, along with the whole 'de la cocina TEX-MEX'. (You'll note I don't use the term 'Tex Mex'. The 'de la cocina TEX-MEX' movement is apparently sensitive to cultural appropriation and also seeks to rehabilitate this particular culinary movement after it was belittled to make way for REAL Mexican food and simultaneously lost in the bastardisation of endless 70's Tex-Mex chains.)

In CCC's case, mega umami underpins the modernist movement here. So along with the tomatoes, caramelised onion and chorizo, we've got Worcestershire sauce and miso, but feel free to get fast 'n' loose by adding soy sauce and mashed anchovies if you want to go all out. You could even chuck in a big chunk of parmesan rind if, like me, you keep a stash of them in your fridge. If you don't, you should. It's a secret weapon deployed more than once in this book.

SERVES: 4 **PREP:** 15 MINS **COOKING:** 1 HOUR

2 tablespoons extra virgin olive oil
1 brown onion, finely chopped
3 garlic cloves, crushed
800 g beef mince
150 g fresh chorizo sausages, meat squeezed out of its casing (or finely diced cured chorizo)
2 tablespoons tomato paste
1½ tablespoons Worcestershire sauce
2 teaspoons ground coriander
1 teaspoon ground cumin
1 teaspoon dried chilli flakes (or ground cayenne, or both for daredevils)
1 teaspoon dried oregano
1 × 400 g can kidney beans, rinsed and drained
1 × 400 g can diced tomatoes
3 teaspoons red miso paste
750 ml (3 cups) beef or chicken stock
3 jalapeno or long green chillies, finely chopped (remove the seeds for less heat)
1 cos lettuce, shredded
4 celery stalks, thinly shaved lengthways
½ bunch coriander, leaves picked
2 limes, quartered
steamed rice, to serve
125 g (½ cup) sour cream, to serve

Heat the oil in a large heavy-based saucepan over medium–high heat. Add the onion and garlic and cook, stirring, for 8 minutes or until starting to soften and turn golden.

Add the beef and chorizo and cook, breaking up any lumps with the back of a wooden spoon, for 4–5 minutes or until browned. Make sure you allow all the liquid to cook out as the meat cooks. Stir in the tomato paste and cook for 4–6 minutes or until it looks like it's almost starting to burn.

Add the Worcestershire sauce, ground coriander and cumin, chilli flakes and oregano and mix through for a minute or so. Add the beans, tomatoes, miso paste and stock and simmer, stirring occasionally, for 30–40 minutes or until the sauce is rich and thick. Stir in the chopped chilli for the last 5 minutes of cooking.

While your chilli simmers away, get the salad together. Combine the cos lettuce, celery and coriander leaves in a large bowl and place the lime wedges on top.

Serve the salad with bowls of steamed rice, sour cream and the steaming hot chilli con carne.

TIPS

Chilli con carne gets better with age so, if you can, make it a day ahead and store in the fridge overnight, then just pop it in a pan and stir over low heat until warmed through. Even better, make it on the weekend, place in airtight containers and freeze for up to 3 months. Thaw overnight in the fridge, then it's ready to warm through for a quick weeknight dinner.

You don't have to serve chilli con carne with rice. It's also great in tacos, in a jaffle, on a baked potato or as a pizza topping. OK, maybe that last one is a step too far – back to the bad old days of 70's Tex-Mex and 90's 'gourmet' pizza restaurants.

Ensalada Cesar

(with the world's longest recipe intro ...)

As you flick through these pages, looking at the pictures and considering what to cook for dinner, you've probably wondered how much research goes into writing each one of those sometimes pithy, seldom witty intros. Well, here's an example of one before it's been artfully cut by my editor.

Success has many fathers, and so it is with America's most famous salad: the Caesar salad. The irony is that this salad, named as the most significant American recipe of the first half of the 20th century at the 1951 Paris meeting of the International Society of Epicures, originated in either Mexico, Italy or Austria, and not the US at all!

The least contentious claim is that it became famous at Caesar's Place in Tijuana, just over the Mexican border from San Diego. Cesare 'Caesar' Cardini was an Italian migrant who, at the age of 20, moved to California from his birthplace on the shores of Lake Maggiore outside Milan. He worked at the Palace Hotel in San Francisco, then in 1919 opened a restaurant in Sacramento called Brown's, before moving to San Diego to open a French restaurant. Prohibition had started to bite, and thirsty Americans turned the dusty Mexican border city of Tijuana into a party town where they could booze and gamble legally. Always one for an opportunity, Cardini opened Caesar's Place on the main strip over the border. It was an instant hit, loved by the Hollywood elite, including Cary Grant, WC Fields, Charlie Chaplin and Jean Harlow. It was at this restaurant that the Caesar salad, assembled theatrically at the guests' tables, got its name.

Now here's the question ... did Caesar himself assemble the first salad to feed a group of hungry 4th of July weekend party-goers, desperate for Sunday lunch, after a particularly big Saturday night had left Cardini with little more than cos lettuce, parmesan, eggs and stale bread in the pantry? That's the story his daughter Rosa used to tell about this auspicious Sunday in 1924. 'Let the guests think they're having the specialty of the house,' it's claimed he said of this makeshift main course that would become the world's most famous salad.

Or was it his brother Alessandro (Alex), the World War I Air Force ace, who claimed he first knocked up the salad in 1926 for a group of US pilots from Rockwell Field base in San Diego who had missed curfew, slept in the restaurant and awoke ravenous. After Caesar's death, he maintained that he had called this the Aviator's salad, and that it was based on a salad their mother used to make back in Italy. At least one ex-airman has claimed that he was there, and this version of events was also supported in 2002 by Jorge Chavez, who now runs Cardini's Hotel. The once-glamorous pleasure dome is faded now, but Jorge bases his support on what his aunt (who worked with Cardini at the time) told him. Even though he hints that she too might have had a hand in the recipe!

However, Paul Maggiora, a partner of the Cardinis, alleged that Alex didn't just steal the recipe but stole the whole story from him too. Paul claimed it was he who made the salad for airmen in 1927, but a young Julia Child – the woman who would go on to be America's most famous cook – remembered eating it, tossed at the table by Caesar himself, in 1925 or 1926, so this claim, and possibly Alex's too, seems spurious. Unswayed, when Alex Cardini moved to Mexico City and opened three restaurants there, each menu offered 'the original Alex Cardini Caesar salad'.

Or was it the help? Italian migrant, 18-year-old Livio Santini worked for the Cardinis in 1924 and 1925 and was partial to a salad his mother used to make when they were exiled to Austria during World War I. It was just soft-boiled eggs, wine vinegar, oil and parmesan thrown over cos lettuce. Speaking in 1984 at Tijuana's first Caesar Salad Festival, Livio claimed that Caesar nicked the idea off him.

Apparently, a rich customer from the San Diego beachside suburb of La Jolla had sprung Livio eating it behind the bar and ordered one of the same from Cardini. A week later, Livio turned up to work to find the maitre d' mixing the same salad at the table for guests and Cardini claiming it as his own.

There are two claims that pre-date these. An Italian cook called Giacomo Junia maintains that he made the first Caesar salad in 1903 at The New York Cafe in Chicago, naming it after Julius Caesar. And Caesar's Grill, a slightly shonky but very popular restaurant in the basement of one of the flatiron buildings in the old Italian quarter of San Francisco, has also been named as the salad's birthplace, before it was closed due to multiple infractions of the Volstead Act during the first years of prohibition.

What is interesting here is that when Caesar Cardini was working at the Palace Hotel in San Francisco, the Caesar Grill – and their salad (if it existed) – was only a 10-minute walk away. Could this have been where Caesar got his inspiration and a late-night beer and salad? Sadly, again, I can find no primary evidence from the time to support this claim, but I think there is something rather delicious about it.

THE SPREAD OF THE SALAD

Controversy aside, there is no doubt that it was from the tables of Caesar's Place that the fame of the salad spread. Hollywood stars returning from weekend trips to Tijuana yearned for it, but it was another Caesar's regular, a screenwriter named Manny Wolfe, who encouraged the hottest restaurants in Los Angeles to put the salad on their menus. By 1948, when *Gourmet* magazine writer Lucius Beebe ate his way round Los Angeles, it was on the menu of every significant restaurant. 'Caesar's salad is as much a part of the Hollywood pattern as swimming pools or Coco Chanel's *new look*,' he wrote.

It was Wallis Simpson who popularised it overseas, demanding chefs in all corners of the world make her favourite salad, as she gallivanted from Europe to China and back, engaging in high-profile affairs before settling down with the future, and soon to abdicate, King of England and other places.

Then there is the dubious contribution of PR huckster Chet L. Switell, who was a passionate supporter of the Cardini legend. Chet was apparently the smart fellow who made up another great culinary legend: that popsicles were first created when Frank Epperson left a paper cup of powdered orange soda and water with a mixing stick in it on a freezing night in Oakland, California.

In the late 1930s Switell tried to get Cary Grant and fellow Hollywood star Irene Dunne to make Caesar salads on screen and credited Wallis Simpson – then big news as the divorcee who had brought down the British monarchy – with giving the salad its name.

By this time, Caesar Cardini had settled in LA. He had left Tijuana in 1935 after the double whammy of the end of prohibition and the Mexican government imposing a ban on border gambling. In July 1936, the *Reno Evening Gazette* reported that 'Caesar Cardini has closed his gay Tijuana cafe forever'. In Los Angeles, Cardini spent the next 20 years running a deli on La Ciegna Boulevard, selling imported food and his proprietary Caesar salad dressings.

The recipe for the salad was first published in 1945 by a San Diego restaurant that had 'adopted' the salad but not the name. Two years later the Waldorf Astoria was inviting New York's food editors to see what all the west-coast fuss was about with its own Caesar salad promotion. By then, the recipe and the name were inextricably united as confirmed by a flurry of cookbooks released over the next decade.

Cardini himself recalled his original recipe in an interview with the *San Mateo Times* in 1952 as 'romaine lettuce, a one-minute egg, garlic croutons, parmesan or romano cheese, lemon juice, garlic, mustard, Worcestershire sauce, whole pepper, pear vinegar and olive oil'. The salad was designed to have the rich creamy dressing clinging to whole leaves, so they could each be eaten with fingers. But it seems it *was* the notoriously 'fast' Wallis Simpson, whose first husband was stationed in San Diego in the 1920s, who suggested Caesar cut up the lettuce so it was easier to eat elegantly with a fork.

Both Santini and Cardini were adamant that no anchovies be used. Caesar classed his as a 'subtle salad', although he did use a splash of Worcestershire sauce. Alex claimed that using anchovy fillets was his idea. It is fair to say that our recipe here does stray a little from these original principles!

One thing I do know for sure: reading that introduction probably took as long as making the salad ... but on the bright side, you now know more about the Caesar salad than 99.999999% of the world's population. If you want to up your obscure food knowledge credentials even further, now turn to page 190 and read the story behind bougatsa.

... and finally the Caesar Salad recipe ...

SERVES: 4 **PREP:** 15 MINS **COOKING:** 10 MINS

8 streaky bacon rashers (or use pancetta)
10 anchovy fillets
2 small garlic cloves, crushed
1½ tablespoons extra virgin olive oil
2 thick slices sourdough, torn into bite-sized pieces
12 cos lettuce leaves
12 radicchio or purple witlof leaves
100 g shaved parmesan

DRESSING

2 eggs, at room temperature – this is critical folks!
80 ml (⅓ cup) extra virgin olive oil
juice of 1 lemon
2 tablespoons Worcestershire sauce
½ teaspoon sea salt
½ teaspoon ground white pepper

Cook the bacon in a non-stick frying pan over high heat for 4 minutes or until crisp on both sides. Transfer to a plate lined with paper towel to drain.

Finely chop two anchovy fillets and place in a small bowl with the garlic and oil. Mash with the back of a spoon until a paste forms (or you can do this using a mortar and pestle). Add the bread and toss to coat in the anchovy paste.

Save washing up and add the bread to the pan you used for the bacon. Cook over medium heat, tossing constantly, until evenly toasted. Transfer to the plate lined with paper towel to drain.

It's now time to make your dressing. Make sure the eggs are at room temperature (if they're too cold they will crack), then gently add to a saucepan of boiling water and cook for 2½ minutes. Immediately remove and plunge into an ice-cold water bath.

Crack the eggs open over a tall jug and use a teaspoon to scoop out all the egg left in the shells. Add the remaining dressing ingredients and blitz with a stick blender until well combined.

Arrange the cos and radicchio or witlof leaves in a serving bowl and add the bacon and shaved parmesan. Top with the remaining anchovy fillets and scatter over the croutons. Drizzle with plenty of dressing.

TIPS

Serve the salad as individual lettuce cups for a smart entree.

Add some poached chicken for a complete meal, or grilled prawns go really well too.

The eggs in the dressing are slightly raw. If you don't like using raw eggs or would prefer your yolks to be a little more firm, cook the eggs for 5 minutes and add a little water to help them blend into the dressing.

Chilaquiles – Chipotle Black Beans & Eggs

I spent years trying to work out how nachos could be classed as a suitable breakfast, only to go to Mexico City (or DF, as the locals still call it; the new acronym CDMX is struggling to take off) and discover chilaquiles. Basically, breakfast nachos!! A true Mexican comfort food!! They've been making them there for years!! And they're a great way to use up leftover tortillas!! Now I'm worried I've used up 26% of the agreed and sanctioned exclamation marks allocated for this cookbook in just one recipe, which will, I suspect, cause issues further down the line.

Chilaquiles are usually cooked in store-bought salsa, but we've kept them out of the sauce to retain the breakfast crunch loved by those of us who hate soggy cereal.

SERVES: 4 **PREP:** 15 MINS (PLUS 6 HOURS SOAKING) **COOKING:** 2 HOURS 15 MINS

400 g dried frijoles negros (black beans)
1 brown onion, coarsely chopped
2 garlic cloves, unpeeled, smashed
1 fresh or dried bay leaf
2 teaspoons sea salt
2 chipotle chillies in adobo sauce
3 teaspoons sauce from your jar or can of chipotle in adobo sauce
1 teaspoon smoked paprika
250 ml (1 cup) tomato passata
1 teaspoon dried Mexican or Greek oregano
400 g good-quality corn chips
1 avocado, thinly sliced
½ red onion, finely chopped
4 eggs, fried (or scrambled if you prefer)
½ bunch coriander, leaves coarsely chopped
125 g (½ cup) sour cream
2 bird's eye chillies, thinly sliced
2 limes, cut into wedges

Place the dried beans in a bowl, cover with water and leave to soak for 4–6 hours. Drain. (Or see TIP.)

Place the beans, onion, garlic, bay leaf, salt and 2 litres water in a large heavy-based saucepan and bring to a gentle simmer over medium–low heat. Partially cover with a lid and cook, stirring occasionally, for 1–1½ hours or until nearly all the liquid has been absorbed. Remove from the heat and use a potato masher to crush some of the beans, leaving half of them whole for some textural variation.

Return the pan to medium heat. Add the chipotle chillies, chipotle adobo sauce, paprika, passata, oregano and 250 ml (1 cup) water and cook, stirring occasionally, for 20–30 minutes or until the liquid has reduced by one-third.

Divide the corn chips evenly among four serving plates or spread on a large serving platter. Top with the black bean mixture, avocado, red onion, eggs, coriander and dollops of sour cream. Scatter with sliced chilli and serve with lime wedges.

TIP

If you don't have time to soak the dried beans, rinse 2 × 400 g cans of black beans, add to the pan with the onion, garlic and bay leaf and reduce the simmering time to 15–20 minutes or until the onion is cooked. Continue with the recipe.

Scallop & Lemon–Mayo Tostadas

I've sat at some bad restaurant tables in my time – in the corridor on the way to the lav, next to the massive speaker at a salsa restaurant, uncomfortably close to a fighting, crying divorcing couple – but my experience at the famous Puyol in Mexico was among the worst. We sat at the long bar for their famous taco tasting menu. That was fine; the problem was that on the other side of the bar there was a sink where sometimes more than two floor-staff at a time stood doing the washing up. All night. I can't think of many more depressing views than watching people endlessly washing up, but contrary to what the late fifties English film and theatre scene would have you believe, there was no drama with this 'kitchen-sink drama'. The only upside of the evening was their version of this dish, which was wonderfully delicious. After our experience that night, I have no compunction about stealing my inspiration from there.

SERVES: 4 **PREP:** 20 MINS **COOKING:** 10 MINS

12 × 10 cm tostadas or 12 small corn tortillas (see page 281)
cooking oil spray
1 lemon
2 tablespoons good-quality whole-egg mayonnaise
¼ teaspoon ground white pepper
sea salt
12 large scallops, roe removed
1 tablespoon extra virgin olive oil
½ avocado, diced
½ cup coriander leaves
black sesame seeds, toasted, to serve

Preheat the oven to 200°C/180°C fan-forced.

First make the crispy tostadas. (If you are using tortillas, cut them into rounds with a 10 cm cookie cutter.) Spread out the tostadas on a large baking tray and spray with oil. Bake for 10 minutes until crisp. Set a timer for 7 minutes so you can check them early, just in case! Set aside to cool.

Finely grate the zest of half the lemon and place in a small bowl. Use a peeler to remove the rest of the peel and any white pith with a small sharp knife. Hold the lemon over the bowl with the grated zest to catch any juices, then segment the lemon, cutting on either side of the white membrane. Chop each segment into small triangles and add to the bowl.

Add the mayonnaise, pepper and ⅓ teaspoon of salt to the lemon and gently mix to combine.

Heat a large non-stick frying pan over high heat until very hot.

Remove any excess moisture from the scallops with paper towel, then place them in a bowl and very gently toss with the oil to coat.

Add four scallops to the scaldingly hot pan and cook for 1 minute each side – they need to be just seared to give them the lightest of golden crusts.

Don't overload the pan, or it will reduce the heat too much and the scallops will stew.

Don't bother the scallops while they are frying.

Do, when you turn them, try to find a hot spot in the pan where a scallop wasn't before!

Repeat with the remaining scallops.

Now cut each scallop into four or five thin slices. Gently fold into the lemon mayo.

Spoon about 1 tablespoon of the scallop mixture onto each tostada and top with the avocado, coriander and sesame seeds. Season well with salt and serve.

TIP

You could make smaller versions of these with store-bought round corn chips.

Lime & Tequila Granita

There is no better way to end a meal than with something mouth-tinglingly refreshing – especially if you can turn it into a cocktail halfway through by adding more tequila. This dessert can be made with super-trendy mezcal, but I'd avoid that and drink it with the meal instead.

SERVES: 6 **PREP:** 15 MINS (PLUS 4 HOURS 30 MINS FREEZING) **COOKING:** 10 MINS

150 g caster sugar
finely grated zest of 1 lime
180 ml freshly squeezed lime juice (from about 4 limes)
100 ml lime juice cordial
100 ml tequila (pick a good one, such as Don Julio)
½ teaspoon sea salt
lime cheeks, to serve

Place the sugar, lime zest and 175 ml water in a medium saucepan over low heat and cook, stirring frequently, for 5–10 minutes or until the sugar has completely dissolved. Remove from the heat and stir in the lime juice, cordial, tequila, salt and another 175 ml water.

Strain the lime mixture through a fine sieve into a jug, then pour into a shallow dish that will fit in your freezer. Place in the freezer for about 1½ hours or until partially set. Remove and use a fork to scrape the top, drawing the granita into the middle. Return to the freezer. Repeat this process twice more until the granita is completely frozen and you have loads of ice crystals.

Spoon straight from the freezer into glasses and serve with lime cheeks.

TIPS

Granitas are fantastic, as you can make them well ahead and store them in the freezer for up to 2 weeks.

This recipe works well with a whole range of different fruit juices and booze. Try fresh blackberry juice or pureed and sieved fresh raspberries instead of the lime juice. A good gin, such as Tanqueray, would be a lovely replacement for the tequila. Add a squeeze of lemon to add a welcome acidic bite.

For something really special, substitute three-quarters of the lime juice with double the amount of pomegranate juice or the same amount of yuzu juice, and use a good vodka, such as Ketel One instead of the tequila.

Emma's Hot Chocolate Torte *with* Sour Cream

Emma Warren is my right-hand woman when we do dinners overseas. As the other half of the Two Warrens, she runs a very tight ship and uses skills that are part steel and part Machiavelli to get disgruntled chefs to surprise themselves with how good they can be. She also writes a mean recipe and, as she's spent much more time in Mexico than me, it seemed wise to ask her to help with this section. Emma is also one of those rare chefs who is strong with both sweet and savoury flavours; and, even rarer, she loves to cook at home. This torte is a constantly evolving work in progress, but one that is pretty close to its pinnacle of ease and deliciousness. Make it once, and I am sure it will become a go-to when you're under the pump and need a crowd-pleaser to finish a dinner in style.

SERVES: 4 **PREP:** 10 MINS (PLUS COOLING) **COOKING:** 40 MINS

250 g dark chocolate (70% cocoa solids, or go even higher if you want), finely chopped
200 g unsalted butter, plus extra for greasing
4 eggs
80 ml (⅓ cup) of your favourite coffee liqueur, plus extra to serve (optional)
100 g (½ cup) raw caster sugar
30 g (¼ cup) almond meal
1 tablespoon plain flour
2 teaspoons dried chilli flakes, plus extra to serve
½ teaspoon ground cayenne
125 g (½ cup) sour cream

Preheat the oven to 190°C/170°C fan-forced. Grease a 20 cm springform tin and line the base with baking paper.

Place the chocolate and butter in a heatproof bowl set over a saucepan of simmering water, making sure the bowl doesn't touch the water, and stir regularly until melted and combined. (Alternatively, place in a microwave-safe bowl and melt in the microwave on high, stirring every 30 seconds.) Set aside for 5 minutes to cool slightly.

Add one egg at a time and stir with a wooden spoon until well combined. Stir in 2 tablespoons of the coffee liqueur, then fold through the sugar, almond meal, flour, chilli and cayenne until well combined.

Pour the chocolate mixture into the prepared tin and bake for 35 minutes or until a skewer inserted in the centre comes out clean. Set aside to cool in the tin for 30 minutes, then release the torte from the tin and transfer to a wire rack to cool completely.

Cut the torte into slices and drizzle with the remaining liqueur. Top each slice with a big dollop of sour cream. If you like, make a well in the centre of the cream and pour in some extra liqueur. Sprinkle with extra chilli flakes and serve.

TIP

If you want to be really organised, bake the torte a day ahead. It will keep in an airtight container in the fridge for up to 5 days. Bring it to room temperature to serve.

Tamale Corn Cake

Tamales are another great Central American street food that hold a special place in the hearts (and hands) of Mexicans, but making them at home is a bit of a pain. Can I suggest you try this giant version instead? It's far quicker and easier to make, but still big on flavour.

SERVES: 10 **PREP:** 15 MINS **COOKING:** 1 HOUR 20 MINUTES

120 g butter, at room temperature
55 g (¼ cup) caster sugar
1 egg
2 egg yolks
1 × 125 g can sweet corn kernels, rinsed and drained
260 g (1½ cups) cornmeal (or polenta, finely blended in a food processor)
80 g plain flour (or masa harina if you happen to have some)
1½ teaspoons baking powder
1 teaspoon sea salt
1 × 395 g can sweetened condensed milk
250 ml (1 cup) coconut milk
90 g (1 cup) freshly grated coconut (see TIPS)
4–5 fresh whole banana leaves (see TIPS)
100 g quince paste (see TIPS), cut into 5 mm cubes
200 ml pouring cream, to serve

Preheat the oven to 200°C/180°C fan-forced.

Place the butter and sugar in the bowl of an electric mixer fitted with the whisk attachment (or use a bowl and electric beaters) and beat until pale and creamy. Gradually beat in the egg and egg yolks one at a time until well combined.

Now get your food processor or blender and add the corn kernels, cornmeal, flour, baking powder, salt, condensed milk and coconut milk. Whiz on high until smooth and well combined.

Slowly pour the corn mixture into the creamed butter mixture, whisking on low speed until a smooth batter forms. Use a spatula or wooden spoon to gently fold in the grated coconut.

Soften the banana leaves by placing them in hot water or the microwave for 1 minute. Line a 24 cm springform tin with the leaves, allowing them to overhang so they can be folded back over the top later.

Pour the batter into the prepared tin and dot with the cubes of quince paste, poking a few of them deeper into the batter. Cover with the overhanging leaves; if you don't have enough to fully cover the top, add an extra banana leaf to make sure all the batter is enclosed. Poke some toothpicks through the top to secure the leaves, then bake for 1 hour 20 minutes or until a skewer inserted in the centre comes out clean. Transfer to a wire rack to cool slightly before releasing from the tin.

Peel back the top of the banana leaves to slice the cake and serve drizzled with cream.

TIPS

You can buy frozen freshly grated coconut from Indian and Asian grocers. If you can't find it, just use moist coconut flakes from the supermarket.

Banana leaves are available at most Asian grocers, but if you don't have one of these handy you can use foil or four layers of baking paper instead.

Try other fruit pastes, such as guava or pear, instead of quince.

This is delicious served with coconut ice-cream. You'll find my super-simple coconut ice-cream recipe online. It's basically just mixing 400 ml coconut milk and 200 g condensed milk in a zip-lock bag and freezing overnight, then breaking into chunks and blitzing into soft serve the next day. Refreeze for a firmer set.

THANK YOU

It takes a village to raise a child, and it takes lots of people far smarter than me to make a book. I'd like to think that I'm the composer or the conductor of this *meisterwerk,* but actually I'm more like the odd angry itch that occasionally gets a scratch.

This is why I firstly need to thank the wonderful team of long-term collaborators who have helped me turn the recipes in this book into something very special through their dedication, skill and knowledge. Marnie Rowe and Kate Quincerot – respectively and very aptly 'M' and 'Q' to my cut-price Bond – have been helping me turn out better recipes with their incredible palates and ruthless perfectionism since the beginning, and I am double #blessed to be supported in this book by rock-solid foundations Warren Mendes and Emma Warren, who are both incredibly knowledgeable and as potty about flavour as me. They have generously allowed their experience to amplify mine. We also enlisted MC alum Karlie Verkerk, who has been working with Warren Mendes and helped with the China chapter. She's done an amazing job. Overseeing all this has been the human culinary encyclopedia that is Michelle Southan, who has tested recipes, suggested changes and made sure all of us deliver impeccable copy. Even me!

Stylish stylist Karina Duncan is as much of a staple in my books as sweet corn or a bad pun. She's worked on all my best cookbooks, but she's reached new heights here. She's also a brilliant and knowledgeable weathervane for good food.

This is my second book working with Lucy Heaver from my publisher, Plum. She has remained my spirit animal and reads my mind in the most worrying (but helpful) way. She is a very special woman. If I am the indolent emperor, then she is the conquering general who actually built the empire. I don't ever want to do another book without her. She has also got incredible 'command K' skills!

Mark Roper took the pictures, and while I still struggle (as I have done for the 16 or so years we have worked together on magazines like *delicious.* and *VE+T*) with the fact that everyone likes him far, far more than they like me (perhaps because he is just so very nice, rather funny and annoyingly talented), his pictures of the food here are quite brilliant. It was great to work together again, old man!

The final part of the panda gang is the talented team in the kitchen, who cooked all the page-lickingly delicious food you see in this book. Led by Caroline Griffiths, with support from Emma Roocke, Seb Nichols and Brea Adams, they provided advice, improvements and more than their fair share of laughs over the three weeks of shooting. Thank you!

Plum's Mary Small and Pan Mac's Ingrid Ohlsson very much helped shape this book, and I am indebted to them both – especially as it takes a brave woman who'll put such trust in me. While formidable glamazon and valued friend Tracey Cheetham, baking wizard Charlotte Ree and the team of Cate Paterson, Kate Butler, Katie Crawford and Ross Gibb made sure you knew about the book and could buy it.

In the engine room, praise needs to be liberally spread among designer Kirby Armstrong, who's also illustrated the recipe titles brilliantly; editor Rachel Carter, who has lived up to the lofty praise she rode into my life on the back of, (that's such clumsy English but she'll fix it); and to our typesetter Megan Ellis. They are the ones who have taken my twisted Gordian knots of words and turned them into something understandable, while Helena Holmgren should be thanked for doing the thankless task of compiling the indexes that are so much a part of the success and useability of this book.

So many of the ideas for this book and its recipes have come from time spent with the inspirational team at *delicious.* magazine, *taste.com.au* and *delicious. on Sunday* in *Stellar*. Thank you so much to Kerrie McCallum, Samantha Jones, Phoebe Rose Wood, Fiona Nilsson, Toni Mason, Brodee Myers-Cooke and Michelle Southan, again! You are still the best in the business. I love you all dearly and it's so much fun 'working' with you.

Yet again, MasterChef has been a huge part of my life while we were pulling this book together, so massive thanks for the support, inspiration and help of Tim Toni, Marty Benson, Maureen Moriarty (aka MoZee McCarthy), Charmaine de Pasquale, DJ Deadly, Bennie and the camera boys, Butch, Roey, Davey the wonder 1st, Tess, the much lamented Sandy Patterson, plus Paul, Beverley, Rick, Anthony, Rob, Carolyn and Voula at Channel Ten. And, of course, above all, the other Two Musketeers, Gary and George, who are the truest sounding boards and the wisest counsel anyone could have. *We few, we happy few, this band of brothers ...*

It's taken me a while, but the dawning realisation over the last five years that none of this means anything without my family is like the best sunrise ever. I am so proud of the smart, engaged and respectful young people my children Jono, Will and Sadie have become, and I love that after 20-plus years 'the woman I love' is still the woman I love. To the moon and back!

I should also blow kisses to my mother and constant inspiration Jennifer and the mob that is Eleanor and Mark, Katie and Paul, Nelly and Gabriel; also my excellent mother-in-law Jude and Sar, Si, Jay, Issy, Ed and Lou. Like I said – I love how family becomes more important not less, and ever bigger, as the years progress.

Of course, that family really includes the people I rely on day to day in my working life. My talented manager, honest friend and total spunk Henrie Stride and her offsider Lena Barridge; David Vodicka and Yasmin Naghavi, who are the wisest counsel a man could ask for; and Aaron Hurle, who just quietly goes about his business of keeping me solvent and honest; while Charlotte James and Catherine Murphy keep the millions who follow me on social media so well informed, and who stop me taking to the trolls who pick on the defenceless out there with the sharpened but brutal ice-axe of my tongue. I so want to ...

PS: CJ and Murph would like me to say: Keep in touch with me on Facebook, Twitter and Instagram at @mattscravat. Send me pics of what you cook from this book. I'd love that!

PANDA POSSE

PANDAS CAROLINE, EMMA & BREA

PANDA MARK

PANDA LUCY

PANDA KARINA

EXTENDED INDEX

START THE DAY BEFORE

DINNER PARTY WINNERS (PERFECT FOR SHOWING OFF!)

DISHES FOR HOT SUMMER NIGHTS

WINTER NIGHT WARMERS

FIRE ME UP – BBQ DISHES

PREP & FREEZE FOR EASE

SIDEKICKS & SAUCES

LIGHT LUNCHES & PERFECT STARTERS

GLUTEN FREE (*GLUTEN FREE IF GF-STOCK IS USED)

VEGAN (*OR CAN BE EASILY CONVERTED)

VEGETARIAN (*OR CAN BE EASILY CONVERTED)

PREP & PUT YOUR FEET UP

MIDWEEK MEALS WHEN YOU REALLY CAN'T BE BOTHERED

LEFTOVERS FOR LUNCH THE NEXT DAY

MINIMAL WASHING UP

INDEX

D

E

F

G

I

J

L

M

N

O

P

Q

R

S

T

Z

A PLUM BOOK

First published in 2018 by Pan Macmillan Australia Pty Limited
1 Market Street, Sydney, New South Wales, Australia 2000

A CIP catalogue record for this book is available
from the National Library of Australia: http://catalogue.nla.gov.au

Designer: Kirby Armstrong
Photographer: Mark Roper
Prop and food stylist: Karina Duncan
Editor: Rachel Carter
Lead home economist: Caroline Griffiths
Home-ec assistants: Emma Roocke, Sebastian Nichols and Brea Adams
Makeup artist: Maureen Moriarty
Colour + reproduction by Splitting Image Colour Studio
Printed in China

10 9 8 7 6 5 4 3 2 1